C000146671

Printing, Propaganda, an
Martin Luther

Printing, Propaganda, and Martin Luther

Mark U. Edwards, Jr.

FORTRESS PRESS
Minneapolis

PRINTING, PROPAGANDA, AND MARTIN LUTHER

Fortress Press ex libris publication 2005

Cover art: "The Dragon of Revelation Wearing the Papal Tiara," from *Luther's German New
Testament*, 1522.

ISBN 0-8006-3739-9
The Library of Congress has catalogued the original publication as follows:

Library of Congress Cataloging-in-Publication Data
Edwards, Mark U.
       Printing, Propaganda, and Martin Luther / Mark U. Edwards, Jr.
         p. cm.
       Includes bibliographical references and index.
       ISBN 0-520-08462-4 (alk. paper)
       Luther, Martin, 1483-1546—Influence.   2. Reformation—Germany.
       3. Reformation—France—Strasbourg.   4. Christian literature—Publication and
       distribution—Germany.   5. Christian literature—Publication and distribution—
       France—Strasbourg. 6. Germany—church history—16th century. 7. Strasbourg
       (France)—Church history.   I. Title.
       BR325.E343   1994
       284.1'092—dc2
       [B]   93-34056
                                                     CIP

The paper used in this publication meets the minimum requirements of American National
Standard for Information Sciences—Permanence of Paper for Printed Library Materials,
ANSI Z329.48-1984.

Manufactured in the U.S.A.

09   08   07   06   05   1   2   3   4   5   6   7   8   9   10

To Lew and Paul

Contents

Illustrations

Tables

Preface

Each term in the title of this book requires some explanation.

Printing takes the pride of place because this book deals exclusively with printed material and with the fact of printing itself, the technology and its limitations and constraints, and what historians may be able to make of it and them. This study depends in no small part on what was printed, where, who may have read it, and how it may have been understood.

This is also a book about *propaganda* in that it is a study of persuasive literature that attempted to redefine a major institution in its social world: the Christian church and its beliefs. I argue that the medium of printing was used for the first time in Western history to channel a "mass" movement to affect change concerning this institution. By using *mass* I do not mean that the whole or even a majority of the population were directly targeted by Reformation propaganda. The majority of the population were at best spectators at this drama, affected but unengaged except, perhaps, for the Reformation's unwelcomed offspring, the German Peasants' War of 1525. I do mean that printing was used to reach an audience far larger than any previous movement reached and one that could not have been reached as quickly and as effectively before printing's invention. Those members of the reading public engaged by the Reformation publicists, or at any case a significant subgroup of them, in turn shared these views orally with a much larger group. Together they inspired the Reformation movement.

I also mean to suggest with the word *propaganda* that the attempt to persuade was not always successful or at the very least did not always coincide with the expectations of the propagandists. In fact, this slippage between those propagandizing and those propagandized is a major subject of the overall work.

Finally, this is a book about *Martin Luther*. Luther is not simply one publicist within a larger constellation. Rather, he was the dominant publicist. And he dominated to a degree that no other person to my knowledge has ever dominated a major propaganda campaign and mass movement since. Not Lenin, not Mao Tse-tung, not Thomas Jefferson, John Adams, or Patrick Henry. Hence an examination of his role in this phenomenon of Reformation printing and propaganda gives us a more secure grasp on the larger whole than the study of any other figure could. He is far from the whole, but the whole would make no sense without him, since he played an inordinate role in its creation and shaping.

This study began in 1984–1985 thanks to a grant from the National Endowment for the Arts. A stint at software development and a few years adjusting to a new position at Harvard Divinity School slowed this study's gestation, but I hope deepened its eventual analysis. While at Purdue University I benefitted greatly from conversation with Les Cohen, John Contreni, and Linda Peck. Here at Harvard, David Hall, Steven Ozment, and Ron Thiemann have given invaluable advice and support. Miriam Usher Chrisman helped me think about the statistics on Catholic controversialists; moreover, her *Lay Culture, Learned Culture: Books and Social Change in Strasbourg, 1480–1599*, and *Bibliography of Strasbourg Imprints, 1480–1599*, both published by Yale University Press in 1982, provided essential background and bibliographic support for my sections on the publications of the Strasbourg press. My research assistant, Mary Jane Haemig, has helped in numerous ways tracking down material that has gone into this book. Finally, without the work and assistance of Hans-Joachim Köhler of the Tübingen Flugschriften Project and his team, this study would have been impossible. To all these scholars, but especially to Hajo and Miriam, I owe a great debt of thanks.

Parts of this study have previously been published. The section in chapter 1 on Catholic controversialists first appeared in "Catholic Controversial Literature, 1518–1555: Some Statistics," *Archiv für Reformationsgeschichte / Archive for Reformation History* 79 (1988): 189–205. Chapter 2 appeared in a slightly different form in "First

Impressions in the Strasbourg Press," in Andrew C. Fix and Susan C. Karant-Nunn, eds., *Germania Illustrata: Essays on Early Modern Germany Presented to Gerald Strauss* (Sixteenth Century Essays and Studies, 1992). Much of the material in chapter 7 appeared in "*Lutherschmähung?* Catholics on Luther's Responsibility for the Peasants' War," *The Catholic Historical Review* 76 (1990): 461–480. Table 5, "Major Evangelical Publicists," is based on table 1 of Alejandro Zorzin's *Karlstadt als Flugschriftenautor*, Göttinger Theologische Arbeiten, vol. 48 (Vandenhoeck & Ruprecht, 1990). I wish to thank the respective copyright holders for permission to reprint these materials.

My wife Linda and my daughter Teon have kept me on an even keel from day to day, and I am deeply grateful. They will no doubt be as happy as I am that this study has finally found its way to print.

I dedicate this work to Lewis Spitz and Paul Seaver, who each in their quite different ways inspired me as an apprentice historian.

I have attempted to preserve the orthography of each source I use. The unusual diacritical marks of the sixteenth century are reproduced except when modernized in the source I quote. Unless otherwise indicated, all translations are my own.

Introduction

The Reformation saw the first major, self-conscious attempt to use the recently invented printing press to shape and channel a mass movement. The printing press allowed Evangelical publicists to do what had been previously impossible, quickly and effectively reach a large audience with a message intended to change Christianity. For several crucial years, these Evangelical publicists issued thousands of pamphlets discrediting the old faith and advocating the new. And they managed to accomplish this with little serious opposition from publicists of a Catholic persuasion. This Evangelical mastery of the press, and the feeble Catholic response, provide the framework for this book and will be dealt with in detail in chapter 1, "Evangelical and Catholic Propaganda in the Early Decades of the Reformation."

Not only did the Reformation see the first large-scale "media campaign," it also saw a campaign that was overwhelmingly dominated by one person, Martin Luther. More works by Luther were printed and reprinted than by any other publicist. In fact, the presses of the German-speaking lands produced substantially more vernacular works by Luther in the crucial early years (1518–1525) than the seventeen other major Evangelical publicists combined. During Luther's lifetime these presses produced nearly five times as many German works by Luther as by all the Catholic controversialists put together. Even if consideration is restricted to polemical works, Luther still outpublished all his Catholic opponents five to three. By Hans-Joachim Köhler's calculation, Luther's works made up 20 percent of all the pamphlets published during the period 1500 to 1530. It is this staggering dominance by one man that justifies the title of this book: *Printing, Propaganda, and Martin Luther*. It also explains the book's focus on Luther.

Within the larger topic of printing and propaganda in the Reformation and the narrower focus of Martin Luther's dominance of the press, this book develops three interrelated arguments on how the history of the early Reformation should be written in light of this Evangelical propaganda campaign. First, any future history needs to bear in mind what most people likely knew of Luther and his message and when they likely knew it. Such an approach yields a narrative that differs in significant ways from the conventional account. Second, the message Luther intended in his writings was not always the message that his various reading publics received, and the discrepancy between the two—message sent and message received—has profound implications for the story of the early Reformation. Third, the medium of printing not only conveyed challenges to traditional authority with particular force but raised in its own right new issues of authority concerning the propriety of public debate on matters of faith, the interpretation of "Scripture alone," and the conferring and deploying of charismatic authority. The medium itself became entangled with its message.

PRINTING AND THE REFORMATION MOVEMENTS

Sited at the intersection of two historiographical debates—one over the history of printing and its role in the Reformation, and the other over the nature and appeal of the early Reformation movement—this book is a contribution to both discussions.

The first debate is over the degree to which the Reformation may be fairly characterized as a "print event." While historians eschew a monocausal technological explanation—"justification by print alone," as it were[1]—strong claims have been made for the importance of printing as a major causal factor of the German Reformation.[2] "Without printing, no Reformation" encapsulates this view.[3] At the other extreme are those who question whether printing can possibly be assigned such a prominent explanatory role, given the very low level of literacy in early sixteenth-century Germany.[4] These skeptics put much greater emphasis on the oral or pictorial transmission of ideas. Some historians even insist that the Reformation movements them-

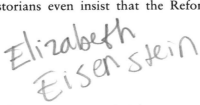

selves engaged only a small minority within the population and were met by the bulk of the largely illiterate masses of (possibly still pagan) Germans with indifference or outright hostility.[5]

The second debate deals with the Reformation message, whether propagated through print or preaching. What was the message or messages that motivated the activists of the various Reformation movements? Was it a form of evangelical theology that resonated with late medieval communalism—either urban[6] or rural or both[7]—or was it a theology that freed laity from the burdens of a monastic form of Christianity[8] or was it simply (or largely) anticlericalism?[9] To what extent did the supporters of the Reformation share Luther's central concerns about justification by faith alone apart from works of the law? What, in practice, did the slogan "Scripture alone" actually entail? Did Christian freedom extend to secular matters, and, alternatively, did divine law properly have binding force in both spiritual and secular realms? These questions arise out of the debate over the content and reception of the printed and preached word.

These two debates overlap not only on the issue of printed propaganda, its message and efficacy, but also on the significance and role of Martin Luther, the foremost author of printed propaganda in the early years of the Reformation movement. Many older accounts have treated the German Reformation as something of a one-man show. As the Göttingen church historian Bernd Moeller put it in a classic 1965 article, "To caricature the common description, Luther generally appears as a great sage, a kind of spiritual colossus, who attains his Reformation breakthrough, draws the broad consequences, and then drags people with him as he strides through history handing out his truths right and left."[10] More recently historians have suggested a much diminished role for Luther, attributing equal if not greater significance to Huldrych Zwingli[11] and to the various local reformers in cities and countryside throughout south and central Germany. How important is Martin Luther really in the history of the early Reformation movements? What authority did his name and his message actually enjoy? Did this change over time? And what role did print play in establishing and propagating this authority?

In addressing the issues of "printing, propaganda, and Martin Luther," this book treats these larger questions of the Reformation as a "print event," the nature and appeal of various "Reformation messages," and the role of Martin Luther among other publicists, preachers, and opinion leaders in the early German Reformation. In so doing, it attempts to explore the dialect between the fixity of print and the fluidity of reception and to probe the role of the medium in not only propagating but even shaping its message.

NARRATIVE FROM THE PERSPECTIVE OF WHAT CONTEMPORARIES KNEW AND WHEN THEY LIKELY KNEW IT

Ironically, most Luther biography and accounts of the German Reformation offer a distorted picture of the attraction and progress of the early Reformation, not because the historian knows too little but because the historian knows too much. Those contemporaries who followed the progress of the Reformation with engaged interest were undoubtedly a small minority within the population of the German-speaking lands. But as events proved, they were an influential minority made up of many leaders, opinion makers, and activists. Yet the great preponderance of even this relatively small group never met Luther face-to-face, never heard him preach with any regularity if at all, and had little or no correspondence with him. They learned of him and of his message through the press or through conversation or preaching. And though there could be several steps in the transmission, the ultimate source for that conversation or sermon was printed material.

We historians loose sight of this fact in our commendable zeal to ferret out as much information about the past as possible. We forget that, except perhaps for a few of Luther's students, no contemporary read Luther's works in light of his pre-Reformation lectures on Psalms, Galatians, and Romans. No member of Luther's reading public was privy to all his many letters, and very few corresponded with him at all. Only a few hundred attended his Reformation lectures at the University of Wittenberg. Merely a handful took their meals at Luther's table and noted down his remarks. Yet modern histories ground much of their presentation and interpretation on these privileged sources of information.

There is another source of distortion that comes from knowing too much. Since historians know how things turned out, we tend to structure our narrative around issues and events that have significance for later developments. But contemporaries did not have such advantage, so they were just as likely to become entranced by historical dead-ends and to be preoccupied by developments or ideas that, as it turned out, had no future. Just because we know, for example, that Luther's three great treatises of 1520—*To the Christian Nobility of the German Nation*, *On the Freedom of a Christian*, and *On the Babylonian Captivity of the Church*—were to become the defining works of the whole Reformation movement, we should not automatically assume that contemporaries would recognize their significance. They had no way of knowing that these treatises marked a parting of the ways. In fact, these treatises were likely to have been understood initially in ways quite different from the meaning they took on in the light of subsequent events.

With these sources of distortion in mind, I attempt in several chapters to reconstruct the progress of the early Reformation as it was likely experienced by the most engaged participants. I attempt to ask what this influential minority could have realistically known of Luther and his message and when they could have known it. To answer this question, I take my clue from what was printed and reprinted, where it was printed and reprinted, and when. This approach yields a narrative for the early Reformation movement that is in some respects strikingly different from conventional accounts.

RECEPTION AND RE-PRESENTATION

Martin Luther attempted mightily throughout his life to dictate how his own writings should be understood. Even though he could normally (but not always) control what was printed under his name, he could not (try as he might) control how he was interpreted by his readers. And when readers became preachers or publicists in their own right, Luther had even less control over the message they associated with his name.[12] They issued their own treatises to explain what he said, what he meant, what people should do. Opponents took to the press as well to decry Luther's message and explain its fallacies and its dangers. Even Luther's allies often disagreed with each other, and with the Reformer himself, in their understanding of what he had said and what he stood for. So, too, did his opponents. Each treatise was received differently by different people, interpreted differently by different audiences. It was the press, then, that both connected Luther with his audience and led inevitably to a divorce between Luther's "intent" and the "meaning" appropriated by various readers.

As distressing as this diversity was for Luther, and as unsettling as it may be for scholars today, we must recognize that the reader and the representer, that is, the *re*-presenter, whether a preacher or an ⟨

invested Luther's publications with meaning drawn from his or her own life experience. In the dialectic of reader and text, there was born myriad interpretations. There was no one "theology" or one correct understanding of Luther's teaching in the sixteenth century. On the contrary, several what we might term "communities of discourse" each read Luther in a different way, with individuals within these "communities" reinforcing each other's particular reading of Martin Luther.

Readers understand what they read from within their own experiences of life. Knowledge and understanding is a cumulative process, a fitting of ideas and impressions into a mosaic made up of the assumptions and beliefs of the larger society and of one's own subgroups within that society and colored and given final arrangement by the experiences of the individual. The mosaic that constitutes understanding varies from individual to individual and from subgroup to subgroup within society. A burgher fitted Luther's message into a quite different constellation than a peasant. A Catholic priest saw things differently than a lay person. And for a variety of accidents of life history, even two members of religious orders could differ widely on their reception of Luther's message: the Dominican Martin Bucer, for example, became a passionate Evangelical, the Franciscan Thomas Murner became one of the Reformation's most determined opponents. Different people reading the same text could come to drastically different understandings. We shall explore this variety and its implications for any account of the early Reformation movement.

THE ROLE OF THE PRESS IN THE DEBATES OVER AUTHORITY

From Luther's first appearance on the public stage, his critics turned the debate towards questions of authority. And when Luther finally responded in the vernacular press, his critics saw him taking an inherently subversive approach to disseminating his dangerously subversive message. To defy the authorities of traditional Western Christendom —the papal magisterium, the decisions of councils, the teachings of the Latin and Greek Fathers, the judgments of universities, and the traditional interpretation of Scripture—made Luther a heretic. To do so by addressing a broad public in the vernacular language through the medium of the press made him a rebel. It was appalling enough to the defenders of the old faith that Luther denounced the papacy, cashiered the spiritual estate of the clergy, rejected monasticism and celibacy, and redefined the sacraments and other practices of traditional Christianity. But Luther compounded his enormity when he disseminated his program through thousands of vernacular pamphlets spread among the common people. Much of the dispute of these early years swirled around the issue of authority: who governs and on what basis, who decides and on what grounds? Printing not only spread the dispute to the far corners of the Holy Roman Empire of the German Nation and beyond, it inherently favored Luther's side of the argument. In a crucial way, it not only conveyed Luther's message but also embodied it.

It is a recurring theme of this book that the printing press played far more than just an assisting role in this many-sided contest over authority. It broadcast the subversive messages with a rapidity that had been impossible before its invention. More than that, it allowed the central ideological leader, Martin Luther, to reach the "opinion leaders" of the movement quickly, kept them all in touch with each other and with each other's experience and ideas, and allowed them to "broadcast" their (relatively coordinated) program to a much larger and more geographically diverse audience than had ever been possible before. Yet, paradoxically, printing also undermined central authority because it encouraged the recipients of the printed message to think for themselves about the issues in dispute, and it provided the means—printed Bibles especially—by which each person could become his or her own theologian.

Under the banner "Scripture alone," Luther and his fellow Evangelicals waged war against the traditional authorities for deciding disputes over doctrine and practice. The propaganda barrage led this charge, dismantling the claims for the papal magisterium, the decisions of councils, and the teachings of scholastics, Fathers, and canon lawyers. The press also offered to its public thousands of copies of the Evangelicals' primary authority, the Scriptures. Yet in an irony that Catholic publicists were quick to seize upon, the press also quickly revealed that the Evangelicals were unable always to agree on the right understanding of their sole authority. The contested authority of Scripture is another recurring subject of the book.

Finally, Luther's enormous propaganda successes gradually conferred on him unusual personal authority. Those impressed by his message tended to think highly of the messenger. Those who fitted his message to biblical prophecies of the Antichrist and the Endtimes were inclined to view Luther himself within biblical categories of prophet and saint. The press, then, allowed Luther to acquire a charismatic authority that could also be brought into play in his publications. Not surprisingly, then, his public authority itself became an object of debate. The development of this personal authority and its deployment are further topics of this book.

SOME METHODOLOGICAL CONSIDERATIONS

This book takes advantage of several characteristics of early sixteenth-century printing. Printers in the sixteenth century were in the business to make money. They might also publish out of conviction and altruism, but they still had to make a profit over time or they would be forced out of business. At the very least, then, we should be able to assume that the *printer* expected that there would be a market for his product. If he were correct in his expectation, then the printing of a work is a valid although indirect measure of public interest. If he was wrong, of course, he took a loss. But if the printer reprinted the work several times, and this is often the case with Luther's works, we may safely assume that he did so to meet the demands of his customers. The printing of a work, and especially the reprinting of a work, then, may be taken by historians as an indirect measure of public interest. This assumption is employed in subsequent chapters to identify those works that likely had the most influence in the Evangelical publishing barrage.

The business side of publishing has other significant implications for the study of printing and propaganda in the early Reformation. In an age well before copyright and with shipping over land expensive and printing relatively cheap, a work generally spread through reprinting. If, for example, there was interest in Strasbourg for a work first published in Wittenberg, it was more common for a printer in Strasbourg to reprint the work than it was for the printer in Wittenberg to ship a large number of copies to Strasbourg. This business fact can also be turned to the use of the historian. Since works were printed with the expectation of sale, the printing or reprinting of a particular work in a particular place may also be an indirect measure of *local* or *regional* demand, and not merely demand in general.

To be sure, a moment's reflection will suggest problems with this approach. Some types of printed material would have circulated more widely than others. For example, there was more centralized production and wider distribution of particularly expensive items such as

Bibles. Yet by concentrating our attention on popular, relatively inexpensive pamphlets, we shall not go too far astray in seeing these works as a rough indication of local interest and demand.

In several chapters, the implication of local production is used to make an otherwise overwhelming task manageable. The media campaign of the years 1518 to 1525 is simply too large for any one scholar to encompass in a reasonable length of time. Even Hans-Joachim Köhler, who directed the Tübingen Flugschriften Project that aimed at collecting and analyzing every surviving pamphlet edition from the years 1500 to 1530, had to settle for a sample when it came to content analysis.[13] Of an estimated 10,000 pamphlet editions produced between 1500 and 1530, and the approximately 3,000 pamphlets actually collected by the project, Köhler used a carefully created sample of 356 pamphlets for the basis of his content analysis. His results will be referred to at several points. I myself have chosen to solve the dilemma in a different way and have in four of the chapters limited my consideration to works published in the city of Strasbourg.

Admittedly, some treatises reached Strasbourg from outside printing centers, influenced the impressions Strasbourgeois had of Luther and his message, and yet were not reprinted in Strasbourg. By omitting these treatises, I add some imprecision to my reconstruction. Having conceded this, I would point out that any treatise that had aroused widespread interest within Strasbourg would likely have been reprinted. The Strasbourg printers were not about to pass up a sure chance for profit. By limiting ourselves to Strasbourg publications, we are in fact unlikely to overlook many treatises that strongly shaped public opinion in Strasbourg. And as it happened, since the vast majority of Luther's early vernacular works were published in Strasbourg, the "outside" publications that might have significantly modified readers' first impressions of Luther would have likely been in Latin. I doubt that this restriction to Strasbourg publications skews the analysis overmuch.

In fact, this focus on vernacular works published in Strasbourg is arguably less artificial than the standard biographical approach that pays little or no attention to evidence that some treatises had much wider readership and impact than others. It may be well and good in a biography to analyze indiscriminately Latin and German works without concern for the different (although overlapping) audiences each addressed. But we need to remember that vernacular publications reached a much wider audience. Furthermore, if we are interested in issues of reception, we risk seriously misunderstanding the historical record if we give to works printed only once the same weight we give to works that were reprinted numerous times and published over a wide geographical area. Some works were simply more significant than others in forming opinion among a significant segment of the population.

Strasbourg, an imperial free city with a population of about twenty thousand, was the third greatest printing center in German-speaking lands, exceeded only by Cologne and Nuremberg. As we shall see in chapter 1, it was a major center during the Reformation for the printing and reprinting of Luther's works, outproduced only by Wittenberg, Augsburg, and Nuremberg.[14] Since I am interested in the media campaign, Wittenberg is obviously not the right place for examining the impression Luther made on his *reading* public since Luther was available to them in the flesh. Among the remaining major centers, I chose Strasbourg over Augsburg and Nuremberg because of the fine bibliographies by Miriam Chrisman and Josef Benzing that make the study of the Strasbourg press easier than for any other major city of the Holy Roman Empire.[15]

It should be stressed, however, that it is the pamphlets that are the "heroes" of this account, not Strasbourg or her printers, not even the various authors of the pamphlets. I am using Strasbourg as a filter, not a focus. For those interested in the history of Strasbourg's printing industry, Miriam Usher Chrisman's fine *Lay Culture, Learned Culture: Books and Social Change in Strasbourg, 1480–1599*[16] is the book to read. Similarly with the authors of the various pamphlets, who are identified in the text but rarely described. Most readers would have known little or nothing about the biographies of the various authors. They would have known only what the authors chose to reveal in the pamphlets themselves, itself an important part of the argument I develop in subsequent chapters. In being faithful to the crucial point of limited information, I do not dwell on the authors or their background.

AN OVERVIEW

After establishing the dimensions of the Evangelical and Catholic propaganda efforts in chapter 1 and situating Luther's own extraordinary contribution into this larger context, the focus turns to the earliest years of the public discussion and debate. Chapter 2 examines the first impression readers were likely to have received from Luther's earliest Strasbourg publications. While pastoral and devotional for the most part, these early treatises nevertheless offered a serious challenge to traditional clerical authority. They also laid the foundation for the special charisma that Luther later enjoyed, establishing him in the public eye first as an earnest and constructive pastor and man of the Bible concerned above all for the religious well-being of the laity. Luther made his appearance in the vernacular press as the angry critic of the papacy only after this first impression had been well established.

When we speak of the message that readers were *likely* to have received from Luther's early vernacular publications, the qualification "likely" is crucial. When we deal with the issue of reception—how people understood what the press had to say about Martin Luther and his message—we rarely have access to the final recipients of the message. Most *heard* the message, and preaching and conversation are ephemeral. Even of those who read his message as it came from the presses, most never put their reaction into a form that historians today can read, except perhaps in the ambiguity of their action. In this and subsequent chapters we do explore how other publicists at least received and re-presented Luther and his message in their own publications. Even this limited information about reception can tell us a great deal about Luther's message and the transformations it underwent.

In the fall of 1520 Strasbourg readers were offered by their presses for the first time a series of polemical writings by Luther attacking the papacy and many traditional beliefs. Strasbourg readers also were able to purchase for the first time locally produced attacks on Luther and defenses of the traditional faith. Chapter 3 explores the ways in which Luther's image and message took on greater, even contradictory valences. Luther was more than an earnest reformer; he was also a rebel, and his rebellion consisted in no little part in his decision to air matters of religion before the "ignorant common people." The authority of Scripture was juxtaposed to the authority of the pope, Scripture was called upon to discredit the papacy and sustain it, and the public debate itself was cast as a challenge to governing authorities. The medium of multiple copies of cheap agitatory pamphlets reinforced the message of lay involvement, much to the distress and disadvantage of Catholic publicists. These defenders of the old faith found themselves propagating the very views that they deplored.

The trickle of published defenses of Luther became a flood in 1521–1522. As Catholic authors took to the Strasbourg press to de-

nounce and debate with Luther, other authors mounted spirited published defenses and reinforced his attack on the traditional church.
Luther was described and redescribed in special terms, drawn from
popular tradition and Scripture. Gradually, he was gaining that special
charisma that would so shape the direction of Lutheranism and Protestantism generally. All these authors understood themselves as
Luther's defenders and supporters, rallying under the banner of Scripture alone and arrayed against a papal tyranny if not in fact a papal
Antichrist. Nevertheless, the message they associated with his name
showed surprising variety and even contradiction. Chapter 4 examines
this early apologetic literature, explores the growing dimensions of
Luther's public persona, and plumbs the depths of the diversity this
early literature illustrates. As we shall see, Luther's early support in
the Strasbourg press depended in no small part on a fateful misunderstanding of what he was all about.

In September, 1522, Luther published his most influential work, his
translation into German of the New Testament. Concerned by what
he viewed as misreadings of the sacred text, and alarmed by the misunderstandings found among those who professed to be his supporters, Luther arrayed within his *German New Testament* a panoply of
techniques to guide the reading of this crucial text. Chapter 5 surveys
the distribution of this publication and explores the techniques of preface, marginalia, translation, and the like, employed by Luther to
guide the reader. The authority of "Scripture alone" was being subtly
subverted by printing itself. Not only was Luther deploying all the
guides he could to the right understanding of Scripture, he was unwit-
tingly inviting a greater diversity in how the Scriptures were read and
understood by making the New Testament and later the Old Testament available to a large reading public. These developments in no
way invalidate Luther's theological conviction that Scripture interprets
itself, but they do point to a central irony in the Reformation redefinition of doctrinal authority, an irony not lost on its Catholic critics.

Propaganda campaigns work best when all the publicists pull
together and the audience does not receive a contradictory message.
Such is the ideal, but reality often falls short. In the fall of 1524,
Luther's colleague and, as the reading public saw it, collaborator,
Andreas Bodenstein von Karlstadt, issued a series of attacks on Luther
regarding the proper understanding of the Lord's Supper. Chapter 6
examines this public rupture within the Evangelical ranks and the various propagandistic strategies followed by the different participants.

In this internecine battle, Luther's authority within Evangelical circles became itself a matter for debate.

As mentioned, the Catholics were badly outpublished by the Evangelicals during the crucial early years of the Reformation. Nevertheless, they did manage to air some serious charges. Chapter 7 probes one of the most telling accusations lodged by Luther's Catholic opponents: that his writings encouraged disobedience and rebellion and were ultimately responsible for the tragedies of the Peasants' War of 1525. This chapter investigates the ways in which Catholic publicists read Luther's writings in ways other than Luther intended but consonant with their own experiences and outlook.

Finally, the concluding chapter attempts a sketch of the revised narrative that results from the "public perspective" on the early years of the Reformation movement advocated by the preceding seven chapters.

lical and Catholic
nda in the Early
of the Reformation

In the spring of 1524 the Leipzig city council petitioned its duke on behalf of its printers. The printers, the council explained, were complaining bitterly that they were in danger of losing "house, home, and all their livelihood" because they were not allowed "to print or sell anything new that is made in Wittenberg or elsewhere. For that which one would gladly sell and for which there is demand," the council continued, referring to the torrent of Evangelical pamphlets pouring from the presses in Wittenberg and elsewhere, "they are not allowed to have or sell. But what they have in over abundance," namely Catholic treatises, "is desired by no one and cannot even be given away."[1]

The Leipzig printers had reason to complain. The empire-wide production of pamphlets had skyrocketed, increasing more than forty-fold since 1517, with the great bulk of this product promoting the Reformation movement.[2] Since 1521 the Leipzig printers had to watch from the sidelines because their staunchly Catholic duke, Georg the Bearded, would not allow the printing of Evangelical treatises in his lands. The Leipzig printers had gone from being the leading publishers of the leading publicist, Martin Luther, to being onlookers.[3] Instead, they were required to produce Catholic rebuttals that by their own report no one wanted and that could not even be given away. They had been shut out of the West's first full-fledged media campaign and cut off from a financial bonanza.

This chapter investigates what the Leipzig printers were missing out on, the attempt by Evangelical publicists led by Martin Luther to use

14

the recently invented printing press to reach as large an audience as possible to persuade them to overturn the old faith and embrace a new understanding of Christianity and the church. It may strike some as anachronistic to speak of a media campaign in the early sixteenth century. But in means, method, and scope, the Evangelical publishing blitz of the early 1520s has all the earmarks of a modern campaign. Some detailed consideration may persuade.

THE MEDIA

The printing press was invented in the Holy Roman Empire in about 1450, seventy years before the outbreak of the Reformation. By 1500 printing presses existed in over two hundred cities throughout Europe. In the Holy Roman Empire and the Swiss confederacy there were some sixty-two presses by 1520 and Cologne, Nuremberg, Strasbourg, Basel, Wittenberg, and Augsburg were the leading publishing centers. With the exception of Cologne, which remained Catholic, the presses of these towns became the nerve centers of the Evangelical media campaign, flooding the cities of the empire with aggressive little pamphlets advocating radical reform.

The Reformation perfected the use of the small booklet or pamphlet as a tool of propaganda and agitation.[4] Frequently in quarto format— that is, made up of sheets folded twice to make four leaves or eight pages—and without a hard cover, these pamphlets were handy, relatively cheap, readily concealed and transported, and accordingly well suited for delivering their message to a large popular audience. They could be easily transported by itinerant peddlers, hawked on street corners and in taverns, advertised with jingles and intriguing title pages, and swiftly hidden in a pack or under clothing when the authorities made an appearance. They were ideal for circulating a subversive message right under the noses of the opponents of reform.

Contemporaries simply called such a pamphlet a *libellus* or *Büchlein*, a booklet or little book. Their nature is better captured, however, in the German term *Flugschriften*, which means literally "flying writings." This designation was first attested in the late eighteenth century (1788) and was borrowed from the French *feuille volante* or "flying (loose) leaves." Although the content and use of these booklets could and did vary widely, the connotations of a *Flugschrift* or "flying writing"—a piece of printed material that is short, spontaneous, often unpretentious, and transitory—fit most of these writings quite well.

The great majority of these pamphlets were brief. Over half of those identified and microfilmed by the Tübingen Flugschriften project under the direction of Hans-Joachim Köhler were less than eight leaves in length—two quarto sheets making sixteen pages. The average was about sixteen leaves—four sheets folded in quarto format to make thirty-two pages. A scant quarter of the pamphlets were longer than this, although a few could extend to book length.[5]

In addition to being short, these pamphlets were generally unpretentious and relatively cheap. Although a few of the pamphlets contained multiple woodcuts, most were unadorned except for the title page, which might display a woodcut border or a single woodcut illustration with, perhaps, some relevance to the content of the pamphlet. The handy quarto size, perfect for cheap but still legible type, the small number of sheets, and the modest decoration (if any) meant that these works could be turned out quickly and cheaply by printers. They did not demand the same heavy investment in paper and multiple sets of type that conventional books did. They also took less time to produce and could therefore be sandwiched between larger print jobs and whipped out quickly to respond to changing events. The small size and ease of production also allowed for relatively inexpensive prices. Although the evidence is sketchy at best, Köhler believes that a good estimate of cost would be one or two pennies (Pfennig) per sheet, which would make for a cost of, say, eight pennies for average pamphlets of four sheets yielding up to thirty-two printed pages. This is about a third of a day's wage for a journeyman artisan, equal to the price of a hen, or a kilogram of beef, or a pound of wax, or the cost of a wooden pitchfork—not insignificant, but certainly within reach of the "common man," the pamphlets' intended target.[6]

The propaganda pamphlet was not new, of course, nor was its use by publicists who wished to sway a large popular audience. From the beginnings of printing there was occasion for short publications of this size and format.[7] In the years leading up to the Reformation pamphlets had been used, for example, in an attempt to mobilize the broader German public in support of Emperor Maximilian's policies. The press was also exploited for its propagandistic potential in the so-called Reuchlin affair, which saw many of Germany's humanists locked in a propaganda struggle with those churchmen, mainly Dominicans, who wished to seize and destroy Jewish writings. Both before and during the Reformation, the printing press was used quite

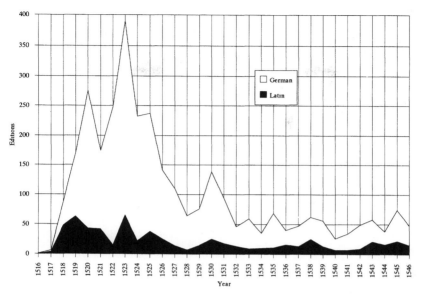

Figure 1.   Editions of Luther's Works by Language

effectively for a propaganda campaign against the Turkish menace in the East.[8] What was new in the Reformation, however, is the sheer scale of the propaganda effort.

Köhler estimates that approximately 10,000 pamphlet editions (first editions and reprints) issued from the presses of the German-speaking lands between 1500 and 1530.[9] Of these almost three-quarters appeared between 1520 and 1526, and most were due to the Reformation movement. Martin Luther alone was responsible for approximately 20 percent of the overall total.

Here are the statistics drawn from the Tübingen project and my own tabulation of the editions of works by Luther (see figure 1 and tables 1 to 4). From 1517 through 1518, the first year of the Reformation movement, there was a 530 percent increase in the production of pamphlets. Production continued to expand rapidly through 1524, increasing nearly eight-fold over this six-year period. Printings of Luther's works also grew rapidly from 87 printings in 1518 to a high of 390 printings in 1523 followed by a gradual decline into the 200 range. The peak year for the overall production of pamphlets came in 1524, which saw the publication of more than 16 percent of the pamphlets produced through the whole thirty-year period from 1501 to

TABLE 1 SUMMARY OF PRINTINGS AND REPRINTINGS OF LUTHER'S WORKS
Published in German-speaking lands, excluding editions of the Bible

	First Editions	Totals (Latin + German)	Latin First Editions	Latin (Totals)	German First Editions	German (Totals)	Percent German of Total Printings
1516	1	1	0	0	1	1	100.0%
1517	3	6	2	4	1	2	33.3%
1518	17	87	11	46	6	41	47.1%
1519	25	170	11	63	14	107	62.9%
1520	27	275	12	40	15	235	85.5%
1521	26	174	6	38	20	136	78.2%
1522	45	248	6	13	39	235	94.8%
1523	55	390	10	44	45	346	88.7%
1524	34	232	4	22	30	210	90.5%
1525	32	237	4	26	28	211	89.0%
1526	26	141	1	20	25	121	85.8%
1527	16	110	1	12	15	98	89.1%
1528	15	64	2	4	13	60	93.8%
1529	12	76	0	6	12	70	92.1%
1530	26	138	3	12	23	126	91.3%
1531	17	94	1	8	16	86	91.5%
1532	12	46	5	13	7	33	71.7%
1533	16	59	0	6	16	53	89.8%
1534	10	35	5	7	5	28	80.0%
1535	19	68	5	10	14	58	85.3%
1536	10	40	5	15	5	25	62.5%
1537	16	47	7	13	9	34	72.3%
1538	18	62	8	22	10	40	64.5%
1539	12	56	3	13	9	43	76.8%
1540	5	26	3	6	2	20	76.9%
1541	7	34	2	4	5	30	88.2%
1542	9	49	2	7	7	42	85.7%
1543	11	58	5	19	6	39	67.2%
1544	7	38	3	14	4	24	63.2%
1545	12	74	3	18	9	56	75.7%
1546	3	48	0	13	3	35	72.9%
Total	544	3183	130	538	414	2645	

All Polemics Against Catholics	German Polemics Against Catholics	Ratio of Reprints to Firsts (Totals)	Ratio of Reprints to Firsts (Latin)	Ratio of Reprints to Firsts (German)
0	0	0.00	0.00	0.00
4	0	1.00	1.00	1.00
38	9	4.12	3.18	5.83
68	28	5.80	4.73	6.64
116	93	9.19	2.33	14.67
114	90	5.69	5.33	5.80
96	88	4.51	1.17	5.03
187	159	6.09	3.40	6.69
89	77	5.82	4.50	6.00
48	41	6.41	5.50	6.54
44	31	4.42	19.00	3.84
40	37	5.88	11.00	5.53
34	30	3.27	1.00	3.62
25	24	5.33	0.00	4.83
84	78	4.31	3.00	4.48
49	47	4.53	7.00	4.38
8	5	2.83	1.60	3.71
23	21	2.69	0.00	2.31
11	8	2.50	0.40	4.60
29	24	2.58	1.00	3.14
7	4	3.00	2.00	4.00
35	29	1.94	0.86	2.78
33	24	2.44	1.75	3.00
24	21	3.67	3.33	3.78
10	9	4.20	1.00	9.00
25	22	3.86	1.00	5.00
21	20	4.44	2.50	5.00
11	5	4.27	2.80	5.50
8	4	4.43	3.67	5.00
40	30	5.17	5.00	5.22
30	23	15.00	0.00	10.67
1351	1081	4.85	3.14	5.39

TABLE 2　PRINTINGS AND REPRINTINGS OF LUTHER'S WORKS
Published in German-speaking lands, excluding editions of the Bible

	1516–1517	1518–1524	1525–1529	1530–1534	1535–1539	1540–1544	1545–1546	Totals 1518–1544	Lifetime Totals 1516–1546
All Printings and Reprintings									
In German	3	1310	560	326	200	155	91	2551	2645
In Latin	4	266	68	46	73	50	31	503	538
Total (German + Latin)	7	1576	628	372	273	205	122	3054	3183
% in German of Total (For Each Time Interval)	42.9%	83.1%	89.2%	87.6%	73.3%	75.6%	74.6%	83.5%	83.1%
Anti-Catholic Printings and Reprintings									
In German	0	544	163	159	102	60	53	1028	1081
In Latin	4	164	28	16	26	15	17	249	270
Total (German + Latin)	4	708	191	175	128	75	70	1277	1351
% in German of Total (For Each Time Interval)	0.0%	76.8%	85.3%	90.9%	79.7%	80.0%	75.7%	80.5%	80.0%

1530. The crucial early years of the Reformation, 1520 to 1526, saw almost three-quarters (73.9 percent) of the total produced in the thirty-year period. Over six thousand editions appeared in this seven-year period, representing conservatively over 6.6 million copies. "The average level of annual production during these seven years was almost four times as high as during the years 1518/19 and 55 times higher compared to the period pre-dating 1518," Köhler observes,[10] adding, significantly, that the production of pamphlets fell off after 1525–1526 but nevertheless remained at a level "almost twice as high as in 1518/19 and more than 20 times higher than before 1518."[11] In other words, the supply of pamphlets continued to be more than adequate to reach a large audience with its message of advocacy.

This outpouring of pamphlets possesses one other characteristic that is decisive for its designation as a media campaign: the drastic turn to the vernacular. Only a small fraction of the population in sixteenth-century Germany could read, and an even smaller fraction could read Latin. So Latin publications were addressed to a relatively tiny learned audience, made up primarily of clerics and members of the learned professions. Vernacular publications could still be read by clerics and learned professionals, but they were also accessible to laity literate in the vernacular. Accordingly, when learned authors wrote controversial treatises in the vernacular, they had a relatively popular audience as their target. We shall have reason to return to this point when we consider the Evangelical and Catholic publicists and their respective audiences. Suffice it to note here that the early years of the Reformation movement saw a massive publication effort in the vernacular. As Köhler shows, the number of pamphlets written in German rose seven-fold from 1519 to 1521, and the proportion of German to Latin pamphlets completely reversed itself, going from about three Latin pamphlets published for every German one to three German pamphlets for every Latin one.[12] In the following year the presses of the empire put out nine German pamphlets for every one Latin pamphlet. Equally telling are the figures for the printing of Luther's publications.[13] In 1518 not quite half of the printings were in German. In 1519 this figure rose to over six in ten, then in 1520 and 1521 around eight in ten, and for the rest of the decade around nine in ten.

It is the magnitude of the effort, and its overwhelming use of the vernacular, that justifies designating this the West's first large-scale media campaign.

TABLE 3   EDITIONS OF LUTHER'S WORKS IN LATIN AND
GERMAN BY CITY OF PUBLICATION
Published in German-speaking lands

	1516–1520	1521–1525	1526–1530
Northern and Central Cities			
Wittenberg	113	300	189
Nuremberg	39	89	100
Erfurt	4	161	41
Leipzig	156	15	8
Subtotal	312	565	338
% of Total Editions (For Each Time Interval)	57.9%	44.1%	63.9%
Southern Cities			
Augsburg	125	272	44
Strasbourg	31	150	25
Basel	40	73	7
Subtotal	196	495	76
% of Total Editions (For Each Time Interval)	36.4%	38.6%	14.4%
Subtotal of Top Seven Publishing Centers	508	1060	414
% of Total Editions (For Each Time Interval)	94.2%	82.7%	78.3%
Other Cities	31	221	115
% of Total Editions (For Each Time Interval)	5.8%	17.3%	21.7%
Total Editions	539	1281	529
% of Total Editions Printed in Luther's Lifetime	16.9%	40.2%	16.6%
Cumulative % of Total Editions Printed in Luther's Lifetime	16.9%	57.2%	73.8%

1531–1535	1535–1540	1541–1546	Totals 1516–1546	Percent of Total
181	142	132	1057	33.2%
45	23	34	330	10.4%
14	5	2	227	7.1%
1	7	21	208	6.5%
241	177	189	1822	57.2%
79.8%	76.6%	62.8%	57.2%	
10	13	26	490	15.4%
6	12	16	240	7.5%
2	3	6	131	4.1%
18	28	48	861	27.0%
6.0%	12.1%	15.9%	27.0%	
259	205	237	2683	84.3%
85.8%	88.7%	78.7%	84.3%	
43	26	64	500	15.7%
14.2%	11.3%	21.3%	15.7%	
302	231	301	3183	100%
9.5%	7.3%	9.5%	100%	
83.3%	90.5%	100%		

TABLE 4 EDITIONS OF LUTHER'S WORKS IN GERMAN BY
CITY OF PUBLICATION
Published in German-speaking lands

	1516–1520	1521–1525	1526–1530
Northern and Central Cities			
Wittenberg	74	266	176
Nuremberg	38	81	92
Erfurt	4	156	41
Leipzig	92	13	7
Subtotal	208	516	316
% of Total Editions in German (For Each Time Interval)	53.9%	45.3%	66.5%
Southern Cities			
Augsburg	109	266	43
Strasbourg	27	117	13
Basel	25	41	6
Subtotal	161	424	62
% of Total Editions in German (For Each Time Interval)	41.7%	37.3%	13.1%
Subtotal of Top Seven Publishing Centers	369	940	378
% of Total Editions in German (For Each Time Interval)	95.6%	82.6%	79.6%
Other Cities	17	198	97
% of Total Editions in German (For Each Time Interval)	4.4%	17.4%	20.4%
Total Editions in German	386	1138	475
% of Total Editions Printed in Luther's Lifetime	14.6%	43.0%	18.0%
Cumulative % of Total Editions Printed in Luther's Lifetime	14.6%	57.6%	75.6%

1531–1535	1535–1540	1541–1546	Totals 1516–1546	Percent of Total
154	102	105	877	33.2%
42	16	31	300	11.3%
14	5	2	222	8.4%
1	6	20	139	5.3%
211	129	158	1538	58.1%
81.8%	79.6%	69.9%	58.1%	
10	13	22	463	17.5%
6	5	12	180	6.8%
1	1	1	75	2.8%
17	19	35	718	27.1%
6.6%	11.7%	15.5%	27.1%	
228	148	193	2256	85.3%
88.4%	91.4%	85.4%	85.3%	
30	14	33	389	14.7%
11.6%	8.6%	14.6%	14.7%	
258	162	226	2645	100%
9.8%	6.1%	8.5%	100%	
85.3%	91.5%	100%		

THE EVANGELICAL PUBLICISTS

In the course of his dissertation on Andreas Bodenstein von Karlstadt, Alejandro Zorzin identified the leading eighteen Evangelicals publishing pamphlets in German during the early years of the Reformation movement (1518 to 1525).[14] In the order of vernacular publications through 1525, both first editions and reprints, Zorzin's statistics, reproduced in table 5, are quite revealing.[15]

The first thing to note from table 5 is the preponderance of clergy. Of the eighteen leading publicists only four were laity: Philipp Melanchthon (who nevertheless taught theology at Wittenberg), Hans Sachs, Ulrich von Hutten, and Hartmuth von Cronberg. Sachs was a shoemaker and *Meistersänger*, and Hutten and Cronberg, disaffected

TABLE 5   MAJOR EVANGELICAL PUBLICISTS, 1518–1525

	German Editions	Total Printings and Reprintings of German Editions
Martin Luther	219	1465
Andreas Bodenstein von Karlstadt	47	125
Urbanus Rhegius	28	77
Philipp Melanchthon	23	71
Huldrych Zwingli	34	70
Johann Eberlin von Günzburg	36	62
Wenzeslaus Linck	26	53
Hans Sachs	15	51
Heinrich von Kettenbach	9	45
Johannes Bugenhagen	14	45
Johann Oecolampadius	19	42
Jakob Strauss	16	42
Ulrich von Hutten	18	41
Hartmuth von Cronberg	15	32
Thomas Müntzer	10	18
Wolfgang Capito	8	14
Balthasar Hubmaier	7	12
Martin Bucer	6	7

SOURCE: Based on Alejandro Zorzin, *Karlstadt als Flugschriftenautor*, Gottinger Theologische Arbeiten, vol. 48 (Gottingen: Vandenhoeck & Ruprecht, 1990), 24.

nobles. In general the authors of the flood of pamphlets were also members of the learned elite. Even most of the pamphlets that purported to be by a "poor unlearned god-fearing layman" were in fact by learned authors, frequently clerics.[16] This pretense is itself revealing because it indicates how, for a few crucial years, the elite not only attempted to reach a broad audience but found it advantageous to pretend that they were speaking for the very audience they were trying to reach.

As Zorzin's statistics show, Martin Luther dramatically outpublished the other Evangelicals in the vernacular during this crucial period. The period 1518 to 1525 saw over eleven times as many printings of Luther's vernacular works as of the next nearest "competitor," Karlstadt. Even the combined production of the other seventeen authors (807 editions) is exceeded by Luther almost two to one. Although I strongly suspect that Luther was outnumbered by the combined total of all Evangelical pamphlets published during this period,[17] there can be no doubt that his was still the dominant voice. This dominance justifies, I believe, a closer statistical look at the printing and reprinting of Luther's works.[18]

The most massive printing and reprinting of Luther's works came in the pioneering years of the Reformation movement. Half of the lifetime printings appeared by 1525 and three-quarters by 1530. This is not to minimize the astonishing productivity of the last fifteen years, but only to put it in perspective. Over eighteen hundred printings of works by Luther had flowed from the empire's presses by the end of 1525. More than an additional five hundred printings had appeared by the end of the decade. Eighty-five percent of these publications were in German. It is also worth noting that two of every five printings through 1525 and one in three through 1530 were sermons, not polemics or theological treatises. The market was seeking out edifying accessible publications. As figure 1 and tables 1 to 4 show, the period of maximum printing and reprinting was the half decade 1520 to 1525. This fact is also reflected in the ratio of reprints to first editions. The ratio was remarkably strong through 1525, with an average of almost six reprints for every first edition. It declined fairly dramatically after 1525, suggesting a waning interest in Luther's works among the buying public. The period 1526 to 1546 averaged only a bit over three reprints for every first edition.[19]

The period of maximum reprints coincided with the period of maximum geographic appeal, measured by where works were reprinted.[20]

In the pioneering years of the Reformation movement (1516 through 1525) over a third of the printings occurred in southern cities, especially Augsburg, Strasbourg, and Basel (see tables 3 and 4). After 1525 Luther became increasingly a regional author, writing largely for central and northern Germany. The printings in southern cities dropped to between a half and a third of what they had been during the heyday of the Reformation movement. The period from 1526 to 1535 also witnessed the fiercest controversy over the Lord's Supper, when the religious leaders of Strasbourg, Augsburg, and Basel were locked in an often vitriolic quarrel with Luther over the proper understanding of Christ's presence in the Supper. Basel, an early and enthusiastic center for the printing of Luther's works, did not join the Wittenberg Concord in 1536 that ended the quarrel between Luther and the south German cities of Strasbourg, Augsburg, and several others. In fact, Basel ended up sheltering Andreas Bodenstein von Karlstadt, Luther's first opponent in the quarrel over the Lord's Supper, until his death in 1541. It is not surprising, then, that after 1525 Basel effectively ceased to publish Luther, especially in German.

But the period after 1525 lies largely outside the ambit of this study. For the crucial early years of the Reformation movement, Luther clearly and decisively dominated the presses of all the German-speaking lands. Since a successful media campaigned normally requires a fairly consistent message, Luther's dominance within the Evangelical publishing effort may have helped provide this essential coherence. In addition, the other publicists saw themselves in substantial agreement with Luther, and often loudly announced their support for his position. As we shall see in subsequent chapters, they were partly mistaken about this, but their intent is still significant. They *thought* that they were all saying much the same thing and attempted as best they could to reinforce each other's message. The divergence only became apparent in late 1524, when splits in the Evangelical ranks were opened by the press to public view, delighting Catholics and distressing Evangelicals throughout the German-speaking lands. It was after this split became apparent to all that reprints of Luther significantly declined and became increasingly restricted to northern and central cities of the empire (see figure 1 and tables 1 through 4).

THE CATHOLIC PUBLICISTS

One of the most striking characteristics of the Evangelical media campaign in the early years of the Reformation is the extent to which the

Evangelical publicists operated almost unopposed. In fact, Catholic publicists were unable to offer a large-scale and credible response to the Evangelical barrage until years if not decades after the Reformation movement got underway.[21] Some statistics should makes this clear.[22]

Comparative statistics based on incomplete data can only be suggestive. Nevertheless, a simple comparison between the vernacular editions of the Catholic publicists and the output of one Evangelical, Martin Luther, suggests the wildly unequal battle for the hearts and minds of literate laity in the first decades of the Reformation (compare table 2 with tables 6 and 8). Over the period 1518 to 1544, Luther's publications (that is, printings and reprintings of his works in German, excluding Bible translations) numbered at least 2551. For the same period the Catholic publicists produced 514 printings (or 542 if all undated printings are to be counted within this time span). In stark terms this translates into about five printings of Luther for every Catholic printing. If consideration is restricted to works by Luther that contained clear anti-Catholic material (that is, if nonpolemical works and polemical works directed exclusively against other Evangelicals are excluded), the ratio drops to about five to three (875 for Luther to 514 for the Catholics), a much lower but still striking difference in output. And of course Luther was seconded by a number of other prolific Evangelical authors. Chapter 3 offers some reasons for the disparity between the publishing effort of Catholics and Evangelicals.

The geographic distribution of Catholic printings presents some additional striking patterns on the matter of influence. Since the shipment of books and treatises was costly and could add substantially to the price of a work, treatises often spread geographically by reprinting. It was normally cheaper, especially for vernacular treatises, to reprint a work in a distant town than to send a large shipment from the place of original publication. This is not a hard and fast rule, and so conclusions based on this assumption must be tentative. Nevertheless, place of publication is not an unreasonable measure of range of influence of a publication.

If the data are broken down geographically and then chronologically, we find the following development (see tables 7 and 8). During the initial years of the Reformation movement (1518–1524), Catholic controversial literature was published in a wide variety of centers, including cities such as Strasbourg and Augsburg, which were later to become Evangelical. Half of these works were in Latin. As the Reformation advanced and Evangelical cities prohibited the publication of

TABLE 6   CATHOLIC CONTROVERSIAL LITERATURE
Published in German-speaking lands

	n.d.	1518–1524	1525–1529	1530–1534	1535–1539	1540–1544	1545–1549	1550–1555	Totals 1518–1555
In German	28	122	188	110	94	34	53	67	696
% of Total (1518–1555)	4.0%	17.5%	27.0%	15.8%	13.5%	4.9%	7.6%	9.6%	100%
In Latin	46	174	194	137	142	111	144	119	1067
% of Total (1518–1555)	4.3%	16.3%	18.2%	12.8%	13.3%	10.4%	13.5%	11.2%	100%
Total (German + Latin)	74	296	382	247	236	145	197	186	1763
% of Total (1518–1555)	4.2%	16.8%	21.7%	14.0%	13.4%	8.2%	11.2%	10.6%	100%
% in German (For Each Time Interval)	37.8%	41.2%	49.2%	44.5%	39.8%	23.4%	26.9%	36.0%	39.5%

Catholic polemical works, two printing centers came to dominate the production of Catholic controversial literature: the western, Rhenish city of Cologne (assisted slightly by its southern neighbor, Mainz) and the two eastern printing centers of Ducal Saxony: Leipzig and Dresden. From 1525 to 1539, when Ducal Saxony turned Evangelical, these two centers accounted for about half of all Catholic controversial literature in general and half of Catholic controversial literature in German. Cologne and Mainz, two ecclesiastical centers, continued to produce works largely for a learned audience; less than a sixth of the controversial works they produced were in German. By contrast, Leipzig and Dresden in the lay principality of Ducal Saxony issued more than three German treatises for every two in Latin. Nevertheless, overall production of controversial literature in German steadily declined throughout the period.

In 1539 the Catholic Duke Georg of Albertine Saxony died; his principality turned Evangelical and Catholicism lost its eastern printing center. Shut off from the presses of Leipzig and Dresden, Catholic publicists turned to Cologne, Mainz, and Igolstadt. Mainz, a minor center up to this point, began producing works in fairly large numbers with about a quarter of the production in German. Ingolstadt, too, began producing in greater numbers with about a fifth of the production in German. But overall, German production still continued to decline. It was not until mid-century that this trend reversed and Catholic controversial writers increased their production of vernacular works.

It is striking that it was a lay principality, Ducal Saxony, and not an ecclesiastical center such as Cologne, that contributed most to the effort to reach a broad, lay audience. In the decade of the 1530s, while Cologne's presses were producing almost exclusively for a learned elite (85 percent of their production was in Latin), over 50 percent of the *total* output of controversial literature in the vernacular for all of Germany flowed from the presses of Leipzig and Dresden! This is no statistical fluke. For the whole period, 1518 to 1555, Leipzig and Dresden accounted for over a quarter of the vernacular printings, despite the fact that not a single Catholic work in the vernacular was published after 1539. At least two factors were at work here. On the one hand, there was the influence both of the patronage of Ducal Saxony's staunch Catholic ruler, Duke Georg, and of the individual efforts of several publicists, especially Johann Cochlaeus. On the other, there was the indifference or even hostility in Catholic ecclesiastical circles towards addressing the laity on religious issues.

TABLE 7 CATHOLIC CONTROVERSIAL LITERATURE IN LATIN AND GERMAN BY CITY OF PUBLICATION
Published in German-speaking lands

	n.d.	1518–1524	1525–1529	1530–1534	1535–1539
Eastern Cities					
Leipzig	7	49	38	58	74
Dresden	2	11	24	26	14
Subtotal	9	60	62	84	88
% of Total (For Each Time Interval)	12.2%	20.3%	16.2%	34.0%	37.3%
Western Cities					
Cologne	4	23	79	62	61
Mainz	0	1	9	7	6
Subtotal	4	24	88	69	67
% of Total (For Each Time Interval)	5.4%	8.1%	23.0%	27.9%	28.4%
Subtotal of Eastern and Western Cities	13	84	150	153	155
% of Total (For Each Time Interval)	17.6%	28.4%	39.3%	61.9%	65.7%
Periphery					
Ingolstadt	0	16	11	9	5
Augsburg	2	22	9	21	9
Subtotal	2	38	20	30	14
% of Total (For Each Time Interval)	2.7%	12.8%	5.2%	12.1%	5.9%
Subtotal of Top Six Publishing Centers	15	122	170	183	169
% of Total (For Each Time Interval)	20.3%	41.2%	44.5%	74.1%	71.6%
Other Cities	11	105	115	34	37
% of Total (For Each Time Interval)	14.9%	35.5%	30.1%	13.8%	15.7%
No Place	48	69	97	30	30
% of Total (For Each Time Interval)	64.9%	23.3%	25.4%	12.1%	12.7%
Total	74	296	382	247	236
% of Total (1518–1555)	4.2%	16.8%	21.7%	14.0%	13.4%

1540–1544	1545–1549	1550–1555	Totals 1518–1555	% of Total 1518–1555	Totals 1518–1539	% of Total 1518–1539
0	1	0	227	12.9%	219	18.9%
0	0	0	77	4.4%	75	6.5%
0	1	0	304	17.2%	294	25.3%
0.0%	0.5%	0.0%	17.2%		25.3%	
31	59	69	388	22.0%	225	19.4%
40	57	42	162	9.2%	23	2.0%
71	116	111	550	31.2%	248	21.4%
49.0%	58.9%	59.7%	31.2%		21.4%	
71	117	111	854	48.4%	542	46.7%
49.0%	59.4%	59.7%	48.4%		46.7%	
41	44	28	154	8.7%	41	3.5%
2	8	7	80	4.5%	61	5.3%
43	52	35	234	13.3%	102	8.8%
29.7%	26.4%	18.8%	13.3%		8.8%	
114	169	146	1088	61.7%	644	55.5%
78.6%	85.8%	78.5%	61.7%		55.5%	
15	19	28	364	20.6%	291	25.1%
10.3%	9.6%	15.1%	20.6%		25.1%	
16	9	12	311	17.6%	226	19.5%
11.0%	4.6%	6.5%	17.6%		19.5%	
145	197	186	1763	100%	1161	100%
8.2%	11.2%	10.6%	100%		65.9%	

TABLE 8 CATHOLIC CONTROVERSIAL LITERATURE IN GERMAN BY CITY OF PUBLICATION
Published in German-speaking lands

	n.d.	1518–1524	1525–1529	1530–1534	1535–1539
Eastern Cities					
Leipzig	2	23	25	32	38
Dresden	2	6	21	24	11
Subtotal	4	29	46	56	49
% of Total (For Each Time Interval)	14.3%	23.8%	24.5%	50.9%	52.1%
Western Cities					
Cologne	0	1	15	7	7
Mainz	0	0	1	3	3
Subtotal	0	1	16	10	10
% of Total (For Each Time Interval)	0.0%	0.8%	8.5%	9.1%	10.6%
Subtotal of Eastern and Western Cities	4	30	62	66	59
% of Total (For Each Time Interval)	14.3%	24.6%	33.0%	60.0%	62.8%
Periphery					
Ingolstadt	0	3	6	6	2
Strasbourg	0	31	6	0	0
Augsburg	2	8	3	8	2
Subtotal	2	42	15	14	4
% of Total (For Each Time Interval)	7.1%	34.4%	8.0%	12.7%	4.3%
Subtotal of Top Seven Publishing Centers	6	72	77	80	63
% of Total (For Each Time Interval)	21.4%	59.0%	41.0%	72.7%	67.0%
Other Cities	3	18	44	11	16
% of Total (For Each Time Interval)	10.7%	14.8%	23.4%	10.0%	17.0%
No Place	19	32	67	19	15
% of Total (For Each Time Interval)	67.9%	26.2%	35.6%	17.3%	16.0%
Total	28	122	188	110	94
% of Total (1518–1555)	4.0%	17.5%	27.0%	15.8%	13.5%

1540–1544	1545–1549	1550–1555	Totals 1518–1555	% of Total 1518–1555	Totals 1518–1539	% of Total 1518–1539
0	0	0	120	17.2%	118	23.0%
0	0	0	64	9.2%	62	12.1%
0	0	0	184	26.4%	180	35.0%
0.0%	0.0%	0.0%	26.4%		35.0%	
5	18	9	62	8.9%	30	5.8%
11	14	22	54	7.8%	7	1.4%
16	32	31	116	16.7%	37	7.2%
47.1%	60.4%	46.3%	16.7%		7.2%	
16	32	31	300	43.1%	217	42.2%
47.1%	60.4%	46.3%	43.1%		42.2%	
8	12	16	53	7.6%	17	3.3%
0	0	0	37	5.3%	37	7.2%
1	0	3	27	3.9%	21	4.1%
9	12	19	117	16.8%	75	14.6%
26.5%	22.6%	28.4%	16.8%		14.6%	
25	44	50	417	59.9%	292	56.8%
73.5%	83.0%	74.6%	59.9%		56.8%	
3	6	11	112	16.1%	89	17.3%
8.8%	11.3%	16.4%	16.1%		17.3%	
6	3	6	167	24.0%	133	25.9%
17.6%	5.7%	9.0%	24.0%		25.9%	
34	53	67	696	100%	514	100%
4.9%	7.6%	9.6%	100%		73.9%	

Duke Georg of Saxony appears to have understood and exploited the press in the Catholic cause more than any other Catholic ruler, including the various ecclesiastical princes. An author of several controversial treatises himself, he also supported the efforts of other publicists.[23] Two of his chaplains, Hieronymous Emser (1478–1527) and Johannes Cochlaeus (1479–1552), made major contributions to the controversial effort, and it seems likely that it was Cochlaeus's published defense of Catholicism that especially recommended him to Duke Georg (and to Emser himself) as Emser's replacement in the post. Cochlaeus in turn, although not without considerable personal sacrifice and numerous pleas for financial assistance to often indifferent Catholic rulers, subsidized the printing of various other Catholic publicists including the Benedictine abbot of Altzelle, Paulus Bachmann (1465–1538), Georg Witzel (1501–1573), who converted to Protestantism for a time and then returned to Catholicism, and the Dominican Johannes Mensing (1480–1541/47).[24]

Not only did one lay principality dominate the Catholic controversial effort in the vernacular, a handful of authors, most of them patronized by Duke Georg, accounted for nearly half of the printings from 1518 to 1555. Witzel, Cochlaeus, Emser, the Ingolstadt theologian Johannes Eck (1486–1543), the Dominican Petrus Sylvius (ca. 1470–1536), and the Franciscan theologian, jurist, and satirist Thomas Murner (1475–1537) produced nearly half of the vernacular printings for this period (see table 9). In all this Witzel and Cochlaeus, both supported by Duke Georg, were the most significant actors. Witzel's out-

TABLE 9   MAJOR CATHOLIC CONTROVERSIALISTS
WRITING IN GERMAN

	Number of Publications 1518–1539	Percentage of Total Catholic Publishing Effort 1518–1539	Number of Publications 1518–1555	Percentage of Total Catholic Publishing Effort 1518–1555
Cochlaeus	67	12.4%	74	10.6%
Eck	38	7.0%	46	6.6%
Emser	37	6.8%	38	5.5%
Murner	29	5.4%	29	4.2%
Sylvius	33	6.1%	33	4.7%
Witzel	47	8.7%	89	12.8%
Others	291	53.7%	387	55.6%
Total	542	100%	696	100%

put accounted for one out of every eight printings from 1518 to 1555. Cochlaeus was second with one printing of every ten. For the period 1518 to 1539, when Duke Georg died and Albertine Saxony turned Evangelical, Cochlaeus was the leading publicist with one out of eight printings. For this same period he accounted for over 20 percent of the literature issuing from Leipzig and Dresden. As already mentioned, Cochlaeus also subsidized the printing of a number of other authors' works.

Were it not for the efforts of Duke Georg of Albertine Saxony and his stable of publicists, the Evangelical media campaign would have been almost unopposed in the vernacular. As it was, the Evangelicals still dominated the presses for several decades. This dominance helps explain the rapid and successful spread of the Reformation.

THE AUDIENCE

"The Reformation was an urban event." Such is the judgment of the historian A. G. Dickens, summing up a wealth of recent scholarship.[25] But to the extent the Reformation was an urban event, it was a minority event as well. About 10 percent of the population of the Holy Roman Empire lived in cities that ranged in size from about fifty thousand inhabitants for a city such as Nuremberg to around two thousand inhabitants, a more typical size for the great majority of towns and cities. These were obviously not the great metropolises we are familiar with today. As is often the case even in major shifts in Western history, the great bulk of the population did not—at least at first—participate actively in the change. It was activists, first of all in the city but also, as recent scholarship has shown,[26] in the countryside, who propagated or opposed the Reformation.

More than an urban event, the Reformation was an *oral* event. Even within the cities, where the literacy rate of perhaps 30 percent greatly exceeded the overall literacy rate of perhaps 5 percent, most urban inhabitants learned of the Evangelical message from sermons and conversation rather than from books, pamphlets, or even pictorial propaganda. So what does it mean with literacy rates so low to speak of the "first Western mass media campaign"? To get a handle on this question we need to explore the issue of literacy itself in sixteenth-century Germany as well as the "two-stage communication process," discussed by the Köhler,[27] by which pamphlets influenced "opinion leaders" such as preachers, teachers, and government officials who in turn passed the message[28] orally to much larger numbers of people.

Obviously only the literate could read these pamphlets for themselves.[29] It has been estimated that overall literacy in Germany in the early sixteenth century was around 5 percent. Although literacy rates were higher in the cities, perhaps in the area of 30 percent for men, cities themselves enclosed no more than 10 percent of the empire's population. In other words, those learned in Latin were a minority among the literate; the literate were a minority within the cities; and the cities enclosed a minority among the empire.[30] The Reformation, then, was a "minority phenomenon," and the audience for the views of the learned may have been small indeed.

These simple statistics have gone a long way to debunking the romantic or confessional myth that Reformation theology galvanized a whole nation. Much to the good, they have also induced some historians to seek other forms by which the ideas of the learned might have been transmitted, such as sermons and other means of oral transmission, and pictures, rituals, and other forms of nonverbal communication.[31] But these statistics may conceal a more complicated situation in which the printed views of the learned reached a larger audience than the literacy statistics suggest.

While we must recognize that the theological concerns of the learned reached the general population through intermediaries and that the message could be transformed in the process of transmission and reception; nevertheless, we should not make the mistake of thinking that a printed message could reach only those who were able to read. It may be a conceit or at least a naïveté of our modern, literate culture to fail to recognize how well the illiterate could get access to the printed page. One reader could share the fruits of his or her reading with hundreds and even thousands of other people. Miriam Chrisman has shown in the case of Strasbourg that during the crucial period 1520 to 1526, the learned wrote large numbers of vernacular treatises aimed at a more popular audience. These and other pamphlets of the early Reformation are replete with suggestions that the reader share his reading with the illiterate. For example, in the dialogue *Karsthans*, examined in some detail in chapter 4, the characters of Murner and Luther both urge Karsthans to have their books read to him, and the character of Karsthans himself speaks of having his son read the books to him.[32] And when the reader was a preacher, the "multiplier effect" could be large indeed. In his *Christian Apology* of 1523, in which he expounded at length on Luther's teachings, the Strasbourg preacher Mattheus Zell stated that he was now putting in writing what he had already taught orally and at length to more than three thousand people.[33] A treatise such as Luther's 1520 *On the Freedom of a Christian* might see twelve reprintings within a year or two of its publication, representing, say, thirteen thousand copies. But one preacher, such as Mattheus Zell, who read this treatise and incorporated its message into his sermons, could multiply its influence many times over.

Even with this, too much may have been conceded to the skeptics. If we assume conservatively that each printing of a work by Luther numbered one thousand copies, we are talking about an output for Luther alone of 3.1 million copies during the period 1516 to 1546. And this total does not include the numerous whole and partial editions of Luther's Bible translation, which, as we shall see in a later chapter, conveyed Luther's central convictions with particular force. Moreover, Luther was only one Evangelical author, albeit by far the most prolific, producing fully 20 percent of the pamphlet literature of the first three decades of the century.[34] If, for the sake of argument, we assume that for every five treatises that Luther published other Evangelicals published an additional four treatises, which is roughly the ratio found in the city of Strasbourg, then we have another 2.5 million copies. Although Catholics were badly outpublished by the Evangelicals in the vernacular—printers produced about five vernacular treatises by Luther to every one Catholic treatise—Catholic authors still contributed at least another 600,000 copies. This all adds up to a bit over six million copies or one exemplar for every two people in the empire, literate and illiterate, or twenty copies for each literate member of the empire.[35] Publication statistics such as these show that we may need to rethink the whole issue of literacy in the sixteenth century.

I have noted before the importance of vernacular publications for reaching a mass audience. Even though only a tiny fraction of the German-speaking people in the early sixteenth century could read, the fraction that could read Latin was much smaller. The mix of Latin and German publications in the overall publishing effort of both Evangelicals and Catholics should tell us something, therefore, about the audience sought by each group of publicists.

In the crucial early years of the Reformation movement, from 1518 through 1524, only two out of every five Catholic controversial works

—that is, works written against Evangelicals and in defense of the Catholic faith—were in German (see table 6). This rose to nearly half from 1525 to 1529, only to fall again in the subsequent decades. For the full period 1518 to 1555, three out of every five Catholic controversial works were in Latin.

This Catholic effort differed markedly from the Evangelical pattern. Consider Martin Luther's production over a comparable period, 1518 to 1544 (see table 2). While Catholics published three Latin controversial works for every two German ones, the ratio for Luther's works was strikingly different, four German works for every one Latin one. In the crucial period 1518 to 1529, when the battle for the minds of the urban laity was at its hottest, more than 80 percent of the overall printings of Luther's works, and nearly as many of those containing anti-Catholic polemics, were in the vernacular. This and the other statistics for the printing of Luther's works exclude the numerous printings of his German translation of the Bible. For the same crucial period, slightly less than half of the Catholic printings were in German.

This comparison suggests some conclusions about the goals, and perhaps the popularity, of the two groups of publicists. The Evangelicals appear to have targeted their argument to a broad audience, including all literate laity. Catholics, in contrast, may have been addressing a smaller audience of what we might term "opinion leaders" such as clerics, councilors, and rulers. This difference may also reflect the more scholastic background of the Catholic publicists. To be sure, Evangelical vernacular publications may have simply sold better, thus encouraging reprints. Recall the petition of the Leipzig council on behalf of its printers with which this chapter opened.

If we can assume that printers in choosing what they published followed not only their personal religious convictions but also the wishes of the market—they were, after all, in the business to make a profit or they did not stay in the business long—this lopsided dominance by Evangelicals of the vernacular market for controversial literature strongly suggests that the literate laity supported Protestantism in far greater numbers than they supported Catholicism. This says nothing about why they supported Protestantism and preferred Evangelical writings to Catholic, but it makes the preference abundantly clear.[36]

CHAPTER TWO

First Impressions in the Strasbourg Press

In October 1520, the successors to the Schürer printing house in Strasbourg issued a collection of Luther's works in German.[1] Among the sermons and treatises by Luther there was a short pamphlet with the long title, *Defense and Christian Reply of an Honorable Lover of Divine Truth [and] the Holy Scripture To Several Alleged Contradictions, With an Indication Why Doctor Martin Luther's Teaching Should Not Be Rejected as Unchristian But Rather Accepted as Christian.* Its author, an unidentified layman, explained that since he had been criticized for his support of Luther and accused of being a disciple of Luther, he wished to explain why he regarded Luther's teachings as in no way improper, and in fact counted Luther among those for whom Christendom in general and the holy Roman church in particular should properly rejoice as "a special, consoling, well-grounded advocate of the holy faith and propagator of holy, evangelical, Christian teaching."[2] This treatise gives us one of the earliest readings we have of the impression Luther was making in the earliest years of the Reformation movement, the topic of this chapter.[3]

When we moderns turn to Luther's early publications, we read them with a perspective that Luther's contemporaries lacked: we know what happened subsequently and are able, therefore, to distinguish the "revolutionary" from the "traditional." Because we are attracted to the drama of Luther's appearance before Cajetan in Augsburg in 1518, when he refused to submit to the pope's representative, and to his fateful debate with Johann Eck at Leipzig in 1519, when he announced that not only the papacy but councils themselves had erred in matters of doctrine, we tend to read Luther's publications and construct our history of the early Reformation in terms of opposition and division. The coming schism from Rome and the clash of irreconcilable theologies we see adumbrated if not clearly exemplified in these meetings, and this knowledge colors our understanding. We are accordingly inclined to single out the published works that most clearly illustrate and embody this parting of the ways, and we tend to read and evaluate these early works in light of the subsequent history of what we now call the Reformation.

But contemporaries had to understand each event, each publication that came to them, without the benefit of foresight. They placed these events and publications into the world as they understood it at the time they encountered them. They had no way of knowing that their world was shortly to undergo so wrenching a shift that in just a few years their view of religion and its institutions would be radically changed. So changed, in fact, that many would be repulsed by the very attitudes and assumptions that they once took for granted. To recapture that "naïve" reading of Luther's earliest publications, we must bracket away our knowledge of what comes after, and focus our attention on the "first impressions" conveyed by Luther's earliest popular publications.

We shall begin with those publications that appeared in Strasbourg before August 1520, when a new chapter in the history of Luther's publications began. On 26 July 1520 Luther's *On the Papacy at Rome, Against the Highly Famous Romanist in Leipzig* left the printing press in Wittenberg. A month later, shortly after 18 August 1520, *To the Christian Nobility of the German Nation* also left the Wittenberg presses.[4] In these two vernacular treatises Luther announced to the world his rejection of the papacy. Both treatises were subsequently reprinted in Strasbourg and elicited passionate rebuttals by the Franciscan friar and author Thomas Murner. For the first time the magnitude of the disagreement between Luther and Rome became widely apparent, thanks to the printing press. The vernacular polemical battle was engaged, and we shall examine this stage of the conflict in the next chapter. From this point forward, Luther was more than a reformer of piety; he was a rebel. This change profoundly influenced how laity subsequently read and understood his works. But by examining in this chapter the works available up to this watershed, we limit ourselves to the works that likely formed the first impression that interested readers had of Luther and his message.

AN OVERVIEW OF THE PUBLICATIONS THEMSELVES

Before the flood of polemics and controversial works appeared in the Strasbourg press in late 1520, Strasbourg readers would have found almost exclusively pastoral and devotional works by Luther available from the local press.[5] In 1519 one sermon on marriage appeared. Two other sermons, one on Christ's passion, perhaps in two editions, and the other on prayer and processions in Holy Week, appeared either in late 1519 or 1520.[6] In the same year there appeared an edition of Luther's *The Seven Penitential Psalms,* originally published in Wittenberg in 1517, and the *German Theology,* a devotional treatise for which Luther had supplied a preface. Only one work, his *Explanation of Several Articles Attributed to Him by His Opponents,*[7] dealt in any detail with the controversy in which Luther was entangled, and that in a very restrained fashion.

In 1520 there appeared eleven sermons (or nine, if two are dated to 1519)[8] and one sermon collection that included a few other treatises, some with mild polemical content.[9] This collection, first published in Basel in May 1520 and reprinted in Strasbourg in October 1520, duplicated several of the sermons that were also published individually.[10] There also appeared four devotional treatises (and perhaps several that I have classified under polemics could equally count as devotional treatises): another edition of the *German Theology,* two different treatises on confession, and a brief exposition of the Lord's Prayer.[11] Finally there were between nine and twelve treatises dealing with the controversy between Luther and the old faith,[12] some of which could also be classified as devotional works with mild polemical content (for example, *On the Freedom of a Christian,* which appeared in one or two editions,[13] and *Doctor Martin Luther's Appeal or Petition to a Free Christian Council,*[14] which appeared in two editions). *On the Papacy at Rome, Against the Highly Famous Romanist in Leipzig* appeared after 26 June 1520.[15] *To the Christian Nobility of the German Nation* appeared after 18 August 1520 in two to four editions.[16] *On the Babylonian Captivity of the Church* appeared in two or three editions, sometime after 6 October 1520.[17] Only one of these polemics, *Doctor Martin Luther's Answer to the Notice Issued Under the Seal of the Official at Stolpen,*[18] may have appeared before mid-year.[19] The rest appeared well after mid-year (since the *terminus a quo* given is the original publication date in Wittenberg), and five or six in the last quarter of the year. So the vernacular writings published in the Strasbourg press through the first half of 1520 were overwhelmingly devotional and pastoral. This alone is likely to have profoundly shaped Strasbourgeois's first impression of Martin Luther and his ideas.

To whom were these treatises addressed? Clearly, the laity. What was their message? That one should humbly rely on God's promise of forgiveness rather than on one's own allegedly meritorious works. Why may this message have appealed to its lay readers and hearers? Because the message explicitly dignified the spiritual status of the laity at the expense of clerical claims and prerogatives.

THE TREATISES ADDRESSED LAY CONCERNS

Even a simple consideration of these vernacular treatises' topics indicates clearly that they were addressed to the laity.[20] There were sermons on each of the sacraments of most concern to the laity—baptism, marriage, the Eucharist, confession, and extreme unction. One treatise instructed the laity on how to pray the Lord's Prayer and another on how properly to confess. A lay ethical concern, usury, was addressed, and lay activities such as processions and brotherhoods were examined from Luther's new religious perspective. Even the more general treatises—one on the seven penitential psalms, two printings of the *German Theology*, and the two mild polemics—dealt, as we shall see, with lay concerns regarding sacramental and popular piety.[21]

The tone of these pastoral works also indicated that their intended audience was the laity. In these writings Luther was, for the most part, not arguing with or even addressing other theologians. He was laying out his understanding of Christianity for his readers rather than defending it from attack by critics. He explained technical issues in simple terms, undergirded with citations of Scripture, and without benefit of the learned distinctions that graced scholastic sermons and treatises of his age. He largely avoided the vocabulary of theological scholarship or, in the few cases where the technical distinction was important, he patiently defined the term for the laity's benefit. He was, in such cases, "popularizing" the scholastic understanding of various issues as a basis, then, for criticism or outright rejection. Throughout, his writings conveyed a tone of moral earnestness.

Before proceeding to the message of these pamphlets, I should say a few words to possible skeptics. These considerations of topic and tone indicate the audience Luther intended to reach, but in no way guarantee in themselves that he was successful in reaching and engaging laity. Many of the purchasers of these pamphlets were no doubt clergy, some of whom, to be sure, we know by their own testamony turned around and shared the message with their lay parishioners.[22] But the number of printings and reprintings, not only in Strasbourg but elsewhere, indicates that laity as well as clergy had to be buying these works. Since Luther's popularity as an author continued to grow for several years beyond this initial period, the natural inference is that readers were at the very least intrigued by what they read. The subsequent Reformation movements in Strasbourg and other cities, involving as they did at least in the initial years significant numbers of burghers outside the narrow ruling circle, suggest that some of this lay readership was more than just intrigued; they were convinced to act on the messages conveyed by these early works. As we shall see in chapter 4, the lay (and clerical) readership did not necessarily appropriate Luther's message exactly as he intended, but they were engaged by his message and in many cases galvanized into taking action on their understanding of its import.

THE CENTRAL THEOLOGICAL MESSAGE OF THE TREATISES

Two interconnected themes run through most of the early works published in Strasbourg: first, that we must acknowledge our own sinfulness and surrender all reliance on our own works, and, second, that we should trust God and God's promise in Christ as our only source of salvation. A few examples, taken from Luther's earliest Strasbourg treatises, should illustrate this well-known theme. Luther's exposition of the seven penitential psalms, which appeared in Strasbourg in 1519, returned repeatedly to our own sinfulness and wretchedness and our total dependence on God for help, strength, and salvation. Punishment came from God to remind us of our true nature, to make us rightly humble, and to prepare us for God's gracious gift of unmerited forgiveness. A good life, Luther explained, consisted not in outward works and appearance but in a sighing and troubled spirit.[23] Yet while his stress on wretchedness, humility, sinfulness, and submission to deserved punishment understandably dominated this work on penitential psalms, Luther still brought in his second theme, as can be seen in a striking commentary on the seventh penitential psalm.

Not in my righteousness for that is sin and unrighteousness. As he says. Graciously make me true and righteous for I see some who wish to be true and righteous through their own truth and righteousness. Protect me from that! They wish to be something when they in fact are nothing, empty, liars, fools, sinners. It should be noticed here that the little word "your truth" and "your righteousness" does not refer to that by which God is true and righteous, as many think, but refers to the grace by which God makes us true and righteous through Christ, as the Apostle Paul, Romans 1 and 2 and 3, calls the righteousness of God and the truth of God, which is given to us through faith in Christ. In addition, God's truth refers not only to the word but more to the work and fulfillment of his word, which is due to this same grace and mercy. And just as a token or a painted gulden is not a true gulden but only represents one, and is indeed an empty thing and a deception if it is given or considered to be a true gulden. But a proper gulden is the truth and without deception. In such fashion all haughty and holy lives and works and righteousness is in relation to the righteousness and work of the grace of God a mere appearance and a deadly, harmful falseness if they are considered true goods where there is no truth. Rather it is God's [truth] which gives the true, substantial righteousness which is the faith of Christ. For this reason the little word "truth" may also be translated from Hebrew *in fide tue*, that is, in your faith.[24]

To a modern ear sensitive to Luther's 1545 autobiographical account of his breakthrough to a new understanding of God's righteousness, this is a paragraph pregnant with significance, closely paralleling his later description of his Reformation discovery.

In his sermon on prayer and procession during Holy Week, Luther stressed from the outset that one had to trust in God's promise. For a prayer to be truly good and heard, one had to have a promise from God. "From this it follows," Luther advised his readers, "that no one obtains something on account of the worthiness of his or her prayer but only on account of the depths of divine goodness which anticipates all requests and desires through His gracious promise."[25] It was crucial not to doubt God's promise.[26] Above all our prayer to God should not rely on any sense of our worthiness. In fact it was our own sense of unworthiness that, paradoxically, made us worthy to be heard "because we believe that we are unworthy and we confidently venture everything on God's trustworthiness."[27] In his sermon on contemplating Christ's passion, Luther located the promise in baptismal faith. Faith, Luther explained, firmly believed that baptism had established a covenant between us and God. For our part in the covenant, we had to fight against sin. For God's part, God had promised to be merciful to us and not count our sins against us.[28] In his treatise on *How One*

Should Confess, published in Strasbourg in 1520, Luther began with the advice that a Christian should ground his confession "on the greatest and fullest trust in the most merciful promise and pledge of God and should firmly believe that almighty God will mercifully forgive him his sins."[29] These examples could be multiplied many times over.

THE APPEAL OF THE MESSAGE: THE DIGNIFYING OF THE SPIRITUAL STATUS OF THE LAITY

What was it about these treatises that may have appealed to their lay readers and hearers? To this question I must side with the historian Steven Ozment in his argument with Bernd Moeller. There was very little in these treatises that, at least on the face of it, would naturally resonate with late medieval communal ideas in the manner Moeller proposes.[30] On the other hand, there was a great deal that, if put into effect, would "liberate" lay people from a clerical form of piety, as Ozment has argued. Or to put it another way, the major themes of humility and promise provided an explicit rationale for dignifying the spiritual status of the laity at the expense of clerical privilege and authority.[31] Luther repeatedly drew these consequences for his readers and listeners.

Luther particularly stressed the value of ordinary lay activities over clerically prescribed "good works." For example, in his 1519 sermon on marriage Luther insisted that married people could do no better work either for themselves or for Christendom than raise their children well. "There is nothing in pilgrimages to Rome, to Jerusalem, or to Saint James [Compostella], nothing in building churches, endowing masses, or whatever works might be named compared to this one work, [namely] that those who are married bring up their children [well]. That is their straightest road to heaven. Indeed, heaven could not be nearer or better achieved than with this work."[32] This was, moreover, the laity's proper and appointed work. In another early sermon, on meditating on Christ's passion, Luther continued this practice of unfavorably contrasting clerically sponsored works with what he saw as true piety. A person who rightly contemplated Christ's sufferings for a day, an hour, or even a quarter hour did better than to fast a year, pray a psalm daily, or even hear a hundred masses.[33]

Luther also insisted on the essential spiritual equality of laity and clergy. For example, in his sermon on baptism he denied that the vows of chastity, of the priesthood, or of the clergy were more significant or higher than baptism. "For in baptism we all vow the same thing: to slay sin and to become holy through the work and grace of God, to whom we give and sacrifice ourselves, as clay to the potter, and in this no one is better than another. But to live according to this baptism, so that sin can be slain, there can be no one way or estate. . . . Thus it is true that there is no higher, better, or greater vow than the vow of baptism."[34]

Luther also undercut the sacramental authority exercised by the priesthood. Consider, for example, Luther's sermon on the sacrament of penance.[35] In this treatise he contrasted the forgiveness of punishment and the forgiveness of guilt. The former, under the control of the church and addressed in part by indulgences, was relatively insignificant in comparison to the latter, which was solely God's gift and reconciled the human with God.[36] To those who thought they might obtain forgiveness of guilt and the quieting of their hearts through indulgences and pilgrimages, Luther wrote,

> All that is for nought and an error. It makes things much worse because God must himself forgive sin and give the heart peace. Some trouble themselves with many good works, even too much fasting and drudgery, so that some have thereby broken their bodies and ruined their minds, believing that by virtue of their works they could do away with their sins and quiet their hearts.

But both approaches—those who sought indulgences and went on pilgrimages and those who disciplined their bodies with fasting and labor—made the mistake of wanting to do good works before their sins were forgiven, while in fact the contrary was necessary, that "sins must be forgiven before good works can occur."[37] The efficacy of the sacrament depended not on the sacrament itself or any human office or authority but on faith in the promise of God.[38] On this basis Luther concluded that the forgiveness of guilt depended on no human office or earthly power, not even the office and power of pope, bishop, or priest, but solely on the word of Christ and one's own faith in that word.

> For he [Christ] did not want our comfort, our salvation, [or] our trust to be based on a human word or deed but rather solely on himself and his word and deed. The priest, bishop, [and] pope are only servants who hold out to you Christ's word on which you should rely with a solid faith as if on a solid rock. In such fashion the word will sustain you and your sins will thereby necessarily be forgiven. For this reason, too, the word is not to be

honored on account of the priest, bishop, [or] pope but rather the priest, bishop, [or] pope [is to be honored] on account of the word, as those who bring you the word and tidings of your God that you are freed from sins.[39]

Luther argued further that in the sacrament of penance and the forgiveness of guilt, a pope or bishop did no more than the lowliest priest, and that when there was no priest, an individual Christian, even a woman or child, could do as much.[40] Luther qualified his pronouncement with the advice that his readers should not despise the established spiritual orders. Nevertheless, the overall thrust of his argument could not but have had the effect of undercutting clerical authority exercised in the sacrament. Subsequent comments reinforced this impression.[41] That priests reserved absolution for some sins did not make the clerical sacrament any greater or better.[42] The keys were not a power but a service.[43] A priest had sufficient grounds for granting absolution when he saw that the penitent desired it. The priest needed to know no more than that. "I say this," Luther explained,

> so that people love and cherish the most gracious virtue of the keys and not despise [them] on account of misuses by those who with banning, threatening, and harassing do little more than make a virtual tyranny out of such a lovely and comforting authority, as if Christ had established the keys only for their wishes and lordship [and] had no idea of how one should use them.[44]

Luther explicitly questioned the need for the priest to inquire into the extent of the penitent's contrition,[45] insisted that because there was no dependable rule for distinguishing between venial and mortal sins, penitents should not attempt to confess all sins but only clearly mortal sins that were oppressing the penitent's conscience at the time,[46] and that the best satisfaction was not assigned prayers but simply to sin no more.[47] Both the treatise and the sermon obviously simplified confession for the laity and undercut some of the conventional claims of the priesthood regarding their own authority exercised in the sacrament of penance. His treatise *How One Should Confess* made similar points.[48]

The sermon on the ban also undercut many clerical claims and thereby elevated the status and power of the laity over their own spiritual destiny.[49] Luther distinguished between inward, spiritual fellowship on the one hand and external communion on the other. No human being, not even a bishop or pope, could give or take away spiritual fellowship. Rather, God through the Holy Spirit poured this spiritual fellowship into the heart of the human being who believed in the Sacrament.[50] Bishops and popes could, however, cut one off from participation in what Luther termed the "external, bodily, and visible fellowship" of participation in the Sacrament.[51]

For lay people, however, the crucial significance of this distinction rested in Luther's assertion that one could be under the ban and still belong to the spiritual fellowship or communion, and vice versa. In an age when lay people often found themselves under the ban for debt or other reasons that struck them as irrelevant to Christian faith, this assertion was undoubtedly consoling. "It may often happen," Luther remarked,

> that a banned individual will be deprived of the holy Sacrament and also of burial [in consecrated ground], and yet still be inwardly certain and holy in the fellowship of Christ and all the saints, as the Sacrament indicates. On the other hand, there are many who freely enjoy the Sacrament without external ban and yet inwardly are completely estranged and banned from the fellowship of Christ even though they might be buried with gold clothes under the high altar with all show, bells, and singing.[52]

At some length through the rest of the treatise, and with occasional heat, Luther criticized clergy who misused the ban.[53]

Several other treatises of a largely devotional or moral character also dealt, at least in passing, with a few issues of clerical authority. Luther's "Sermon on the Sacrament of the Body of Christ," for example, advocated that a general council should mandate that all Christians receive both the bread and the wine in the Sacrament as the priests currently did.[54] In his morally earnest small sermon on usury, Luther attacked the clerical use of "*Zinskauf*," a form of purchase of an annuity, "in the service of God." "To serve God," Luther explained with some evident exasperation, "means to keep his commands and not steal, take, charge interest, and the like, but rather to live and lend to the needy. Would you tear down such true service of God in order that you might build churches, endow altars, and have [masses] read and sung, none of which God has commanded you [to do]?"[55]

In sum, these early Strasbourg treatises urged readers to rely neither on their own efforts nor on the mediating power of clerics or clerically sponsored works but to trust solely in God and God's promise. They questioned clerical claims to jurisdiction and to power, and specifically to mediation between the laity and God. The clergy were to preach the word of God, and only to that extent could they be considered intermediaries. The overarching message in these writings was that the religious destiny of lay Christians was in God's hands rather than their

own. It certainly was not in clerical hands. The laity were freed from
the standards of clerical piety, freed from such a thoroughgoing reliance on clerical mediation in their relations with God, freed, above
all, from concern about their own worthiness and spiritual efforts.

THE QUESTION OF RECEPTION

This was what was presented and why it might have appealed to the
laity (and sympathetic clergy). Was it, however, the message received?
One measure of reception is the degree to which this message was
picked up and repeated by other publicists. Unfortunately in this regard, it is difficult to measure the influence of these early treatises
apart from the effect of the great vernacular polemics of late 1520
since most of the few treatises published in Strasbourg in 1520 or early
1521 that either characterized Luther or his teachings came after, and
even in response to, the great polemics of the last quarter of the year.
Still, a brief survey is not out of place.

Ulrich von Hutten published a number of treatises in Strasbourg in
the early years of the Reformation.[56] Three of them appeared in
late 1520.[57] In these three treatises, Hutten ferociously attacked the
Roman papacy, the clergy, and various abuses within the church, and
in two of the three Hutten made brief mention of Luther. In the *Complaint and Warning Against the Excessive Unchristian Power of the
Pope at Rome and the Unspiritual Clergy*, Hutten mentioned Luther
only once explicitly, in a marginal note that likened the treatment
afforded both himself and Luther with that meted out to Jan Hus.[58]
The treatise itself was an anticlerical, antipapal poem or song that
accused clergy of everything from gluttony to sexual misconduct, attacked ecclesiastical practices such as indulgences and dispensations,
and advocated a nationalistic attack on the papacy. In his short treatise
*Indication of How the Roman Bishop or Pope Has Acted Against
the German Emperor*, Hutten excerpted various accounts of papal
betrayal of the German emperor and warned the emperor to take heed
of how his predecessors had been treated and not to expect any better
from the current pope. Luther was mentioned only once, on the last
page, when Hutten claimed that his and Luther's writings had to be
acknowledged to benefit and honor the emperor and the whole German nation.[59]

As these brief summaries indicate, Hutten's writings do not help
us much with understanding how Luther's writings may have been

understood by his Strasbourg readers. At the very least, we can
reasonably infer that Hutten himself understood Luther to be an ally
in his fight against Rome and against clerical abuses. But since Luther
was mentioned only twice in these treatises, once in a marginal note in
Complaint and Warning and again in the concluding remarks of *Indication*, it is difficult to demonstrate that other readers would have
made the same identification

On the other end of the spectrum from Hutten, the Franciscan and
satirist Thomas Murner of Strasbourg published five polemical works
against Luther in the waning months of 1520 and early 1521.[60] But
since all of these treatises by Murner responded to polemical works
published by Luther *after* midyear, they cannot really be used to determine how Luther may have been understood in Strasbourg through
mid-1520. Still, it is worth mentioning that Murner did single out for
extensive criticism many of the reforms that we have characterized as
dignifying the spiritual status of the laity at the expense of the
clergy.[61] I shall have considerably more to say about Murner in the
next chapter.

Slightly more useful for our purposes is Laux Gemigger's *To the
Praise of Luther and to the Honor of All Christendom*.[62] Published in
two editions towards the end of 1520 or early in 1521,[63] this verse
treatise praised Luther as "a light of Christendom" chosen by God "to
tell us your divine word." Unfortunately for our purposes, it was never
very specific about what Luther had accomplished except to speak the
"divine truth,"[64] reveal the papal and clerical rascality, teach "good
morals," and question indulgences.[65] At one point, however, Gemigger
suggested that Luther had taught "Christ's teaching," namely, "how
we have turned from good to evil," and had laid out the "teaching of
the evangelists ... without additions." Luther had also explained
"God's word and increased faith in Christ." Luther had driven out the
"evil spirit" (the origin of vices, which taught human laws rather than
God's Word), established different clerical "sects," and attributed un-
warranted power to indulgences in order to deceive people out of their
money. "For this reason Luther was sent by God to teach us God's
word and good morals and to drive out the Antichrist here on earth,
also to see to it that God's word not be fully spoiled and that the
Roman tyranny be recognized, that they should have no kingdom here
on earth.[66]

Readers might have inferred from Gemigger's attacks that Luther
had also criticized noble families for making monks and nuns of their

children and had raised questions about the accumulation of property in noble hands through this action,[67] had attacked the ban, and had challenged clerical greed. "It is the penny's shine," Gemigger explained at one point, "that accounts for the treatment of the pious Luther, who is unjustly and improperly treated because he reveals to us the Roman rascality as well as their great heresy."[68] They even sought Luther's life. "He who now dares to tell the truth must turn himself over to death," Gemigger claimed, explaining, "If speaking kindly makes good friends, then saying the truth makes great enemies. It is because Luther has proclaimed to us the divine truth that people are so hostile towards him."[69] On several occasions Gemigger labeled the papacy the Antichrist and suggested that the clergy needed to be reformed with "cold steel."[70] Gemigger also identified Hutten and Sickingen as supporters both of Luther and of the truth.[71]

The strongest evidence in the early Strasbourg press that at least one lay person received Luther's message much as I have summarized it comes from an anonymous work by the Nuremberg city secretary, Lazarus Spengler.[72] He was the anonymous author of *Why Dr. Martin Luther's Teaching Should Not Be Rejected As Unchristian But Rather Be Regarded As Christian*, with which this chapter began. First published in late 1519 in Augsburg,[73] this defense was reprinted in Strasbourg in October, 1520, in a collection of Luther's works in German.[74] In the work Spengler enumerated six basic reasons for this conclusion that Luther was "a special, consoling, well-grounded advocate of the holy faith and propagator of holy, evangelical, Christian teaching."[75]

First, Luther's teaching and sermons were Christian and wholesome as well as consistent with Christian order and reason because they were based on the Holy Gospel, the prophets, and St. Paul.[76] Second, Spengler would let each reasonable, pious person determine whether Luther's teaching was consistent with Christian order and reason. For himself, Spengler remarked, "No teaching or preaching has seemed more straightforwardly reasonable, and I also cannot conceive of anything that would more closely match my understanding of Christian order as Luther's and his followers' teaching and instruction."[77] Spengler claimed not to be alone in this opinion. "Up to this point," he remarked, "I have also often heard from many excellent highly learned people of the spiritual and worldly estates that they were thankful to God that they lived to see the day when they could hear Doctor Luther and his teaching."[78] Third, Luther's doctrine, teaching, and instruction promoted Christ and salvation rather than Luther's own advantage. The indulgence preachers did just the opposite.[79] Fourth, any reasonable and truthful person who had heard Luther or his followers had to acknowledge that his troubled conscience had been relieved of many scruples and doubtful errors.[80] Fifth, since Luther was a monk, preacher, and doctor and required by his office not to keep silent about Christian teachings but rather to venture even his life on their advocacy, it was proper, appropriate, and necessary for Luther to speak out against indulgences and other errors and scandals of Christendom once he became aware of them.[81] Sixth, and finally, Luther had to the best of his ability and in accordance with his conscience, based his teaching on the gospel set forth in Holy Scripture. He was willing, however, to be better instructed by German or French universities on the basis of the truth, or by papal judgment, or by the church.[82]

It is under points two and four that Spengler asked a number of rhetorical questions that should be of interest to us. Under point two he asked with some heat whether it was not the case that "fairy tale preachers" had disquieted the consciences of "many simply unlearned people," directing them "to rely more on their works than on the grace and love of God." Hadn't these preachers urged people to rely more on external ceremonies such as rosaries, the praying of psalms, pilgrimages, fasting, the lighting of candles, reliance on holy water, and other external works than on faith, more on law than on grace, more on the flesh than on the spirit? "Hadn't these same teachers," Spengler asked, "caused us countless scruples in our hearts simply with the wide-ranging, clumsy institution of confession?"[83]

This led into a sharp criticism of indulgences. Hadn't these teachers, Spengler asked, elevated the indulgence and its utility above grace and the treasure of faith and the blood of Christ? Hadn't they turned indulgences and all the sacraments into a business? In addition, Spengler was ashamed to report, these teachers had sold for money souls in heaven and misled "poor ignorant people" into believing unquestionably that, thanks to the sole power of indulgences, they were freed from their sins and thereby delivered unto salvation.[84]

Hadn't these same preachers put forward so many ecclesiastical laws that they had thereby completely tossed out the commands of Christ? Spengler continued with his rhetorical questions. Wasn't a person who ate meat on Friday considered more reprehensible than an adulterer or blasphemer of God? Spengler added to this indictment the misuse of the ecclesiastical ban.[85] "In my opinion," he concluded,

"Luther has cleaned up these scruples and errors by means of well-grounded Christian references to holy divine scripture so that every reasonable person can easily understand. For this reason, we should more properly commend, thank, and praise him for [what he has done] than to denounce him as a heretic and enemy of the church. And yet except for some shadow boxing nothing solid, based in Holy Scripture, has been offered against [Luther's arguments]." But Luther's opponents tried to use force rather than reasoned arguments to combat him.[86]

Under point four Spengler asked whether "our preachers" had not sought to ensnare consciences by multiplying sins and by offering a false reassurance through indulgences. "In this manner the human being is made more anxious than comforted, more led into doubt than refreshed, more led into excessive fear than into love and trust of God, despite the fact that according to the holy gospel the yoke and way to salvation is completely sweet and wholesome and is to be achieved more through an orderly well-founded trust in God than in these deceptive sermons."[87]

This treatise presented Luther as an opponent of those who advocated external works over an inward trust and reliance on God's grace revealed in Christ. Luther came off, above all, as a critic of indulgences. His criticism was based, Spengler claimed, solely on Scripture. Luther's concern was to reassure consciences troubled by those who advocated external works, a burdensome form of confession, and indulgences for both the living and dead. Luther's opponents responded to Luther with force, Spengler claimed, rather than with reasoned arguments grounded in Scripture.

CONCLUSION

In this age when the hermeneutics of suspicion are almost axiomatic, it may seem hopelessly naive to argue that it was the correspondence between the content of Luther's message and the concerns and interests of laity that best accounts for its appeal. I am persuaded of this, however, by several straightforward considerations. First, as we saw in the last chapter, the publication statistics for Luther's works show large and geographically widespread demand for these early works, and especially for those works that were more pastoral than polemical in nature.[88] Second, as we shall see in subsequent chapters, the issues advocated or attacked in these publications are just those issues Ozment has identified, especially the issue of Christian freedom and the spiritual dignity of lay status. The works by Hutten, Gemigger, Murner, and Spengler illustrate this reception at a very early period in the reform movement. Third, and perhaps most to the point, if one assumes that behavior is a good indirect measure of which ideas people found appealing, then one needs to look at what really changed in the sixteenth century. When life before and after the initial decades of the Reformation is compared, what actually changed corresponded closely (although not, of course, exactly) to those changes that Luther and other reformers had advocated on the basis of their new, learned understanding of Christian theology.[89]

We need to be much more careful than we have in the past to determine what actually was read, how many people read or heard it read, the message contained in these treatises, and—often not the same thing—the message that different readers actually appropriated from their reading or listening. It is perhaps the fourth point—the message actually acquired by different readers or listeners—that is the most important. For the early period of the Reformation movement the evidence for these first impressions is slight. The remarks by other early Strasbourg publicists, although each complicated by a publication after mid-1520, suggest that Luther's message of reliance on God's promise rather than human effort, a reliance that dignified the spiritual status of the laity often at the expense of clerical privilege and authority, got through at least to other publicists. Subsequent chapters will explore the further development of this attractive, and ultimately ambiguous, message.

CHAPTER THREE

The Catholic Dilemma

For almost two years the vernacular press of Strasbourg had been virtually silent on the growing estrangement between Luther and the papacy. The silence came to a strident end in the fall of 1520. In a series of vernacular pamphlets Luther rejected the authority of the papacy, claimed that pope and curia had perpetrated a series of frauds on Christendom, and called for Christendom's liberation from a papal captivity that distorted the sacraments and subordinated the laity to a clerical tyranny. In rebuttal an anonymous author issued a series of counterattacks that portrayed Luther as "the destroyer of the faith of Christ," and as "a seducer of simple Christians,"[1] seeking to overturn all authority in society by inappropriately involving the common people in a debate over traditional belief and practice. The propaganda battle was joined, and at its crux lay the issue of authority: who was to decide the true content and character of Christendom. From the outset the Catholic apologist was at a serious disadvantage in this battle, for both the medium and the message favored the Evangelical position.

By their very nature as objects, vernacular pamphlets were the physical embodiment of a message. Multiplied by the art of printing into hundreds of exact copies, cheap to buy and handy to pass around, these pamphlets were in some sense what they contained: an address to the laity to become involved in an unprecedented way in their own religious destiny. Anyone could buy a pamphlet. And anyone who could read it, or have it read, became a participant in the debate and was asked to take sides. A pamphlet was not privileged communication. It circumvented discussion and decision in narrow circles—it opened to scrutiny papal fiat, conciliar decrees, city council rulings, and princely mandates—and asked the public to make up its own mind. Even if it urged ultimate deference toward hierarchy and authority, as most of these pamphlets in fact did, by presenting the issues to the public it implicitly invited the public into the discussion to a degree unprecedented in Western history.

In Luther's case, there was a congruence between the means—pamphlets addressed to the laity of the empire—and the message—that lay people should not allow the clergy fraudulently to claim that they mediated between the laity and God. By their very nature as an address to a large (and largely lay) audience, they were subversive of the hierarchical views of many contemporaries. And their message reinforced that potential, for it urged an end to the many distinctions that had grown up between members of what were termed the "spiritual" and "worldly" estates, the clergy and the laity.

It is this subversion of traditional views of authority, both by means of pamphlets and by means of the pamphlets' message, that became the target of the Catholic counterattack. Yet by a subtle irony, the very means chosen to rebut Luther—vernacular pamphlets attacking him and his message—undercut the message the authors intended to convey, namely, that it was dangerous and inappropriate to air before the "common people" disputes over religion. By their very existence the Catholic pamphlets did what they argued should not be done.

The rebuttal itself posed a further dilemma, for to refute Luther Catholic controversialists had to describe the position they opposed. The controversialist would of course present Luther's message in unfavorable terms. But even in the most damning of presentations, readers would learn of Luther's radical reformulation of Christian teaching and practice. In the early years of the Reformation movement, Luther needed above all to get his message out. Even a distorted account could peak interest and lead readers to seek out the source of the dangerous but nonetheless intriguing ideas. Inadvertently and ironically, the Catholic counterattack necessarily helped propagate the very message it wished to expunge.

Not to reply was to surrender much of the vernacular reading public to Luther and his friends. To reply was to further by both message and medium the position of the Evangelicals. This was the Catholic dilemma.

THE FALL PUBLICATIONS

The first person to reply to Luther in the Strasbourg vernacular press was the Franciscan jurist, theologian, and satirist Thomas Murner. In quick succession he issued five anonymous treatises, the titles of which illustrate the progression of Murner's concerns. His first treatise suggested in its title both qualified deference to the "highly learned doctor" and a concern that at least in regards to the Mass, Luther had parted company with common Christianity: *A Christian and Fraternal Admonition to the Highly Learned Doctor Martin Luther of the Augustinian Order at Wittenberg, That He Distance Himself From Several Statements He Made Concerning the New Testament of the Holy Mass and That He Join Himself Once Again With Common Christianity.* It left the press of the Strasbourg printer Johannes Grüninger on 11 November 1520.[2]

This treatise was in fact largely a reply to Luther's *A Sermon on the New Testament, That Is, On the Holy Mass,* his *To the Christian Nobility of the German Nation,* and his *On the Papacy in Rome, Against the Highly Famous Romanist at Leipzig.* Murner's first effort generated sufficient interest to warrant a second, slightly revised edition, that appeared on 21 January 1521. His next treatise, *Concerning Doctor Martin Luther's Teaching and Preaching, That They Are Suspicious and Not To Be Considered Completely Trustworthy,* was published on 24 November 1520.[3] Its title alerted readers to approach Luther and his teachings with caution. The treatise itself was largely a response to an anonymous defender of Luther whom we know was the Nuremberg city secretary Lazarus Spengler and whose treatise we examined in the last chapter.[4]

The third treatise, *Concerning the Papacy, That Is, the Highest Authority of Christian Faith, Against Doctor Martin Luther,* issued from Grüninger's press on 13 December 1520.[5] A reply to the Latin *Luther's Resolutions on the Power of the Pope* of 1519, and to the German *To the Christian Nobility* and *On the Papacy at Rome,* its title indicated that Luther opposed the papacy. The fourth treatise of this anonymous series appeared in 1520 around Christmas and was entitled *To the Most Mighty and Enlightened Nobility of the German Nation, That They Protect the Christian Faith Against the Destroyer of the Faith of Christ, Martin Luther, a Seducer of Simple Christians.*[6] Its title summed up the underlying message Murner was attempting to convey to the reading public in all his treatises, namely, that Luther threatened the destruction of Christian authority through a seductive but heretical appeal to "simple Christians." The concluding and somewhat anticlimactic treatise of Murner's series, *How Doctor M. Luther, Moved by the Wrong Reasons, Has Burned the Canon Law*, appeared on 17 February 1521, and attacked Luther's justification for this act of defiance.[7]

The treatises to which Murner replied were for the most part published in Strasbourg, and it is quite possible that Murner was using Strasbourg editions in preparing his rebuttals. Luther's *A Sermon on the New Testament, That Is, On the Holy Mass* was reprinted in Strasbourg sometime after July 1520.[8] In it he challenged the traditional understanding of the Mass and offered an alternative vision that undercut many traditional practices and seriously enhanced the religious status of the laity at the expense of the clergy.[9] In *On the Papacy at Rome, Against the Highly Famous Romanist in Leipzig*, printed sometime after the Wittenberg first edition of 26 June 1520,[10] Luther disputed the assertion that the papacy was of divine institution and that those who did not adhere to Rome were necessarily heretics and schismatics. It was followed by *To the Christian Nobility of the German Nation, On the Improvement of the Christian Estate*, which appeared first in Wittenberg on 18 August 1520. In this impassioned treatise Luther attacked the "Romanists" for claiming that the "temporal power" had no jurisdiction over them, that only the pope might interpret the Scriptures, and that no one but the pope could call a council. It aroused such interest among the reading public that it was immediately reprinted in Strasbourg at least once and perhaps as many as three times in the space of just a few months.[11] Sometime after 6 October 1520 this treatise was joined by two or three printings of a German translation of *On the Babylonian Captivity of the Church*.[12] As the title suggests, it argued that the church was being held prisoner in exile like the people of Israel. Luther proceeded to free it from its captivity by assailing the institutional church's claim to act as a sacramental mediator between God and humanity.[13] Surprisingly, given Murner's published views about exposing Luther's subversive ideas to the general public, it was Murner himself who apparently translated this treatise into German! Two of these treatises—*To the Christian Nobility* and *On the Papacy at Rome*—may also have appeared sometime in the late fall in a collection that included Luther's *A Sermon on the New Testament, that is, the Holy Mass*.[14]

It is striking that Murner chose not to reply to, or for that matter even to mention, the highly influential *On the Freedom of a Christian*, which appeared in Luther's own German translation in one or two printings in the last month or so of 1520 (and several subsequent printings in 1521, 1522, and 1524).[15] I have no explanation for this remarkable omission.

"MATTERS OF FAITH SHOULD NOT BE DISPUTED BEFORE THE IGNORANT COMMON FOLK"

Murner generally replied point-by-point to Luther's arguments. For our purposes, however, the details of his refutation are less important than the general message he attempted to convey. That message can be briefly summarized and broken into several components. Luther was a religious demagogue whose writings challenged traditional authority and threatened to overturn the established order. First, although Luther was a highly learned and skilled theologian, his theology offered a mixture of truth and falsehood that could easily mislead "simple Christians" not only into religious error but also into rebellion against authority. Second, despite his claims to the contrary, Luther would not submit his theology to any authority, be it the papacy, ecumenical councils, the Greek or Latin Fathers, scholastic theologians, or ecclesiastical law. This unwillingness promoted a disregard for authority among the common people. Third, Luther attacked a number of widely recognized and deplorable abuses within the institutional church, but the existence of these abuses did not justify his changing the traditional faith. His attack on abuses did, however, gain Luther a popular following that could easily be incited to violence and rebellion against proper authority. Fourth, Luther was attempting to subvert the traditional order of society and promote rebellion when he challenged the authority of the papacy and when he asserted that the distinction between the spiritual and temporal (worldly) estate was a deceit intended to enrich the clergy at the laity's expense and that, in fact, all baptized Christians were priests.

With each of these four points Murner emphasized the effect of Luther's teachings on the common people. It was highly inappropriate and dangerous, Murner insisted in each of these treatises, that Luther was involving what Murner termed the "rebellious and ignorant commoners [*gemein*],"[16] the "unlearned and rebellious commoners [*gemein*],"[17] or "Karsthans"—the eponymous hoe-carrying peasant[18] —in a debate over religious issues. Commoners could not separate the "sound and Christian" from that which was "false and mixed with poison [and] also pungent with acidic comments [*auch vff den essich stechend*]."[19] The "pious simple Christian" did not understand how subtly falsehood [*vnwahrheit*] is mixed with truth and the devilish angel transforms itself into the angel of light."[20] Even worse, a public debate encouraged the commoners to take matters into their own hands, thereby subverting proper authority and promoting rebellion. Even legitimate reforms, as some of those Luther listed in his book "to the German nobility," Murner insisted, should not be paraded before the ignorant common folk, who might, like the Bohemians before them, attempt to undertake the reforms themselves and end up murdering priests and monks, whom Luther had sharply criticized.[21]

So concerned was Murner about the subversive potential of airing such disputes in vernacular publications that he devoted a whole section of *Concerning Doctor Martin Luther's Teaching and Preaching* to the proposition that "matters of faith should not be disputed before the ignorant common folk."[22] In this section he marshaled the objections also found scattered through his other treatises. He started with a blanket assertion. Whether Luther's teachings were true, as Spengler in his *Defense* asserted, or false, as Murner was convinced, they should not in principle be discussed before the common people because they dealt with matters of faith. To defend this principle, he offered the analogy that city councils should not discuss their business publicly even though they dealt with issues touching on the welfare of all.[23] Imperial law forbade open discussions of faith because, among other things, "such public justification of the faith causes great scandal among Jews and other unbelievers" and also caused "great scandal and disobedience among ignorant Christians." "As we unfortunately now can clearly see," Murner continued, "not many Christians have been moved to reverence by doctor Martin's teaching but only to rebellion [and] to stealing two of the pope's crowns," that is, to a denial of papal authority in both spiritual and temporal realms. The "ignorant Christians" had been moved "not to obedience but rather to despise the ban along with the bishops, to electing bishops themselves 'behind the oven and over wine' [that is, informally and frivolously], [and] to priests marrying their maids in a thievish fashion." To put the matter briefly, people had now turned away from the good, paid no attention to bishops or anyone else, and simply announced, "I no longer obey anyone, I am a good Lutheran." That was the end result of Luther's teachings. That was its fruit. And for this reason everyone should be kept from teaching such things publicly. "I am concerned that Luther's teaching will soon prove with deeds whether it is of God or of the devil," Murner wrote, "for the teaching of God serves peace and unity and [the teaching] of the devil [promotes] contempt of authority with rebellion."[24]

Murner had put the Catholic case clearly. Matters of faith should be left to proper authority to decide. To bring the common people into the debate, even on legitimate reforms, was to subvert proper authority and to promote rebellion. Murner was especially upset that Luther had decided to air these issues in the vernacular. "Previously you have published Latin books that have brought you much fame," Murner wrote at one point, "But now you have begun to answer every cuckoo in its own terms, to repay each insult with an insult, to speak slanderously and unworthily of the pope and the highest authorities of faith in Europe, to your own disgrace, so that I pity you greatly that you have so completely forgotten your moderation.[25]

This concern for the deleterious consequences of vernacular pamphlets in which religious issues were debated runs like a red thread through Murner's treatises. It is a concern voiced repeatedly by other Catholic publicists in subsequent years,[26] a concern that made the Catholic counterattack in the press so conflicted. We may wonder what the "common people" thought of this argument when they read or heard it in the vernacular. Even if they agreed with Murner or the other early Catholic controversialists in principle, in the very reading or hearing they were violating this principle. The medium subverted the message.

THE CATHOLIC DILEMMA, PART TWO

We have already noted the irony that by entering the public arena to refute Luther's views, Murner and other Catholic publicists ran the risk of promoting and propagating what they opposed. To refute Luther, first Catholic publicists had to explain what Luther was about. In so doing, they conveyed information that might actually attract readers rather than repel them. This has important implications for the historian attempting to understand the progress of the Reformation movement. It is common in historical accounts to start with Luther's treatises and then describe the Catholic replies. But if we ask how

Luther's contemporaries learned of his views, we cannot assume that they always started with Luther's own works. To be sure, publication statistics—the large number of printings and reprintings—suggest that as a matter of probability most readers did start with Luther's own publications. But some Strasbourg readers may have first learned about the substance of these challenging new publications not from Luther but from his anonymous critic.

Historians also need to remember that to live in the middle of great events is to live in confusion. It takes time to separate the significant from the unimportant, the lasting from the ephemeral. Accordingly, we need to be careful not to allow the knowledge of the outcome of these crucial months to get in the way of recapturing the shock and surprise of late 1520, the feeling that things could go in many directions, the uncertainty about how the public controversy would be resolved. The Strasbourg reading public and those with whom they shared their reading were sufficiently taken with several of Luther's treatises that their demand prompted several reprints. But they did not know, as we know now, that three of these treatises—*To the Christian Nobility of the German Nation, On the Babylonian Captivity of the Church*, and *On the Freedom of a Christian*—would be among the most important treatises Luther ever published. They did not know, as we know now, that these treatises marked a turning point, perhaps *the* turning point that led to the Reformation movement and the eventual foundation of Protestantism. They did not know that the anonymous author who replied to Luther was the Franciscan author, satirist, and doctor of theology and both laws, Thomas Murner.[27] They did not know who would prevail in this public confrontation, whose words would last and whose words would soon be forgotten. They did not know which position would be more appealing or convincing until they read or heard about Luther's views and read or heard about the views of his challenger.

Even if Murner's rebuttals were a reader's first detailed introduction to Luther, the reader would have nevertheless learned a great deal about Luther and what he stood for, albeit through a hostile lens. Consider, for example, Murner's first treatise, *A Christian and Fraternal Admonition*.[28] If readers had gotten no further than the foreword,[29] which was addressed to Martin Luther, they would have still learned several things about Luther. For example, they would know that Luther had recently published some theses. He had repeatedly appealed to the pope, to a better informed pope, and to a council, and had then criticized even the council's authority. He had issued "one book after another."[30] In these books he attacked abuses in the church, arguing, among other things, that it was better to believe Christ than the pope and better to accept the Bible alone than the decisions of councils or church fathers. Others, under Luther's influence, had also been publishing on these issues.[31] In the body of the treatise, readers would learn that Luther taught that the community could select its preacher and that once the priest gave up his office, he was no longer a priest.[32] Luther attacked abuses in the holy Christian church,[33] and in his book *To the Christian Nobility* he offered numerous suggestions for reform of the papacy.[34]

Since it was the target of a large section of the treatise, readers would have learned that Luther had written a treatise about the Mass, which he called the "new testament." In this work he apparently suggested that priests had fabricated their view of the Mass simply to gain money, that the Mass was no good work, and that masses read for their benefit were in fact of no value to the living or the dead.[35] The Gospel and its words, Luther argued, should be preferred over honorable custom or tradition.[36] He criticized "human additions" to the Mass and would allow people to participate without the traditional preparation.[37] He favored using German in the Mass.[38] He charged that it was the devil that inspired the silent recitation of the canon of the Mass.[39] He argued that the Sacrament should be used in an assembly of Christians to strengthen and awaken faith, to admonish one another, to promote the "new testament" concerning the forgiveness of sins; in so doing each Christian acted as a priest or priestess.[40] The Mass, according to Luther, was neither a sacrifice nor a good work of use to another.[41] He objected to withholding the cup from the laity.[42] Finally, Luther advocated a "spiritual" church with Christ at its head rather than the pope.[43]

The trick for the reader of *A Christian and Fraternal Admonition* or any of Murner's other pamphlets was, of course, to separate the relatively neutral information from the heavy freight of his criticism. It was an even greater challenge for the reader to see through the distortions that may have entered into Murner's re-presentation. A few examples on a common theme may illustrate the difficulties as well as the possibilities.

The three major targets of Murner's disapproval—*A Sermon on the New Testament, On the Papacy at Rome,* and *To the Christian Nobility*—have one important motif in common: each insisted that since faith alone saved, every baptized and believing Christian was a true priest and there was no difference between Christians in this regard. Accordingly, Luther denied the validity of the contemporary distinction between the spiritual and secular (lay) estate and argued that it served only to allow the clergy to take advantage of the laity.

In re-presenting this argument, Murner confused Luther's distinction between the two realms—that is, the two ways in which, Luther said, God ruled the spiritual and secular world—with the traditional distinction between the two estates, laity and clergy. It cannot be determined whether this confusion was willful or inadvertent, a polemical distortion or a "natural" misreading due to Murner's particular mindset. It was a confusion, however, that allowed Murner to conclude that Luther was attempting to do away with the clergy and overthrow all distinctions of rank and hierarchy.

On the matter of the priesthood, consider what Luther said in *A Sermon on the New Testament, That Is, the Holy Mass*. Here he explained to his readers that in the Mass God offered a divine promise of forgiveness. For their part, human beings simply had to accept this gift and faithfully believe this divine promise.[44] Therefore Luther insisted that the Mass was a sacrament, not a sacrifice offered by the priest. To be sure, Christians offered through Christ a sacrifice of prayer, praise, and thanksgiving and their very selves.[45] "Thus it becomes clear," he concluded, "that not only the priest offers the sacrifice of the Mass but each one [offers] his own faith." This was the true priestly office, through which Christ was offered before God as a sacrifice. Therefore, everyone was equally a spiritual priest before God.[46]

In his restatement Murner understood Luther to say that the sacrament of the Mass should be celebrated "in an assembly of Christians to strengthen and awaken their faith in the promise of Christ, to admonish each other in this regard, and to promote the testament regarding the forgiveness of sins." The reader of Murner would get this part of Luther straight, but that was about all. It did not follow from this, Murner continued, that everyone was a priest or priestess. Only consecration made a priest. "Therefore you have misused in an incomprehensible way the words priest and priestess with the result that the laity has become highly angry about the matter and already thinks that priests are no longer necessary for the practice of the Sacrament."[47] Consecration was of course, from Murner's perspective, the way a person moved from the laity, the secular estate, to the ordained clergy within the spiritual estate. A person was in either one estate or the other. So it seemed nonsensical to him to assert that lay people were priests, even "spiritual" priests. Murner and Luther were using the distinction spiritual and secular differently, but Murner did not acknowledge this. Perhaps he was not even aware of the equivocation. If readers were first introduced to Luther's priesthood of all baptized Christians through Murner's re-presentation, they would have learned that Luther taught that all Christians were priests, but they would likely have been at a loss for Luther's rationale.

Murner was even more upset by the way in which Luther drew the consequences from his conviction that faith alone made the true priest. In *A Sermon on the New Testament*, Luther asserted, for example, that "all Christian men are priests, all women priestesses, be they young or old, master or servant, mistress or maid, learned or lay. Here there is no difference, unless faith be unequal."[48] In *To the Christian Nobility*, Luther declared even more pointedly that all Christians were of the spiritual estate and there was no difference among them except one of office, because all Christians had the same baptism, the same gospel, and the same faith, which alone made a spiritual and Christian people.[49] "Thus it follows from this that there is basically no other difference than one of office or task, and not of estate, between laity, priests, princes, bishops, and, as they say, spiritual and worldly [estates], for they are all of the spiritual estate and true priests, bishops, and popes but not with the same tasks."[50] From passages like these Murner concluded that Luther sought to erase all social distinctions. As he explained to the emperor in his *To the Most Mighty and Enlightened Nobility of the German Nation*, Luther was a rebel who stirred up civil uprisings and promoted the downfall of the fatherland, setting "father against his child, brother against brother, subjects against their authorities" and so mixing things up "that neither pope, emperor, king, bishop, bath attendant, or pig-herder will any longer be distinguishable" one from another.[51] Murner urged the emperor and German nobility to forestall the incipient rebellion and to protect "our faith" against Luther, "who has robbed you all of your noble estate and turned you into priests."[52] Whether a willful distortion or a misreading that is explicable given Murner's clerical point of view, this re-presentation bears little resemblance to Luther's position.

In *On the Papacy at Rome*, Luther treated at length "what 'Christendom' and 'head of Christendom' mean" and, in the process, concluded that Christendom was an "assembly of all believers in Christ throughout the earth."[53] This was a spiritual rather than a physical assembly; the "natural, real, right, essential Christianity exists in the Spirit and in no external things, whatever it may be called," Luther insisted.[54] The visible church including pope, bishops, priests, monks, nuns, and other members of the "so-called spiritual estate" and the external worship they produced was *not* Christendom, although this community and these estates would always contain people who were true Christians, keeping the visible church spiritually "alive" just as a soul animated the body.[55] It was faith that made true priests and Christians in the soul, not membership in the "so-called spiritual estates" or the institutional church.[56] Murner once again either did not understand or would not accept Luther's redefinition of the spiritual-secular distinction. "In the same manner in which you [deal with] the spiritual church," Murner wrote, "you also deal with the spiritual Mass [claiming] that it was an assembly of Christians [gathered] to observe the passion of our lord in a strong faith, to promote the new and eternal testament concerning the forgiveness of sin." And this led to a false dichotomy. "You sever the spiritual Mass from all bodily and external things, as if we had no need of bodily ordained priests but rather baptism has made us all priests and priestesses."[57] Murner of course identified the true church with the institutional church with the pope as its head. To speak of "spiritual Christendom" was to mislead people into believing that they could ignore the authority of the actual, institutional church and its leaders. Murner's reworking would, once again, leave his reader with the bare substance of Luther's position but rather in the dark about Luther's theological reasoning.

So it would appear that readers who were first introduced to Luther through Murner's writings would likely come away with a severely skewed view of some central tenets such as the priesthood of all baptized Christians. They would learn that Luther claimed that all Christians were priests through their faith, but they would have at best a distorted grasp of Luther's rationale. On other, perhaps less theological matters, the readers of Murner's treatises might neither need nor particularly care about the underlying justification—the position itself would be sufficient. Consider two examples: Luther's violent opposition to the papacy and his appeal to the laity to take matters into its own hands.

Luther's three treatises gave Murner considerable reason to conclude that Luther had rejected papal authority. While all three treatises named various abuses within the church and proposed reforms that drastically challenged current church practice, *On the Papacy at Rome* and *To the Christian Nobility* went on to attribute many of these abuses to the papacy. In *On the Papacy at Rome*, Luther stated openly that "all evil examples of spiritual and worldly knavery flow out of Rome and into all the world as if from a sea of all wickedness."[58] The papal claims to be of divine order were made for the sake of money, from confirming bishops and priests to issuing indulgences.[59] "Because money is involved, whatever they think must be of divine order."[60] Luther attacked, among other thing, the papal demand for clerical celibacy, papal laws regarding fasting, papal claims of superiority over temporal authority, and papal misuse of the keys.[61] Christ's command to "tend my sheep" meant "in Romanish,"

> to oppress Christendom with many human, destructive laws; to sell the bishop's cape for as much as possible; to rip annates from every benefice; to take to themselves all foundations; to turn all bishops into [their] servants through horrible oaths; to sell indulgences; to tax the whole world with letters, bulls, lead [and] wax [seals]; to forbid the preaching of the Gospel, to occupy the whole world with knaves from Rome, to gather all quarrels to themselves [for adjudication], [and thereby] to increase disputes and quarrels. In short [they] do not allow anyone to come to the truth or have peace.[62]

In *To the Christian Nobility*, Luther escalated his attack against the "Romanists." He accused them of cleverly constructing three defenses against reform, thus greatly damaging Christendom. He rejected as "a fine fabrication and hypocrisy" [*ein feyn Cōment vnd gleyssen*] the Romanists's first defense, their claim to be the "spiritual estate" distinct from the laity and with special privileges.[63] The Romanists' second defense—their claim that only the pope could interpret Scripture and in so doing, could not err—he labeled a "wanton, made-up fable" contrary to Scripture.[64] To the third defense—that only a pope could convene a council—he replied that when the pope acted contrary to Scripture, he was to be reproved and corrected by authority of a council.[65] "It is the power of the devil and the Antichrist that resists that which serves to improve Christendom," Luther stated. "Therefore it is not at all to be followed but rather resisted with body, goods, and all that we are capable of."[66]

Luther's conclusion was stark. "With this I hope that the false, lying terror with which the Romans have long intimidated us and confused our consciences should lie defeated," he said, adding that he hoped that they would be made subject to the temporal sword "just like the rest of us," stripped of the power to interpret Scripture "on the basis of mere force without skill" and unable "to fend off a council or to bind or obligate it according to their whims and take away its freedom." Until these changes were made, the Romans were "truly of the fellowship of the Antichrist and the devil" and had "nothing of Christ except the name."[67]

From the pope's ostentatious style of life to the various ways that the papacy gained control of and taxed benefices and sold dispensations of all sorts from its own canon law, the theme running through the remainder of his treatise was that the papacy was fleecing the Germans and that reforms should be instituted to reduce Rome's centralized authority and to stop the flow of gold from Germany to Rome.[68] Luther had frequent occasion to characterize the papacy as a band of robbers doing the devil's and perhaps even the Antichrist's work. "Since, then, such devilish rule is not only public robbery, deceit, and the tyranny of the portals of hell, but destructive to the body and soul of Christendom," he summed up, "it is our responsibility to spare no effort to fend off such affliction and destruction of Christendom." He even posed the rhetorical yet still threatening question, "If we properly hang thieves and behead robbers, why should we allow Roman greed to go free, since it is the greatest thief and robber that has or could come to earth, and [it does] all [of its robbery] in the sacred name of Christ and St. Peter?"[69]

Murner's description of these attacks is reasonably faithful to bare charges while putting a quite different interpretation on the motives underlying the attacks. According to Murner, Luther's attack on abuses within the institutional church and the papacy was a pretext to stir up the common people. Luther, Murner remarked, "under the cover and appearance of doing away with the many abuses in the Christian churches wishes to lead the poor simple [people] into an erroneous faith and errors in Christian truth."[70] Murner could no longer stand by and watch. Instead, he had "to spring to the rescue and protection of the pious simple Christian man."[71] Luther and his supporters claimed that they only sought to lighten the monetary burdens imposed by the papacy on the German nation, but in fact they made accusations against the papacy about burdens and exactions in order to protect and maintain among the commoners error and falsehood concerning the Christian faith and to promote disobedience against authority.[72]

Murner's recurring refrain was that Luther sought to promote rebellion by abusing the clerical estate in writings aimed at the common people. "There are many who think that you thirst for the blood of the clergy since you have thrown such great and, as they say, undeserved ill-will, suspicion, and hatred on them." Luther did not publish anything that did not "slander and abuse the pope, all the cardinals, archbishops, and bishops along with the whole clerical estate."[73] If, as Luther recommended, the cloisters were closed, churches destroyed, and endowed masses ended, and people deprived thereby of their property, "we would throw things into such confusion that a child would slay or strangle its parents, one brother, the other, a friend, his friend."[74] The Hussites and their bloodshed served as an admonitory example, and the author repeatedly suggested the parallels between Luther and his followers and Hus and the Hussites.[75]

Murner certainly did not misread Luther's desire to incite the laity, or at least the lay rulers, to action against the institutional church, although Murner placed it in a most unfavorable light. In *On the Papacy at Rome*, Luther announced that he would "tolerate" letting kings, princes, and the rest of the nobility keep the "knaves of Rome" from their streets and prohibit papal fees for new bishops or benefices.[76] In his *To the Christian Nobility* he announced in its very title that lay temporal authorities had to reform the Christian estate. As he explained in his prefatory letter to the Nicholas von Amsdorf, he was bringing together various suggestions for Christian reform and laying them before the Christian nobility of the German nation in the hope that God might help his church through the laity since the clergy, to whom the task more properly belonged, was faithless and negligent.[77] The priesthood of all the baptized gave them the right to act since the clergy would not. The temporal authorities were "fellow Christians, fellow priests, fellow members of the spiritual estate [*mitgeystlich*], and fellow lords [*mitmechtig*] in all things" and were therefore in the best position to call a free council.[78]

All this was rather heady stuff. No wonder Murner concluded that Luther was attempting to incite the laity to action against the church. He was. But for Murner this was the wrong way to go about reforming abuses. It not only bypassed legitimate authority, it directly subverted that authority. It violated the distinctions of rank and responsibility that Murner believed society depended upon and advocated that the laity leave its proper sphere and interfere in the spiritual estate. As

Murner put it, Luther "has also misused his noble skill and understanding and the Holy Scripture for a rebellious, unpeaceful also unchristian purpose," namely, to use the German nobility "to seduce
the other poor sheep of Christ into unbelief."[79] Worst of all from
Murner's perspective, it invited the "rebellious and ignorant common
people" to become involved in a debate that was properly the private
business of their "betters."

In the early years of the Reformation movement, even many literate
people would have had only a vague notion of why Luther opposed
the papacy. If Murner was one of their original sources, especially on
Luther's opposition to the papacy and to many traditional beliefs and
practices of the Western church, they would have learned quite a bit
about his positions, albeit in a hostile and frequently distorting light.
Still, even a distorted picture could intrigue readers and lead to further
exploration in Luther's own writings. And some of the very issues that
distressed Murner—Luther's attacks on the papacy and the clergy, and
his appeal to the laity—may well have actually recommended Luther
to those members of the laity who were themselves hostile towards the
papacy or clergy or both. The hook could be set by anti-Roman, antipapal, and anticlerical appeals, and the theological rationale could follow afterwards as the reader explored what was behind the attacks.

ON THE BABYLONIAN CAPTIVITY OF THE CHURCH

Readers of Murner's treatises would have had to puzzle out Luther's
views from Murner's re-presentation. Their challenge would depend
upon the issue. Certainly most nuances would be lost. The rationale
underlying various theological positions would also be obscured.
But the positions themselves would to varying degrees probably get
through, although assuredly in a form far less convincing than Luther
would have wanted. Still, in the early stages of a media campaign, the
proponents of change would likely benefit from the further propagation of even a distorted message and the acknowledgment that the
message was serious enough to warrant refutation. Murner's voice colored but it did not completely obscure Luther's program. This was the
predicament that all Catholic publicists faced when they chose to respond to Luther's writings.

But what are we to think of the remarkable decision by Murner to
translate Luther's *On the Babylonian Captivity of the Church* from
Latin into German? By Luther's charge—in print—and by Murner's

own admission—also in print—it was Luther's "poisonous friend," Thomas Murner, who did the German translation. Luther claimed that Murner had done the translation in order to "disgrace me." Murner rejoined that he had done the translation to the best of his abilities without any falsifications. If the book was a disgrace to Luther, Murner wrote, then Luther had disgraced himself because Murner was not the author but only the translator. The Evangelical publicist Michael Stifel, discussed in the next chapter, disputed this in print, arguing that he had seen Murner's manuscript and that Murner had falsified more than translated. Whatever the truth of this accusation—and Stifel, as one of Murner's most vociferous opponents, was hardly an impartial observer—the published translation followed Luther's Latin treatise fairly closely. Stifel himself conceded that the falsifications did not make it into the printed work, although he of course gave Murner no credit for this. To the extent that Murner's translation made it into print unchanged, the only notable deviation from the Latin was the occasional use of colloquial terms that were slightly stronger than the Latin original.[80] The printed version is, on the whole, a reasonably faithful translation.

For our purposes the interesting question is why Murner chose, by translating it into German, to make broadly available one of his opponent's most important treatises. As we have seen, Murner sharply criticized Luther for discussing matters of faith before the common people in German. Yet in this case, Luther had chosen to limit his critical discussion of traditional sacramental theology to those who could read Latin. It was Murner, then, who opened the debate to the broader reading public. Why did he do this?

Michael Stifel suggested that he did this for money (seven guldens' payment) and to bring Luther into disrepute through mistranslations and falsifications.[81] Murner himself denied any falsification and contended that any disrepute that accrued to Luther was Luther's own fault as the treatise's author. I am inclined to find Murner's own explanation plausible. He apparently believed that Luther condemned himself with his own words. From Murner's perspective, that is from the context in which he read Luther, the message of this treatise did more harm than good to Luther's cause. But of course many people read Murner's translation and were convinced rather than offended. This is the seemingly paradoxical outcome when we consider not what Luther intended but how he was understood, when we consider how a treatise was variously received by the reading public. Catholic publicists could propagate ideas they deplored in the mistaken belief that that which repelled them would repel others. This irony was another element of the Catholic dilemma.

In *On the Babylonian Captivity of the Church* Luther attacked that aspect of the institutional church probably nearest to the laity's everyday experience, the institutional church's control over and claims for the sacraments. Of the seven traditional sacraments, the Mass, confession, and marriage (or at least the rules surrounding the sacrament of marriage) most influenced laity on a daily basis. But all the sacraments with the possible exception of the sacrament of orders were important to laity at one point or another during their journey through life. Several of the sacraments—especially baptism, the Mass, penance— were represented by the institutional church as crucial to lay salvation and under the discretionary control of the church. To be saved, the lay person needed the sacramental mediation of the institutional church.

Luther challenged this claim. He denied that there were seven sacraments. At first he argued that only three of the traditional seven— baptism, the Mass, and confession—were established by Jesus and possessed the requisite sign and promise. By the end of the treatise, however, Luther had concluded that confession was not a sacrament since it lacked a visible sign. Instead, Luther subsumed the sacrament of penance under the baptismal promise to which the penitent repeatedly returned.

When he turned to the sacraments themselves, Luther began with the Mass and devoted the most attention to this sacrament. The Mass impinged on the lay life in a variety of ways. From daily masses in the local churches to private and votive masses for the living and the dead, from Corpus Christi processions to the restriction of lay communion to the bread (with the wine reserved for the priest), and in the large clerical population needed to staff this multiplication of masses, the Mass was the sacrament that most clearly exemplified clerical claims, justified a large clerical population, and reminded laity of their dependence on the institutional church. Luther effectively demolished this whole structure. He charged that Rome had subjected the sacrament to three captivities: the tyrannical withholding of the cup from the laity, the insistence on the doctrine of transubstantiation, and the claim that the Mass was a good work and sacrifice. Underlying his attack on these three "captivities" was the insistence that the Mass or sacrament of the altar was "Christ's testament that, dying, he left behind him to be distributed to his faithful."[82] The Mass "is a promise of the remission [*ablassung*] of sins done for us by God, which promise was confirmed by the death of God's son."[83] Since the Mass was a promise, access was gained "with no works, no powers, no merits but only with faith."[84] On this basis Luther attacked the claims of priestly mediation and all the institutions that sprang from this claim. "Therefore it is a manifest and wicked error," Luther insisted,

> that the Mass should be sacrificed [*geopffert*] or done for sins, for satisfaction, for the dead, or for any other of our needs. You will easily understand this to be true if you firmly hold that the Mass is a divine promise that cannot be of use to anyone else, cannot be provided to anyone else, cannot help anyone else, cannot be commonly shared with anyone else except only those who believe with their own faith.[85]

With this insistence on personal faith, the traditional claim of the mediatory role of the priesthood was severely compromised and the wealth of traditional practices surrounding the Mass, not to mention the employment of many priests, was thrown in question.

In the course of his treatment of the remaining six traditional sacraments, Luther challenged a range of other established practices and argued for positions more congenial to lay concerns. He insisted, for example, that in baptism Christians were freed and should not have new spiritual obligations imposed upon them. He attacked the customary practices of confession for stressing the human acts of contrition, confession, and satisfaction and suppressing the promise of forgiveness. He proposed relaxing the degrees of relationship that prohibited marriage between even distant relations, and he argued for divorce or even extramarital relations in certain situations. He argued that ordination was not a sacrament and left no indelible mark on the person ordained. All who were baptized were equally priests, and those to whom the public ministry was committed by the consent of the community or by the call of a superior were no different from any other Christian. Their public ministry was to preach the Word. Those who failed to preach the Word—whatever else they might do reading hours or saying mass—were no true priests. Priests should be permitted to marry. These are but a few of a range of challenging assertions this treatise contained.

If Murner translated *On the Babylonian Captivity of the Church* in the belief that Luther's own argument would bring him into disrepute, which of these many challenges did Murner see as most discrediting? This can only be inferred, but as we shall see in a later chapter, there are two themes in this treatise that were singled out for the most attention by Catholic writers, namely, Luther's position on the Mass and his position on the priesthood of all baptized Christians. Both arguments undercut the traditional authority and status of the clerical estate, especially the priesthood. This would certainly offend some of the clergy, but did Murner really expect laity would also take offense? Apparently so, which raises once again the fascinating question of how Murner could have read Luther as he did. Did he view matters from so clerical a perspective that he failed to realize that the laity might actually be attracted to this frontal assault on clerical authority? Such naïveté would have been incongruous for a publicist who designated Luther as a "seducer of simple Christians."

Be that as it may, by translating *On the Babylonian Captivity of the Church* into German, Murner also assured that some laity would be convinced by Luther's position once given the opportunity to become acquainted with Luther's view of the sacraments. Given the numerous reprints of this German translation, it seems likely that it found more interest (and approval) among the reading public than Murner would have preferred.

THE CATHOLIC CONTROVERSIAL EFFORT

Murner was only one Catholic publicist among many, but the dilemma he faced was also faced by his colleagues. In entering the publishing arena, he worked, as we have seen, at a substantial disadvantage. Both the medium and his message cut against his cause. He received no support from Catholic authorities and only ridicule and abuse from the various Evangelical publicists who sprang to Luther's defense.[86] While he continued gamely on for a time, he eventually had to quit Strasbourg and henceforth found it extraordinarily difficult to have any of his works published. His fellow Catholic publicists fared little better.

In the crucial early years of the Reformation, suggestions for a coordinated and well-financed effort to answer Evangelical publications were made but found no response from higher ecclesiastical authorities. Four of the six leading Catholic publicists (see table 10) were supported not by ecclesiastical authorities but by the layman Duke Georg of Albertine (Ducal) Saxony. Other authors outside Albertine Saxony did not do as well. The Catholic historian Hubert Jedin has detailed the difficulties of early Catholic publicists in gaining occasional support or even attention from higher Catholic authorities.[87]

Although several proposals were made in the mid-1520s to support Catholic publicists, none were put into effect. The papal legate Girolamo Aleander (1480–1542), for example, recommended in 1523 that a list of Catholic controversial writers be compiled for each diocese and that benefices or other forms of remuneration be found for these men.[88] But his advice was not followed. Similar suggestions in 1524 by the Breslau Bishop Jakob von Salza and in 1525 by the vicar-general of the diocese of Constance, and later bishop of Vienna, Johannes Fabri (1478–1541), met with similar inaction.[89] Citing Aleander's disparaging evaluation of the Catholic controversial writings published up to 1523,[90] Jedin observes that this view seems to have been shared by the curia and its representatives throughout the reign of Pope Clement VII (r. 1523–1534). Although they occasionally rewarded the Catholic publicists, for the most part they held them and their services in contempt, and nothing was done to promote or coordinate the Catholic response to the Evangelical use of the press.[91]

It was under Pope Paul III (r. 1534–1549), more than a decade after the beginning of the Reformation movement, that Catholic publicists first received some regular support from the central authorities of the church. In expectation of the upcoming council, the papal nuncio to Germany, Pietro Paolo Vergerio (1498–1565), requested Pope Paul III at the end of 1534 to choose three or four Catholic theologians skilled in writing who could use their great knowledge of Lutheran writings to refute the heretics.[92] As a result, the Ingolstadt theologian Johannes Eck, the Saxony publicist Johannes Cochlaeus, the onetime Evangelical Georg Witzel, and several others received pensions.[93] The new nuncio Giovanni Morone was also instructed to support Fabri, Eck, Cochlaeus, Witzel, and several lesser writers.[94] Yet in 1540 Fabri could still opine that the Lutherans had won the upper hand

> because little or no attention had been paid to the scholars. The capable and steadfast are for the most part dead. Only a very few remain who are able and dare to resist; and those who are able to contradict [the Lutherans] or rather to prevail over them scarcely have the means to feed themselves not to mention the means to pay the printers.[95]

Cochlaeus, who underwrote the efforts of several Catholic publicists as well as himself, had repeated difficulties receiving support for his printing efforts.[96]

Although consistent support for Catholic controversial writers may have begun under Pope Paul III, this support did not immediately translate into an appreciable increase in publications. The printings or reprintings of Catholic controversial works, especially in the vernacular, remained relatively low through mid-century. It was not until the second half of the century, with the end of the Council of Trent and the efforts of the Jesuits, that the institutional church began an organized effort to counter Evangelical controversial writing. A variety of reasons can be advanced to explain this significant lag.

The Roman Catholic church saw itself as the only legal institution of religion. It represented the status quo, and its opponents were rebels, heretics, and outlaws. Moreover the Roman Catholic church possessed both the juridical power and ample precedent to condemn its opponents and hand them over to secular authorities for appropriate punishment. The Peasants' War gave added legitimacy to this view of their opponents and to the conventional method for dealing with such opponents.

Given this "law-and-order" conception of affairs, it should be no surprise that in the early decades when Catholics reflected on the Evangelical propaganda barrage and how to counter it, they thought mainly in terms of intervention by authorities. As Paulus Bachmann, abbot of Altzelle, saw it, it was the authorities' negligence or connivance that allowed the Evangelicals to fill the markets with anti-Catholic writings.[97] It was up to the authorities to remedy the situation. Even the publicists were slow to realize that more than censorship was called for.[98] As Jedin pointed out, Eck made no proposal for a program of published replies to the Lutherans in the first draft of his famous memo to Pope Adrian VI (r. 1522–1523).[99] Instead, he proposed that Lutheran pamphlets should be burned and inquisitors should be established. He also made no mention of publishing duties for the theologians whom he proposed should be taken on as advisors by the bishops. In the second edition of his memo, probably directed to Pope Clement VII, he recommended that scholars should be commissioned to refute the Evangelicals using the Scripture, Fathers, and church councils, but not scholastic theology. They would provide an official justification for the new bull condemning Luther. But even here there is no thought of a comprehensive program of published responses.

Cochlaeus, more than Eck, seemed aware at an early date of the need for a coordinated response to the Evangelical barrage of publications. In his memo of 1522, Cochlaeus in no way precluded the intervention of the authorities, but he also suggested a greater role for publications. He recommended both the assembling of a compendium of Evangelical error with appropriate Catholic refutations and the composition of books dealing with individual controversies. The counteroffensive, he felt, should not be confined to refutations of the opponents. At least as important was the circulation of German treatises dealing with the Mass, the sacraments, the veneration of Mary and the saints, as well as the explanation of other ceremonies in the worship service. As Jedin noted, this last proposal, to offer the people catechetical and educational literature, found acceptance only decades later.

In evaluating the tardy Catholic response to the Evangelical propaganda effort, it is important to remember that in the early years of the Reformation Catholics were laboring under a severe disadvantage that only time could cure. Unlike their Evangelical opponents, who, at least for the first couple decades, could appeal to ideals and "Scripture alone" without bothering overly much about the intractable reality of real institutions and real people, Catholics were defending, more or less, an existing institution, whose faults and flaws were apparent and had been experienced by their readers. It took some time for the Evangelicals to build their own imperfect institutions and thus become vulnerable to the criticism that reality differed significantly from the ideals they espoused. When this finally happened, Catholics, not surprisingly, took some delight in pointing out the inconsistency between Evangelical theory and practice.

It should also be kept in mind that for the Roman church to engage in organized, "official" polemics with the Evangelicals, it would have to acknowledge that there was something to debate.[100] Normally one does not even argue with outlaws, which was what the Catholics considered Evangelical publicists to be. The Roman church had acted with authority (*auctoritas*) when it had condemned Luther and his teachings. Further debate only gave apparent legitimacy to the Evangelical claim that there was something to debate. A similar logic lay behind the reluctance of the papacy to convene a general council to decide the matters at issue. Such an action gave at least the impression that papal decisions were not final.

Moreover, the Catholics were understandably loath to accept the Evangelical contention that beliefs and ceremonies that had, the Catholics believed, existed in the church for centuries should now suddenly be open to question. As the Dominican Johannes Mensing remarked in his defense of the Mass, "It should not be necessary for us now, after so many hundreds of years, to prove the validity of our holy sacrifice of the Mass, held in simple faith by all our predecessors, both the Greek and Latin Fathers, from the time of the twelve apostles to today, as the heretics demand of us."[101] The very act of defending and justifying long-standing Catholic practices seemed to some Catholics to acknowledge the Evangelical claim that such practices were subject to the "test of Scripture" rather than to the judgment of the Church.

Evangelicals, on the other hand, had everything to gain by polemics. They had to convince people to change their minds and change their allegiance. To accomplish this, they had to convey to people their new understanding of the Christian gospel. It appears from the sixteenth-century literature, and especially from the very belated introduction of Catholic catechisms to counter Evangelical ones, that it took Catholic authorities some decades to realize that it was not enough to counter Evangelical attacks. They had to match the Evangelical educational enterprise with one of their own. Intriguingly, it was a former Evangelical, Georg Witzel, who was one of the pioneers in producing basic, positive summaries of Catholic theology for the use of simple laity.

The propaganda campaign itself posed a considerable dilemma for Catholics, at least in the initial years of the Reformation movement. For Catholics such as Murner and his fellow controversialists, who opposed in principle the public discussion of matters of faith, to enter the vernacular pamphlet war was to risk compromising their own position, for the medium subverted a crucial part of their message. Authority lodged in the hierarchical church and its head, the pope. Common people had no right even to discuss, much less to debate, matters already decided by the institutional church. Yet those who could get their hands on these angry little booklets were brought into the debate, exhorted to make up their own minds, and urged to take action. Is it any wonder, then, that the dissonance between the medium—hundreds of easily circulated pamphlets—and the message—common people should not discuss matters of faith since such discussions subverted proper authority—may have inhibited the Catholic response?

The Catholic dilemma extended further. The controversialist had to describe the views that he was refuting. The readers of Murner, for example, would have learned a great deal about Luther from Murner's own treatises, and there was no guarantee that they would be offended by what they learned. Murner read and re-presented Luther from his own, hostile point of view. But as his decision to translate *On the Babylonian Captivity of the Church* so dramatically illustrates, material that Murner understood as bringing Luther into disrepute could have just the opposite effect. That which repelled Thomas Murner could ironically intrigue if not actually attract his readers. In the early years when the Evangelical message was just being disseminated and people were just learning what the debate was all about, even a hostile presentation helped propagate the Evangelical message and invited readers and hearers to think about the novel understanding of Christianity that Luther and his supporters were offering.

Finally, there may be some merit to the suggestion that, in a fundamental way, the Evangelical message was more easily propagated by the press than the Catholic message. Evangelical emphasis on the word, and especially the word of Scripture, lent itself to written argument. Catholicism, in contrast, was more "visually" and "ritually" oriented. As Paulus Bachmann put it, "The written word of God, as the Lutherans call the Gospel, cannot always be productively presented to the simple folk according to its bare words or literal meaning but rather requires interpretation and the addition of commentary [menschlicher wort]."[102] It was accordingly not a good idea, Bachmann believed, to present everything in German.[103] Explanations from the Scriptures were suitable for the learned, while those of "little understanding" were best nourished by external pomp and ceremonies.[104] Perhaps more to the point, much of the Western church's practice and ritual had developed over centuries, often arising first among the common Christians and only later receiving theological explanation. That is, practice preceded theology. To defend theologically practices that had first arisen apart from strictly theological concerns was a difficult task unless one had recourse to the authority of tradition itself. Whatever its ultimate cogency, the argument from tradition was not easily defended solely on the basis of Scripture, which was the only authority that Evangelicals accepted.

THE PUBLIC IMAGE BY THE END OF 1520

The last chapter examined how the vernacular treatises of Luther's published in the Strasbourg press through July of 1520 were resolutely addressed to the laity. The central message of these early treatises was clear: Christians should humbly rely on God's promise of forgiveness rather than on the mediating power of clerics or clerically sponsored works. In a more speculative vein, I argued that these treatises likely appealed to their intended lay audience because their message explicitly dignified the spiritual status of the laity at the expense of clerical claims and prerogatives. The laity who took the message of these early publications to heart were freed from the standards of clerical piety, freed from a thoroughgoing reliance on clerical mediation in their relations with God, and freed from concern about their own worthiness and spiritual efforts.

Luther's Strasbourg publications in the fall of 1520 continued these themes. They remained primarily addressed to the laity and, in fact, exhorted the laity (or at least the lay temporal authorities) to undertake religious reforms on their own authority. The central theological message had also not changed though it had been elaborated. As he would for the rest of his lifetime, Luther continued to insist that Christians must through faith rely solely on God's promise of forgiveness. He attacked priestly claims to mediation, and he vociferously assailed the notion that good works, even clerically approved good works, could save. He now added that since faith alone saved, every baptized and believing Christian was a true priest. Accordingly, the existing religious, social, and political distinctions between the temporal and spiritual estates—that is, between the laity and the clergy— were at best inappropriate and at worst a fabrication intended to enrich the clergy at the laity's expense. This new emphasis on the spiritual equality of all believing and baptized Christians only deepened the potential appeal of his message for lay Christians.

There is, of course, a crucial difference between these two sets of publications. While the earlier publications presented Luther as a *pro*ponent of the lay religious life, these later publications added the image of Luther as the *op*ponent of the papacy and of many practices of the institutional church. For some readers such as Thomas Murner, these new publications exposed Luther as an opponent not only of the spiritual estate but of social order generally. For all his worthy concerns and great gifts, Luther was at bottom a rebel and "seducer of simple Christians."

CHAPTER FOUR

Luther's Earliest Supporters in the Strasbourg Press

In his path-breaking study *For the Sake of Simple Folk: Popular Propaganda for the German Reformation*, Robert Scribner examined the ways Luther was depicted in woodcuts and engravings during the early years of the Reformation movement.[1] He showed that with slight variations the three recurring signs in all pictorial depictions of Luther were monk, doctor, and man of the Bible. To these central signs were added other signs such as a dove, which symbolized the Holy Spirit and suggested that Luther had been enlightened or inspired by God, and the nimbus of sainthood, which suggested that Luther had saintly qualities or could be considered to be like a Father of the church or both.[2]

As it happens, all of these signs were deployed on the title page of a Latin account of Luther's appearance before the Diet of Worms, issued by the Strasbourg press of Johann Schott (see plate 1).[3] The woodcut presented Luther as a monk (monastic habit), doctor (doctoral beret), and man of the Bible (held in his hands) who was inspired by God (the dove of the Holy Spirit and the nimbus of a saint). The woodcut was reused in 1522 when Schott issued a German translation of the same account.[4]

This constellation of visual signs constituted the skeleton of Luther's public persona among at least some of his supporters. But it left undisclosed the specific content of each sign. What did the doctor teach? What did being a man of the Bible entail? In what way was he inspired by God and to what purpose? In what did his sanctity con-

Plate 1. Luther as Monk, Doctor, Man of the Bible, and Saint. Woodcut to *ACTA ET RES GESTAE, D. MARTINI LVTHERi, in Comitijs Principu Vuormaciae* (Strasbourg: Johann Schott, 1521).

sist? Answers to these questions must draw on social expectations and stereotypes, and Luther's own actions and the reactions of others. The other Reformation publicists who were published in Strasbourg through 1522 may help us to see how this worked.[5]

MONK, DOCTOR, AND MAN OF THE BIBLE

The relevant authors who published in Strasbourg were all aware that Luther was an Augustinian friar, but the sign of Luther as monk was probably the least developed in the text of the Strasbourg pamphlet literature. It may, of course, underlie the frequent comments on Luther's piety. For example, the character Karsthans (a stereotypical hoe-carrying peasant) in the treatise of the same name remarked that he had heard much good said of Luther, that he was "a pious Christian man."[6] Similarly, in *A Beautiful Dialogue and Conversation Between a Pastor and a Mayor Concerning the Evil Condition of the Clergy and the Evil Dealings of the Worldly*, probably written by the Dominican and future reformer of Strasbourg Martin Bucer, one character spoke of "the pious Luther" and another characterized him as "pious and right."[7] Such comments may have been inspired by Luther's monastic vocation, but they may just as well be linked to other signs such as "man of the Bible" and "inspired saint."

Luther's learning attracted considerably more attention than his monastic status, which is hardly surprising when one considers that many of the authors of this early pamphlet literature in defense of Luther were themselves humanists who greatly prized learning, both Luther's and their own. In *Karsthans*, Karsthans' son reported that the Dominican "Master of Heretics," Jakob von Hoogstraten (1454–1527), thought it a bad idea to dispute with Luther and his adherents because they were "too learned."[8] This was, of course, a tie-in to the earlier Reuchlin controversy, when a group of prominent humanists took on Jakob von Hochstraten and the other Dominicans who were attacking Johannes Reuchlin (1455–1522) for his defense of Jewish literature. In *A Beautiful Dialogue*, the priest said that he had heard that all the learned were on Luther's side.[9] Finally, in *Declaration of the Celebrated University of Erfurt In Defense and Protection of, and Administration of Justice Concerning, the Christian Servant of God and Teacher, Doctor Martin Luther*,[10] the translator Wolfgang Rüßen, in his letter of dedication described this formal document as showing that the University of Erfurt had concluded "that the writings of Martin

..er are just and Christian,"[11] and he termed Luther "an incisive and precise theologian," an "Evangelical teacher," and an "innocent revealer of truth."[12]

The one theological issue that all Luther's defenders agreed on, and uniformly approved, was that Luther based his teachings on Scripture alone. Luther's image as a "man of the Bible" was ground on this insistence. In *Concerning the Conformed-to-Christ and Properly Grounded Teaching of Doctor Martin Luther*, the Augustinian Michael Stifel (1486/87–1567) announced in the title, for example, his conviction that Luther's teaching was conformed to Christ and properly based on Scripture alone. He concluded his verse pamphlet with the ringing challenge,

> The truth is revealed
> [And] in no way divided
> If Luther is a heretic
> Then who on earth writes properly?
> If then the Scripture is false, incorrect,
> Then that confirms the screams of its enemy.
> But the Scripture is true, constant, firm
> Made lustrous by Christ himself.
> In comparison to which all human trifles are lies
> Without Scripture, sent by the devil.
> 'Scripture, Scripture!' cries Luther publicly
> And risks his head, neck, and skin on it.
> Do you wish to silence Luther? Give him Scripture,
> Otherwise your teaching is pure poison.[13]

In *Karsthans*, the character "Murnar" admitted that he had hoped by the use of sneering words not to be defeated by Luther in disputation, but Luther wanted to evaluate everything according to the gospel and the letters of Paul, which "Murnar" had not much studied.[14] A bit later "Karsthans" expressed the opinion that Luther was a "thousand times more skilled telling the common, natural meaning of Scripture than Murner."[15] The author of *A Beautiful Dialogue* grounded his whole argument on the insistence that Scripture was the sole judge of right belief. One of his characters stated at the outset that Luther "grounds all his writings in right faith and out of the holy gospel and out of Saint Paul's teaching and leads us out of many entanglements into which the clergy has for a long time gotten us on account of money and goods."[16] In *A Pleasant Christian and Godly Reminder*, the nobleman Hartmuth von Cronberg insisted that Luther's position was clearly based in Scripture while the pope had no Scripture with which to refute Luther. Even he, a layman and one of those of little understanding, could prove this on the basis of Scripture.[17] In the anonymous *A Pleasant Argument, Conversation, Question and Answer of Three Persons, Namely a Curialist, a Nobleman, and a Burgher*,[18] the curialist in the dialogue, of all characters, repeatedly insisted that Luther's teachings were grounded firmly in Scripture.[19] Luther always wished the argument to be based on Scripture and proved his positions with Scripture.[20] In his *Against Murnar's Song*, Michael Stifel wrote that Luther insisted vehemently that one abide by Christ's words and understand them the way they were spoken.[21] And he summed up the conviction of all these authors when he wrote, "Luther speaks well when he says that one should judge all books according to the Scripture, [to determine] whether they are right or not."[22]

THE CHRISTIAN ANGEL

Several of the publicists depicted Luther in largely mundane categories, but the hovering dove and glowing nimbus also had their verbal equivalents in some of the publications. For example, in his *A Pleasant Christian and Godly Reminder and Warning To the Imperial Majesty, Sent By One of His Imperial Majesty's Poor Knights and Obedient Servants*, Hartmuth von Cronberg spoke with some moderation of "the true servant of God, Doctor Luther" and characterized Luther as one who had led thousands of people to the true spring, Christ Jesus.[23] But in his *Rejection of the Alleged Dishonor Attributed By Many To the Pious and Christian Father, Doctor Martin Luther of the Augustinian Order, In That He Called Our Father the Pope a Vicar of the Devil and Antichrist*,[24] Cronberg went on to say that there had "undoubtedly not been a truer more Christian teacher living in a thousand or more years than this doctor Luther."[25] In his *To the Praise of Luther and To the Honor of the Whole of Christendom*,[26] the student Laux Gemigger thanked God for bestowing his grace "upon us poor sinners" and sending into the world "the well-born doctor Martin Luther, whom you have chosen as a light of Christendom" to tell of God's divine word and reveal the state of the present world, much to the displeasure of the pope and his supporters who desired to pervert the world, "which the pious Luther will never permit."[27] Escalating the rhetoric even further, the oft reprinted *Passion of Doctor Martin Luther*, written by "Marcellus," called Luther a "preacher of truth" and "doctor of the writings of St. Paul,"[28] but the treatise as a whole described Luther's appearance at Worms in a narrative modeled explicitly on Christ's passion—with Luther taking the role of Christ!

While this last comparison was obviously extreme, in his *Concerning the Conformed-to-Christ and Properly Grounded Teaching of Doctor Martin Luther, An Extremely Beautiful and Artful Song Along with Its Exegesis*,[29] Michael Stifel claimed with all evident sincerity that Luther was the angel of the apocalypse come to reveal the Antichrist. The signs laid down in the Bible concerning the last times led Stifel to conclude with Luther that the time was near for the persecution of the Antichrist against the truth of God. "I believe," he wrote of Luther, "that this man is sent to us by God, ordained and raised up in the fervor of the spirit of Elias."[30] With direct reference to the angel of Revelation, he explained that "the undertaking and purpose of this pamphlet is to certify and prove the teaching of the Christian angel, Martin Luther, and [to show] how his writings flow directly from the ground of the holy gospel, Paul, and the teachers of the Holy Scriptures [that were] sent and certified by God."[31] In explaining how he could make this bold claim, Stifel also made a pun on Luther's name that was frequently used by these early authors. "Yes, even now I wish to name this angel," Stifel wrote, "He is called Martin Luther. And [his teaching] is also so clear or pure [*luter*], that I believe that he has this name as a sign for us of God's order." Stifel went on to explain that his readers should not be bothered that an angel or spirit did not have flesh and bone, yet Martin Luther had flesh and bone as a human being. "For one finds in the Holy Scripture that holy men who teach the way of God are called angels." After giving several examples from Scripture, Stifel concluded, "An angel is also called a messenger of God, which without doubt Luther is, proclaiming the word of God so clear [*luter*] and purely."[32] Other treatises also played on Luther's name and the German word for pure or clear to associate Luther with the preaching of the pure gospel.[33]

In only one of these treatises, the anonymous *A Pleasant Argument*, was Luther himself criticized even as his teaching was being affirmed. This treatise showed a remarkably clear grasp of Luther's central concerns, but the anonymous author reacted badly to the more extreme claims made by Luther's supporters. The curialist in this dialogue, who most likely represents the author's own point of view, commented at the outset that the Germans honored "their idol Luther" as if he were God rather than just a saintly man.[34] He reported that he had heard it said in Rome that, although Luther touched on the fundamental issues, he did not do so out of love of God but out of jealousy. This jealousy was revealed in his books, in which he said that if the Romanists had not written against him, he would not have written against the papacy. From this admission, those at Rome wished to argue that he was provoked not by the love of God but by human writings directed against him. They concluded that it was pride that motivated Luther and made him want to be prominent in the university and teach something new. Their judgment, the curialist went on, was sustained by the sharp, abusive, slanderous, and foolish words that Luther employed in his writings.

Interestingly, the curialist was willing to ignore these considerations as long as Luther's teachings continued to be scriptural. "All that I let be as it may be," he wrote, concluding this recitation of the Roman view. "Whether Luther writes out of God or out of the spiritual deceit of the devil, his teaching pleases me very much. And since [he] does not deal with these matters contrary to the Scriptures, I will continue to be pleased with them."[35]

This is an instructive example of how expectations and experience could clash, making it difficult to settle on a coherent public persona. On the one hand, the author standing behind the curialist regarded Luther as a "saintly man" who thus far had taught in accordance with the Scriptures. But he was put off by Luther's supporters' characterizations of him, and he harbored serious questions about Luther's motivations. He was also offended by Luther's violent and abusive language and by what he saw as Luther's willingness to use force to bring about reforms.[36] This abusive vehemence, questionable motivation, and willingness to use force all accord poorly with the socially defined role of the "saint" or "man of the Bible." Most of the defenders either shrugged this dissonance off or did not even make mention of it. But in A Pleasant Argument the conflicting attributes are held in fascinating tension. Given the normal course of psychological dynamics, it is highly unlikely that many of Luther's supporters would have maintained this tension very long. The tension was eventually resolved either by going wholly over to Luther's side and finding rationalizations for his angry temperament or by returning to Catholicism in the conviction that Luther's aggressive temperament disclosed his true subversive nature.

THE PAPAL ANTICHRIST

Culturally determined expectations or stereotypes were at work in most of these pamphlets. When Stifel said that he believed Luther was "sent to us by God, ordained and raised up in the fervor of the spirit of Elias,"[37] he was tapping into the popular legend that Elias and Enoch were the two prophets sent by God to reveal the Antichrist.[38] Stifel also likened Luther to the angel of the apocalypse, another role associated with the fight against the Antichrist.[39] Here is the predominate source of the nimbus and hovering dove. Luther was more than a monk, doctor, or even man of the Bible. He was God's specially chosen instrument to combat the papal Antichrist.

Chapter 2 argued that readers of Luther's works printed in Strasbourg would have seen Luther as a learned doctor and engaged pastor who based his teachings solely on Scripture and whose appeal to the laity (and sympathetic clergy) was that his message enriched and dignified the laity's religious status. Chapter 3 explored how in the fall of 1520 Luther's public persona gained new dimensions with his published attacks on the institutional church, especially the papacy. With the treatises of the late fall Luther had presented himself as an impassioned critic of clerical fraud and papal tyranny. He had even suggested that the papacy might be the Antichrist spoken of in Scripture.

Most of the pamphlets published in Strasbourg accepted Luther's drastic depiction of the papacy.[40] In the very title of one of his treatises, for example, the nobleman Hartmuth von Cronberg defended Luther against the charge that he went too far in calling the pope a vicar of the devil and Antichrist (*Rejection of the Alleged Dishonor Attributed By Many to the Pious, Highly Learned and Christian Father, Doctor Martin Luther of the Augustinian Order, In That He Called Our Father the Pope a Vicar of the Devil and Antichrist*).[41] Cronberg considered Luther's charge to be the irrefutable truth.[42] The pope and his supporters, by relying on human wisdom rather than the two great commandments to love God and neighbor, were taking a "devilish and most dangerous way" and misleading countless people from the true way of Christ into the path to hell.[43] In another treatise, *A Pleasant Christian and Godly Admonition and Warning* addressed to Emperor Charles V, Cronberg rather improbably urged the emperor to lead the pope out of brotherly love to the "divine spring" by showing the pope "on the basis of the Holy Scripture that he truly is a vicar of the devil and Antichrist, that truly the papal law is thought up by human minds without any proper basis, and that such things are nothing less than a stinking piss [*pffitz?*] of the devil." People had been "wickedly misled" into "our own self-conceived devilish way" and thereby hindered "from coming to the wholesome spring, which, by the great grace of God, has been so truly and clearly expressed by the teaching of doctor Luther so that anyone who has eyes and ears clearly sees and hears the same."[44] In Marcellus's *Passion of Doctor Martin Luther*, Luther was challenged with having taught that the Council of Constance had erred and that the papacy was the Antichrist. Luther replied, "You have said it. Nevertheless I say to you, I can prove it with divine Scripture [as well as] that which I have written in books. And unless I am overcome with divine Scripture, I will not recant or speak against my books."[45]

The grounds given for Luther's opposition to the pope varied from treatise to treatise. Cronberg saw Luther's opposition coming from the pope's imposition of human laws rather than the divine law expressed in the two great commandments. In *Karsthans*, the objection arose in relation to the scriptural basis for papal authority.[46] This line of argument was continued in *New Karsthans*.[47] The treatise also defined "Antichrist" as one who was "against Christ" [*gegen-Christ oder Wider-Christ*] and explained that "there has never been, and there may never be, a greater Antichrist than the pope at Rome, who completely perverts the gospel and positions himself against Christ in all things."[48]

Several authors took issue with various claims that the pope either could not err or if he erred, could not be corrected by anyone but God. Here they were echoing Luther's arguments, especially in his *To the Christian Nobility*.[49] For example, Karsthans in the pamphlet *Karsthans* criticized Murner's claim that no one might punish or judge the pope unless the pope erred publicly in matters of faith. Citing Luther, Karsthans sarcastically observed that as far as the pope's defenders were concerned, unless the pope worshipped the golden calf nothing he did would be considered an error of faith.[50]

Others, for example the anonymous author of *A Beautiful Dialogue*, were seriously upset by the claim that it was the clergy, at least in the first instance, who made up the church. In this *Dialogue* the "priest" charged that what Luther wrote was against the Christian church and against ecclesiastical law. The character of the mayor asked, "Who is the Christian church?" The priest replied, "Haven't you often heard it from me in the sermon?" The Christian church was "the pope and his cardinals, all the bishops and prelates." This the mayor could not believe. He had heard it said that the pope himself had established the ecclesiastical ("spiritual") law and that he might make the law to be whatever he wished. The mayor was concerned that there was little of "God's law" in the ecclesiastical law that he had heard at home from his student. For if the Christian church consisted only of the pope and his adherents, "then we poor Christians have lost the game." If the pope and his people could also not err or sin and yet little good could be said about him, what good should the mayor think of him? "Have you not heard what Doctor Martin Luther has written about them all," the mayor asked, "what a great, wicked thing they do at Rome with buying and selling benefices, with exchanging, changing, [and] despoiling [benefices] and not being in residence nor serving and many other things, how they also eat meat during periods of fasting and all times and forbid us all sorts of things, and how they are up to their ears in shameful matters? In addition, all their affairs are aimed at extracting piles of money from us."[51] In this one example we see the full range of the attack, from theological considerations to anger over abuse and fiscal extortion. Luther, as this example also illustrates, was the cited authority on papal tyranny and abuse.

Most of Luther's defenders had been convinced by Luther that the papacy was in fact the Antichrist. This accomplishment put Luther in a special position within sacred history and legend. He was spoken of in biblical terms, taking on the attributes of the prophesied opponents of the Antichrist. He was not just any monk, doctor, or man of the Bible, however learned. Fitted to the role of revealer of the papal Antichrist, he possessed an authority and inspired a deference that no other man of his age could claim, at least in the religious realm. No wonder the other publicists rallied to his side to attack the papal tyranny.

THE DYNAMICS OF POLARIZATION

In the fall of 1520 Luther's public persona was challenged by the anonymous counterattacks of the Franciscan Thomas Murner. If Luther presented himself as an impassioned critic, Murner depicted him as a dangerous rebel seeking to overthrow all legitimate authority through a seductive appeal to "simple Christians." For the most part, however, Luther's supporters had been convinced by Luther that his criticism was more than warranted. The battle had taken on apocalyptic proportions, and in the war between light and darkness the supporters of darkness deserved all the abuse that could be heaped upon them. The dynamics of polarization were at work. The polemical and psychological pressures all drove Luther's supporters to maximize Luther's virtues as their leader against the Antichrist, to minimize or discount his vices, and to see nothing but self-seeking and wickedness among their opponents.

Thomas Murner was mercilessly satirized in treatises such as *Karsthans*, and his name was invariably changed to "Murnar" to play on the German word *Narr*, "fool."[52] He was also likened to a cat, just as Emser was depicted as a goat, Eck as a pig, and popes and clergy in general as ravening wolves. In the *Declaration* of the University of Erfurt, the translator, Wolfgang Rüßen, called the bull excommunicating Luther "the trumped-up Eckian bull" and labeled it "heretical and unjust."[53] Eck and the other sponsors of the bull were called "ungodfearing" and "hypocrites" doing the work of the devil, and the bull of excommunication was termed the "tyrannical and more than devilish papal ban."[54]

Several of the treatises emphasized Luther's learning and the learning of his supporters and characterized his opponents as ignorant and unlearned. For example, in *A Good Coarse German Dialogue*, there was an exchange between the characters Peter and Hans. Peter said that he could tell that Hans thought "there is no one wiser than Luther and those who protect him and his undertaking." But Peter would not be swayed, for the "great lords, which are the cardinals and bishops" were not well disposed toward Luther. "So say the canons at the chapters, for one, and various other clergy and several learned people besides, how he is a wicked, perverted monk." It was no wonder that he had misled the whole world since, by all reports, he had in his books "so wickedly attacked the pious man, the pope." The character Hans found this funny, suggesting that these friends of Peter should have been absolved for slander. Rebutting Peter's charges, Hans insisted, one found "many pious people" among Luther's supporters, and the most learned members of the chapters and cloisters were "well disposed towards him and highly praise his teaching."[55]

In *A Beautiful Dialogue* the priest who by pamphlet's end was brought around to Luther's side said that he wished henceforth "to agree with the pious Luther and have nothing more to do with these blatherers," Luther's opponents. Instead, he wished in future "to rely entirely on his teaching and lead you as a true pastor. For I hear," he continued,

> [that] there are in fact many learned people on his side, especially Doctor Erasmus [of] Rotterdam, a strong cornerstone of the Scripture, the same [is true of] Doctor Andreas Karlstadt, a crown of the Holy Scripture, also Oecolampadius and still many more. For I understand [that] these highly learned men are well practiced in the true kernel of the good books— Greek, Hebrew, Latin, and perhaps Chaldean—out of all that has appeared in recent years. [In this] lies, as I hear, the true treasure of the Holy Scripture.[56]

So Luther and his supporters were all learned men. It was only "the unlearned and the greedy," as *A Good Coarse German Dialogue* put it, "who are his enemies and those who are involved with Roman business and those who nourish themselves with deluded judicial quarrels [*verplentem haderwerck ð recht*]. But those who promote justice and love listen to him gladly."[57]

While Eck and his supporters were "the unlearned and the greedy," Luther was not only learned but motivated solely by Christian zeal. In the anonymous *A Good Coarse German Dialog Between Two Good Journeyman*, the character Hans insisted that Luther had done nothing for money, regardless of what the character Peter had heard. "He has not in fact retained a penny." Hans said, "He also does not seek worldly honor. He could have had a bishopric and a great prelacy but he did not wish it. How can he be accused of pouring out poison [when in fact he has been] with great effort championing the proper teaching of God day and night?"[58] This report of an attempted bribe appeared elsewhere. The anonymous author of *A Beautiful Dialogue* had the mayor insist to the priest that Luther "is pious and right [and] does nothing for money. In fact the pope had wanted to give him a bishopric so that he would no longer write against him. Luther would not do this for he would rather be poor than abandon God's truth."[59] By way of contrast, among other harsh accusations, the *Declaration* of the University of Erfurt suggested that Eck and his supporters were in the pay of the Roman bishop.[60]

Luther's supporters generally agreed that Luther had been set upon because he threatened clerical income. The student Laux Gemigger stated that God had sent Luther to reveal the current state of the world, which greatly displeased the pope and his supporters. It was "the penny's shine" that prompted the injustice done to Luther "because he tells us about Roman rascality and also their great heresy."[61] A touch of xenophobia could also creep into the explanation. For example, in *Karsthans* the character Luther, when asked by Karsthans what brought him to do what he was doing, answered that it was the simplicity of the German people who were of such little understanding that they did not question what was presented to them and were thus deceived and made fun of by foreigners.[62]

As these several examples illustrate, popular stereotypes were working to enhance Luther's status and demean the status of his opponents. In the natural polarization of polemical characterization, Luther took on all the attributes of goodness and virtue and his opponents, the attributes of evil and vice. So Luther's selfless concern for Christianity is juxtaposed with papal hirelings like Eck or greedy clerics, who fleeced Christ's sheep or tore into them like ravening wolves. He and his supporters were learned, his opponents ridiculous and ignorant. And so on.

These Strasbourg publications also made much of the contrast between Luther's alleged willingness to be instructed and the alleged unwillingness of his opponents to give him a hearing or overcome him with Scripture, for the contrast fit perfectly into their authors' view of Luther and the struggle in which they were all engaged. In *Karsthans*, for example, Karsthans' son reported that the Dominican "Master of Heretics," Jakob von Hochstraten, had said that "it is not good or certain to dispute with such people or to give them a hearing or to follow the law [in dealing with them] because they are too learned and have often disgraced the master of heretics."[63]

This was a message of several of the treatises: Luther had risked his teachings through public disputations and hearings and had not been overcome. Michael Stifel said that Luther had appeared among his enemies three times now and requested a discussion of his teachings at Augsburg, Leipzig, and Worms. Those who took up the challenge were disgraced; the rest avoided disputing. It was a scandal, Stifel wrote, that members of the universities called Luther a heretic and yet not one of them would come forward to dispute with Luther.[64] In *A Beautiful Dialogue* it was reported that Doctor Eck of Ingolstadt disputed with Luther at Leipzig and "carried away a great sow," the traditional prize for last place in horse racing.[65] In *Karsthans* the student reported that Eck had gained neither much honor nor victory in his disputation with Luther.[66] Hartmuth von Cronberg spread the blame even further. "One says that the wise do not commit small follies," he wrote in his *Rejection of the Alleged Dishonor*. "This may also happen to our geniuses [*hochwysen*] who acted so childishly at the last imperial diet in the matter of doctor Luther, for there has undoubtedly not been a truer more Christian teacher living in a thousand or more years than this doctor Luther."[67] Cronberg went on to say of Luther at Worms that "this doctor rejoiced that he was honored by God in being condemned and banned by men for the sake of the truth. He would much prefer to suffer death and all the horrors of the pope than to keep silent concerning the truth, and in that fashion he shows forth [his] great Christian brotherly love towards the pope and all human beings."[68]

The anonymous author of *A Pleasant Argument* summarized well a point made by several of the pamphleteers. The nobleman in the dialogue asked the curialist why they had not appointed "learned people" to refute Luther "with divine Scripture" and "show him his error," for Luther "wishes nothing else and has offered gladly to be corrected and to give up if he is overcome with Scripture." If this were done, the curialist and his people "would receive great praise" and secure the allegiance of the laity "so that we would believe and persevere more strongly than ever. But when we see that you do not wish to do this but only wish to proceed against him with force you arouse in us a suspicion that you have not shown us thus far the right way to eternal life but rather are misleading us."[69]

The other side of the claim that Luther was willing to be instructed was that it was his opponents who had refused to enter into proper measured debate on the basis of Scripture. Instead, they had started the public battle in the press and then, unable to overcome Luther's arguments, had resorted to force. The burgher of *A Pleasant Argument* became upset with the curialist's criticism of Luther's polemics. While he agreed that some of the pamphlets used "improper ridicule and insulting words" that were inappropriate for "Christian people or doctors" to use, he asked, "But who started this in the first place? Indeed, you Romans! For when Luther first wrote against you in Latin and warned you in a friendly fashion, you would not tolerate any criticism from him. Instead you insulted him so badly [by calling him] a heretic and [attacked him] with such inappropriate treatises that you gave him great cause to write in German."[70] Michael Stifel in his *Against Doctor Murnar's*[71] *False Made-Up Song Concerning the Downfall of Christian Faith*[72] essentially agreed with the burgher's remark. To Murner's charge that Luther had awakened rebellion in the land, Stifel replied that it was widely known that Luther had written that he had often wished to withdraw from the public battle but that his opponents had not allowed this. Instead, they had attacked him with their "insane bacchanalian writings" so that "no pious Christian could have tolerated such sacrilegious falsifying of the holy word of God" that his opponents had practiced. The conflict had been forced by the opponents. "Murnar" called it rebellion, but he needed to know that Christ and Paul had undertaken the same "rebellion."[73] In the introduction to *Karsthans*, the author also claimed that it was Murner who had replied in German to Luther's Latin publications.[74]

Several of these treatises expressed the conviction that Luther's opponents were applying brute force, book burning and the like, because they were unable to defeat Luther in debate or refute his claims with Scripture. In Marcellus's *Passion of Doctor Martin Luther*, it was Luther's books that were burned at Worms rather than Luther himself. Hutten's books were burned to the right of Luther's, Karlstadt's to the left. And following the passion narrative, Marcellus claimed that a portrait of Luther was also consigned to the flames. Over it stood the words "This is Martin Luther, Doctor of divine truth." The portrait would not burn, however, until covered in pitch.[75] Perhaps less fanciful was the account in *Karsthans* that in Mainz in 1520 the papal legate, Aleander, had attempted to arrange that Luther's books be publicly burned. "When everyone was assembled on the square and was awaiting the event," the pamphlet reported, "the executioner asked whether a legal judgment had been given that the books should be burned. When no one could attest to this, the lowly man did not want to execute the judgment and went away. O what great shame and disgrace was thereby shown the legate!"[76] The author of *New Karsthans* had Karsthans report that the emperor was a good papist and accordingly had had Luther's books burned and "placed under the ban with a ferocious, sharp mandate"—the Edict of Worms. Karsthans said that Hutten was being persecuted as well.[77]

Luther was willing to enter into debate on the basis of Scripture; his opponents refused. He had sought to resolve their disagreements peacefully and quietly; his opponents had taken to the press and smeared his name and lied about his teachings. He had been forced to respond to defend the truth and expose error. He had courageously testified to his faith in Leipzig, Augsburg, and now Worms. But instead of offering him the instruction he requested, his opponents resorted to force, condemning him with an unjust ban and burning his books. But just as his picture failed to catch fire, he too, like Christ, would rise up to continue to testify to the truth. These were the stereotypical characteristics of a humble yet learned man of God.

LUTHER'S MESSAGE

If there was a consensus in these pamphlets that Luther insisted on Scripture alone, there the theological consensus largely ended. To the extent that readers in Strasbourg and its environs might be interested in the detail and grounding of Luther's position, they would discover real variety in this literature. To put this another way, the authors of these pamphlets did not themselves agree on what Luther taught or, at the very least, chose to emphasize in their own publications—in their own "re-presentations" of Luther's position—significantly different points. The general agreement on Luther's public persona could stretch to fit a variety of specifics, yet each of these authors thought he was supporting Luther and furthering his theological and reform program.

Some of the Strasbourg pamphlets treated Luther's theological concerns only in passing and in vague terms. Marcellus's *Passion of Dr. Martin Luther*, for example, mentioned only that Luther was a teacher of truth, that he proved his teaching from Holy Scripture, and that he would not recant unless he was shown on the basis of Scripture that he had erred. Of course, the whole *Passion* informed its readers that Luther was at odds with the leadership of the church. Other treatises dealt at length and in detail with the full range of Luther's program. The most remarkable treatise in this group is the anonymous *A Pleasant Argument*, which combined an uncommon familiarity with Luther's positions with a judicious wait-and-see attitude towards Luther himself. Challenged by the curialist in the dialogue, for example, the nobleman listed the things that Luther had taught the laity. The noble's list is quite comprehensive and so worth quoting at length. He had learned from Luther, he said,

> first, that I should not spend so much on indulgences and he shows me that I cannot purchase grace with money since no one can give grace except God. Item, that it would be better with fewer prelates and bishops; that the pope is nothing more than another bishop. Item, that the curialists are rogues involved in fraud—the trickery of simony regarding benefices with absenteeism and reservations has become so flagrant that the village priests have learned [how to do it] and laity can now purchase benefices for their children and friends [*frainden*?] only one may not call it a purchase. Item,

Luther teaches me further that I need not, as was previously the case, confess all the particulars of [my] sins to the priest—it is sufficient that I confess properly to God and briefly to the priest. Item, that when I stand before the mass and the priest elevates the Sacrament, it is sufficient for [the forgiveness of] all my sins to hope with great seriousness and to believe firmly as God has exhorted us [to do] for he must forgive me as he has promised. Item, he teaches me [that] there are no more than three sacraments. Item, he teaches me that the laity are as much clergy [pfaffen] as the priests [priester] and he well establishes this for me from the Bible. Item, he teaches me [that] it is not necessary to sacrifice or do pilgrimages for it is futile to dash off to foreign churches from one's own parish where God also acts and [that] the clergy have thought this up on account of their greed. Item, he teaches me that I no longer need to inquire after [the extent of my] contrition for my sins, as our clergy had heretofore preached. Item, he also teaches me that when we are baptized we are nonetheless still in sin, [that is,] the taste or dregs of original sin are left. That is what Luther has taught me and much more.[78]

Luther, one may speculate, would have been pleased by this list. But such detailed knowledge of Luther's teachings was the exception rather than the rule for these early years.

Some of Luther's distinctive teachings were "re-presented" by only a minority of these authors. Perhaps the most interesting of these other, distinctive teachings was Luther's position on the priesthood of all baptized Christians.[79] We have seen how vehemently Murner objected to this teaching. What did the Evangelical publicists think of it? Karsthans in the pamphlet *Karsthans* attacked Murner for his criticism of Luther's use of Scripture to show that all Christians are priests. Karsthans found Luther's scriptural proof convincing.[80]

The anonymous author of *A Pleasant Argument* explained Luther's position carefully, answering various objections and trying in the process to reconcile much of Luther's position with traditional teaching. The curialist explained how through faith and baptism Christians were incorporated into Christ and Christ shared all that he had with them. Christ was the true high priest, interceding with the Father and offering himself for them. "But since now a lay person can believe, pray, and sacrifice as well as a priest," the curialist explained, "thus he is also just as much spiritually a priest before God as a learned person. Conversely, a consecrated priest and also a lay person are equal spiritually or internally to a king, prince, and temporal lord because God has subject everyone to his faith."[81] "But if we wish to speak of the external priesthood, regarding only the external work, clothing, and tonsure," the curialist continued, "we must speak differently about this since, in fact, Doctor Luther does not say that the laity are priests but rather the priests are appointed ministers or servants of the laity or of the Christian church, that is, of all people who believe in Christ." These appointed ministers are "servants in that they should pray, sacrifice, sing, read, and distribute the sacrament." So in respect to the office of the priesthood, there was a great distinction between laity and priests. The laity also did not have the right at their own pleasure to appoint or remove these same servants "as now the ignorant laity say and contend."[82] "All this," he asserted, "is also Doctor Luther's basic opinion, especially in his pamphlet that he wrote to the pope concerning Christian freedom."[83]

But *A Pleasant Argument* was the exception rather than the rule. What is the significance of the fact that most of the treatises published in support of Luther in 1521–1522 have so little to say about the specifics of Luther's theology? There was consensus on only three points: first, on the principle of Scripture alone and, second, that the papacy was a tyranny and needed reform if not to be abolished outright. The third point that found rather broad re-presentation was that "human" law had no place in religious matters. We examine this in the next section, since it illustrates rather dramatically the theological variation encompassed by Luther's one public persona. But these findings raise an intriguing question. Could it be that it was just these two powerful principles—Scripture alone and the rejection of "human" laws in religion—and the general attack on the papacy and clerical exploitation—anticlericalism, perhaps—that accounted for much of the support Luther received in the early years and not, or rather not yet, the many specific theological positions that we associate with Lutheranism? The works of these early publicists suggest that this may be the case.

HUMAN LAW AND DIVINE

The variety in the representations of Luther's position is nowhere more apparent—and more significant for our approach to Luther's influence and image in these crucial early years—than in the treatment of law and works, for on this issue the Strasbourg publications offer a seemingly contradictory reading of Luther's position.[84] At the heart of Luther's understanding of law and works lies the paradoxical notion of Christian freedom. This is best expressed in Luther's remarkable "best seller," *On the Freedom of a Christian*. Although Luther himself prepared both a Latin and a German version, the Strasbourg printers chose only to reprint the German version. Two editions appeared in 1520, another in 1521, another in 1522, and the last Strasbourg printing in 1524.[85] So Strasbourg readers had ample opportunity to read this important treatise.

Luther began with the paradox itself: "A Christian is a free lord over all things, subject to no one. A Christian is a subservient servant of all, subject to all."[86] One half of the paradox meant, Luther said, "that a Christian has enough with faith [and] needs no works to make him pious; [and] if he no longer has need of works, then he is certainly unshackled [empunden, "set free"] from all commands and laws; [and] if he is unshackled, he is free indeed."[87] It is this paradoxical freedom from the law and submission to the law that many of our authors failed to understand or accept even as they wrote in support of Luther and his program. Luther explained this freedom clearly. "One should know," Luther wrote,

> that the complete Holy Scripture is divided into two words, which are commandment or law of God, and promise or pledge. The commandments teach and prescribe for us various good works, but they are not thereby accomplished. They indeed point the direction, but they do not help [with accomplishment]. They teach what one should do but give no strength for the doing. Therefore they are only established so that the human being can see from them his inability to do the good and learn to doubt himself.[88]

That was the function of the law, to humble a person and reveal the human incapacity to fulfill the law. "Then comes the other word," Luther explained,

> the divine promise and pledge. And [it] says, if you wish to fulfill all the commandments [and] be freed from your evil desires and sin as the commandments compel and demand, look at this! Believe in Christ, in what I [Christ] promised you, all grace, righteousness, peace, and freedom. If you believe, then you have [it]. If you do not believe, then you do not have it. For it is impossible for you [to achieve this] with all the works of the commandments, which are numerous but are of no use. But you will easily and quickly [achieve] it through faith.

Therefore the promise of God gave what the commandments required, and accomplished what the commandments commanded. Everything belonged to God—commandment and fulfillment. "He alone commands; he alone also fulfills."[89]

Luther went on to explain that once freed from the law by grace through faith, Christians voluntarily subjected themselves to the law for the sake of the neighbor and undertook service to others, not for any reward that such service might be thought to merit, but out of spontaneous love in obedience to God. At the same time that Luther taught the voluntary submission to the law, he also concluded that a wide range of clerically imposed "human" laws were not just unnecessary and fraudulent, fabricated in order to enrich the clergy, but positively sinful since they motivated people to trust in their own efforts rather than to accept God's free gift of forgiveness.

Significantly, many of our authors adopted Luther's insistence that Scripture should be the sole authority and his concomitant rejection of "man-made" laws that conflicted with Scripture, but they did not share his understanding of the inability of human beings to fulfill the law, even the divine law. Instead, they rejected "man-made laws" but insisted on the fulfillment of "divine law." For example, the author of *New Karsthans* severely criticized the clergy because they did not live according to the pattern set by the early church or in accordance with the teachings of Christ; that is, they did not conform to Scripture. Papal law was contrasted with Christ's commands. For example, the character Karsthans responded to a recitation of 1 Timothy 4:1–4 with the comment, "These words are against the papal law, in which, as I hear and the clergy preach, it is forbidden to eat meat, eggs, and milk on fast days and [it is stated] that clergy should not have wives." The character Sickingen agreed that the words of 1 Timothy 4 were indeed opposed to the papal law. Unfortunately, however, "it has come to the point where more attention is now paid to what the pope institutes than to what Christ himself says with his own mouth and [what] the apostles have said and written. And the pope is served with greater fear than God Himself." That was what the clergy believed and taught, Sickingen asserted, and they thereby perverted "the legitimate Holy Scripture with their human, indeed devilish decretals."[90] At another point Sickingen observed that, although the papal law was illegitimate and should be rejected, it was given precedence over the commands of God. Christ himself had excoriated the Jews for just such a practice of violating God's commandments for the sake of human laws.[91] Further on Sickingen deplored the fact that the papal law was considered to be completely firm and constant while the gospel and Christ's teaching was given little respect. One could see this in the widespread opinion, he remarked, that to eat meat on Friday was an "unchristian, evil thing," although this was not God's prohibition but rather the pope's.[92]

This attack is strongly reminiscent of Erasmus's insistence on a simple, scripturally based Christianity. This impression is reinforced by a prototypically Erasmian attack in *New Karsthans* on external ceremonies. They were unnecessary, the author observed. Christians should rather serve God spiritually and confine their external activity to good works.[93] The author of *New Karsthans* was still operating with traditional categories, although in a humanist vein. His objection was not to a reliance on law per se but only to a reliance on false, man-made laws and especially ecclesiastical law. In fact, he sought above all to champion "divine law and commandments," which he equated with God's "wholesome faith."[94] Tradition or custom was rejected in favor of the teachings of Christ and the apostles.[95] Christ was a teacher and example to the clergy.[96] Divine law was not to be sullied by human additions; but the role of the divine law was viewed in completely positive terms. The problem was the burden of ecclesiastical law, not law generally. God was implored to rescue them from the "papal oppression and the wantonness of the clergy, who with their arrogant, irritating life have scandalously suppressed your divine word and sacrilegiously taken from us the wholesome food for souls [and who] have laid upon us an unbearable burden in the place of your light yoke."[97] This "light yoke" was the teaching and example of Christ, the "divine law." It is crucial to note that the author did not offer his readers Luther's condemnation of *all* works done in anticipation of reward. More importantly, he did not offer the word of promise as the answer to the challenge of the law, even (or perhaps especially) the challenge of "divine law."

Other treatises also took this more "humanistic" than "Lutheran" approach to law and works. The author of *A Beautiful Dialogue*, who may be the same person as the presumed author of *New Karsthans*, namely Martin Bucer, used Scripture to criticize the clergy and the institutional church, for Scripture was seen as the source of divine law, which took precedence over all human laws of the church. When he stated that Luther "grounds all his writings in right faith and out of the holy gospel and out of Saint Paul's teaching and leads us out of many entanglements into which the clergy has for a long time gotten us on account of money and goods,"[98] the clerical entanglements that he had in mind was the ecclesiastical law, concerning which he remarked, "I am concerned [that] there is little in it of God's law."[99] On this basis he proceeded to criticize the clergy and many clerical practices.

The student Laux Gemigger suggested that Luther had taught "Christ's teaching," namely, "how we have turned from good to evil," and had laid out the "teaching of the evangelists . . . without additions." The additions were, of course, human laws. Luther was "sent by God to teach us God's word and good morals and to drive out the Antichrist here on earth, also to see to it that God's word not be completely spoiled and that the Roman tyranny be recognized, that they should have no kingdom here on earth."[100]

While *New Karsthans, A Beautiful Dialogue*, and Laux Gemigger's *To the Praise of Luther* did not even mention salvation by faith alone, Hartmuth von Cronberg's *Rejection* did attempt to explain the relation between salvation by faith alone and good works. Luther had given everyone the power to become a child of God and an inheritor of his eternal kingdom, Cronberg began, because

> he who believes that is assured and his God will lead him and keep him on his way. There may be no doubt: no one who believes in Christ rightly may be ungrateful for such magnificent grace. For this reason we wish to be thankful to our Lord Christ for the magnificent grace that he has shown to us his unworthy creatures. Therefore we must be attentive to the works that please the Lord God the most and on which the whole Christian foundation stands. That is to love God with all the strength of body, mind, and soul and [to love] the neighbor as our selves.[101]

But as this excerpt shows, Cronberg was still operating largely with a contrast between the divine law of love and human laws. Cronberg set the two great commandments taught by Christ against the ecclesiastical laws of the pope. If the pope could be led from "human wisdom" to the "true wisdom," "the divine Christian wisdom," he would virtuously desist from "all unchristian laws." All self-seeking would be transformed into "the most sweet brotherly love" based on the love of God and neighbor. Justice would be instilled into human hearts and consciences, and there would be less reliance on juridical books because "Christian brotherly love cannot tolerate the interminable legal dealing [*Juristery*]."[102] God, for Cronberg, "does not regard the multiplication of external works of pageantry or longer prayers. He wishes that [one] have a good heart. This is what is truly called seeking the kingdom of God."[103]

If in their defense of Luther Cronberg, Gemigger, and the author or authors of *New Karsthans* and *A Beautiful Dialogue* viewed the contest largely in terms of "divine law" or Scripture versus "human law," Michael Stifel and the anonymous author of *A Pleasant Argument* read and represented Luther differently. For them, as for Luther himself, the law disclosed human unworthiness and drove one to God's unmerited gift of forgiveness. "See now, dear man," Stifel wrote, "thus

Luther teaches us to fear God through His law so that we can in no way by our own efforts fulfill the law without His grace." Fear induced humility and a great desire "to run after the grace of God." "But observe what clumsiness is in our doctors," Stifel exclaimed. They raised the cry that Luther "disparages God, the wicked heretic! He says that God demands more from us than we are able. If that were the case, God would be unjust for condemning us on account of that which was beyond our power." "O blindness!" Stifel replied, "Take notice, dear lay person, dear peasant, how these big cheeses understand nothing about either the law of God or His grace!"[104]

Stifel went on to state that Luther taught that the Christian was not bound to do good works but, in the freedom of faith, did good works joyfully. Christian freedom "joyfully fulfills the law." For this reason, Stifel explained, Luther said of the righteous man in Psalm 1 that he was not bound to any work nor to any time. Rather he freely did what the law required. "That is truly the correct teaching of the spirit of freedom," Stifel insisted, citing 1 John 2 and 2 Corinthians 3. There was freedom where there was the spirit of the lord. "From this it follows that a work done in the conviction that it is necessary . . . is a work contrary to Christian freedom. It is a work of presumption. It goes against the Holy Spirit."[105]

To be sure, Stifel explained, Luther was criticized by his enemies because he taught that good works outside of grace were sins, but for Stifel salvation itself hung on this point. "Everything that occurs before grace is sin and nothing good because it is mere human work which God does not reward other than by appearance." Stifel explained that just as such works had an appearance of goodness, God gave for them temporal reward, that is, an appearance of a reward. "But in truth it is more a punishment," he said, "since the human being misuses it as all other things before he is in grace." But now that Luther had taught such things, his enemies cried against him "as the Jews did against Christ." The Jews said that Christ could not be sent from God because he broke the Sabbath. In the same way, Luther's opponents said that Luther could not be a messenger from God because he rejected praying, fasting, the giving of alms, and so on. He was a heretic. "God willing," concluded Stifel, "may I die on account of the confession of such a heresy, namely, on account of the honor of God and His Grace."[106] Stifel seemed relatively unconcerned about the confusion and outrage that was occasioned by this rejection of works apart from grace.

Not so the author of *A Pleasant Argument*. He took some pains to lay out his understanding of Luther's position and to protect it from misunderstanding. In the dialogue, the nobleman challenged the curialist. "Doctor Luther teaches that one may not do good works because one may not earn heaven though good works. Also, that one can do no good work without sin. If this is the case, why are you always talking about good works?"[107] The curialist replied that the nobleman had not understood Luther and was doing him an injustice. Luther never forbade people to do good works. "If you wish to read him, you must understand him correctly for Luther is never against the Gospel and Paul, who teach us that we should do good works."[108] When challenged by the burgher to make sense of this, the curialist urged the burgher and nobleman to read Luther's *Instruction Concerning Several Articles That Were Attributed To Him By His Opponents*. "There you will find that he thinks a great deal of good works and although it is indeed true that one cannot come to salvation through works, nevertheless works are necessary for salvation, for Christ has commanded us to work in his vineyard."[109] The curialist then went on to explain Luther's position as he understood it. Luther's opinion was that "external works such as fasting, going to church, giving alms, doing pilgrimage, endowing masses and benefices" were insufficient in themselves for salvation. The human being was unable to become holy through such things, however many of them he did. "This must be understood," the curialist said, "for good works do not make the human being justified (because a wicked, lost person can also do good works)." If the human being wished to be saved, he had to be just beforehand. This could not happen through works but only through God's grace, which relieved the human being. "And it is indeed a false delusion," the curialist said, "when one takes it upon oneself to earn God's favor and grace through one's good works, for the grace of God comes solely from the free inspiration of God without our merit but rather out of His mercy."[110] The curialist went on to say that once we had grace, that grace worked in us so that we did good works. So people did Luther an injustice when they said that he rejected fasting, confessing, alms giving, and the like.

VARIETY AND RECEPTION

We see in these writings some significant variety in the ways in which different authors read and re-presented Martin Luther and his writings. These authors all wrote in support of Luther and his teachings, as they each understood it. Underlying this support was both consensus and divergence.

The authors agreed among themselves on a few crucial items about Luther's character and his message. They all saw Luther as a learned doctor and an engaged pastor dedicated to teaching "Christian truth." They also agreed that Luther's teachings set him in conflict with the institutional church and especially the papacy. Most important of all, these authors agreed that Luther insisted that "Christian truth" could be establish only on the basis of "Scripture alone." The historian and bibliographer Hans-Joachim Köhler has examined a representative sample of 356 pamphlets that closely resembled the major characteristics of the larger universe of approximately 10,000 pamphlets published between 1500 and 1530. He found that nearly all the pamphlets dealt in one way or another with the issues of theology and the church. "Only six of the 285 German pamphlets in our sample," Köhler remarks, "do not touch upon theological topics—and likewise only three of the 71 Latin texts."[111] Of the five major thematic groupings Köhler constructed—theology and the church, the economy, politics and law, learning and education, and society and culture—theology and the church was the most popular topic, found in 98 percent of the pamphlets. Issues of the economy were least popular, found in only 43 percent of the pamphlets.

Köhler's results go beyond these gross categories to identify the most important subtopics within this pamphlet literature. Once again, it was a religious issue, or to be more precise, a Reformation issue, that dominated these publications. The one issue that excelled all others, the one issue that received the greatest attention, was the principle of *sola scriptura*, Scripture alone. In other words, two-thirds of the pamphlets, both Catholic and Evangelical, dealt in one way or another with the claim that Scripture should be the sole source of faith. In the period 1520 to 1526, this Reformation topic was dealt with by more than 70 percent of the authors.[112] Perhaps not surprisingly, then, this was also the one issue on which all these defenders of Luther agreed.

If our authors agreed on Luther's vocation as a teacher and on his insistence on Scripture alone, they disagreed (without probably being aware of the disagreement) on his larger role and on the crucial conclusions he drew from Scripture alone. Some of our authors still presented Luther as primarily a teacher and theologian seeking to reform

the institutional church. He was a highly learned theologian and a trenchant (and perhaps excessively vociferous) critic of abuses within the
church. But others saw Luther in a larger, possibly apocalyptic role.
To view Luther as a special instrument of God—as an "Elias" or
"Christian angel," as Stifel did—invested his message with special authority. We see in this public persona the beginnings of Luther's peculiar personal authority among his followers.

When we turn from Luther's person to his message, only a minority
of these authors picked up on some issues of central interest to Luther
himself, such as the priesthood of all baptized Christians.[113] In fact,
the majority of Luther's defenders published in Strasbourg were still
reading Luther within a context strongly shaped by humanistic and
specifically Erasmian concerns. This context inclined these authors to
assimilate Luther's scripturally based criticism of human laws to the
Erasmian attack on the "superstitions" of external observance that
lacked spiritual grounding. For a time—a crucial time for the fledgling
Reformation movement—Luther was read and re-presented in these
Erasmian terms. It took time for these authors to realize that more
was at stake, that Luther's radical understanding of commandment
and promise was corrosive not only of "man-made laws" but of reliance on law in any form in the process of salvation.

CHAPTER FIVE

Scripture as Printed Text

For both Catholics and Evangelicals Scripture was *the* premier author-ity. All parties agreed that the church and its beliefs rested ultimately on Scripture.[1] At issue, then, was not the authority of Scripture but its authoritative interpretation. Who had the right to say definitively what Scripture taught when church Fathers could be cited on both sides of an issue, when university theological faculties divided into opposing camps, and when academics could not convince each other of the cor-rectness of their reading? Catholics answered that the pope or an ecumenical council or both had that right. But at Worms Martin Luther made his stand against these authorities in favor of Scripture alone. "Unless I am overcome through testimony of Scripture or through evident reasons (for I believe neither the pope nor the council alone because it is apparent that they have erred repeatedly and con-tradicted themselves), I am overcome by the Scripture that I have cited and my conscience is captive to the word of God."[2] Scripture was the sole authority. It was even the authority on its authoritative interpreta-tion. Scripture, Luther insisted, interpreted itself.

Whatever the cogency of this position from a theological stand-point,[3] in practice Scripture did not interpret itself. Human beings interpreted Scripture, and they disagreed. The inability of Catho-lics and Evangelicals to reach the same interpretation of Scripture was readily explicable to both sides and caused little anxiety among Evangelicals, who on the whole shared the reading of Scripture that con-demned the papacy and many traditional practices and beliefs. But it

Plate 2. *Das Newe Testament Deûtzsch*. Title page to the first edition ("September Testament") of Luther's *German New Testament* (Wittenberg, 1522).

was another matter entirely once Evangelicals began to disagree among themselves. Unless the conflict was over a matter of no great importance, Evangelicals were inclined to attribute their opponents' misreading to a lack of the Holy Spirit, which guaranteed a proper understanding. The fault must lie in the man, not in the text.

Even so, Luther decided in issuing his German translation of the New Testament[4] that it was necessary to fit out the text of Scripture with aids to its interpretation. "It would indeed be right and proper for this book to be issued without any prefaces and foreign names [attached] and for it to bear only its own name and to speak for itself," he wrote in the preface to the first edition, expressing his view of the theoretical ideal. "But because various wild interpretations and prefaces have so confused Christians that one no longer even knows what 'Gospel' or 'law,' 'new' or 'old testament' means, necessity demands a notice and prefaces to be placed [in this book] so that the simple person will be led from his old delusion on to the right way and instructed in what he should expect in this book so that he not seek commandments and laws where he should be seeking Gospel and the promises of God."⁵

Using forewords and introductions, marginal glosses, polemical illustrations, rearranged paragraphing, and a theologically inspired translation, Luther sought to assure that at least the *printed text* of Scripture interpreted itself. Let us see how he went about helping the "simple person" out of his "old delusion on to the right way," and how Luther instructed him in "what he should expect in this book."

PRINTED AIDS TO THE "RIGHT" UNDERSTANDING OF SCRIPTURE

In the very first paragraph of his preface, Luther identified his central concern, namely, that the readers of the New Testament be instructed so that they could rightly distinguish "laws and commandments" from the "Gospel and promises of God." This was no simple matter. As the last chapter showed, a majority of those authors publishing in Strasbourg in defense of Luther in 1521–1522 failed to distinguish law and gospel in a manner consistent with Luther's own concerns. While Luther believed that Scripture testified to the inability of human beings to fulfill any law, human or divine, many of the Strasbourg publicists appealed to Scripture alone to invalidate human laws, but went on to insist that Scripture demanded the fulfillment of divine law. To rectify such confusion Luther deployed a range of arguments.

After maintaining that there was but one gospel found in both Old and New Testaments,[6] Luther turned to his central concern that the reader "not make a Moses out of Christ, or a book of law or teachings out of the gospel." For the gospel, Luther insisted, "does not in fact demand our works so that we become pious and holy through them." In fact, it condemned such works. Rather it demanded only faith in Christ, faith "that he has overcome sin, death, and hell for us and thus made us righteous, alive, and saved not through our own works but through his own work, death, and suffering so that we may take on his death and victory as if we had done it ourselves."[7] To be sure, Christ, Peter, and Paul issued commandments and expounded doctrines. But to know Christ's works and his history was not the same as knowing the true Gospel that Christ had overcome sin, death, and the devil, and hearing the voice that says, "Christ is your own with his life, teaching, works, death, resurrection, and all that which he is, has, does, and can do."[8]

The gospel was not a law book "but only a sermon on the benefits of Christ as shown to us and given to be our own as we believe."[9] No law was given to a believer because he was "justified, alive, and saved through faith." Nothing more was necessary for him except that he should prove this faith. Without explicitly mentioning the Catholic accusation that his teaching undercut good works and promoted antinomianism, Luther offered a retort. Believers who were saved by faith could not in fact restrain themselves from doing good works and showing love towards their neighbors, following Christ's example. In this way one could recognize who Christ's disciples and true believers were, "for where works and love do not break forth, there faith is not right, there the Gospel has not yet taken hold, and Christ is not properly recognized." "Take note," Luther admonished in closing, "apply yourself to the books of the New Testament in this fashion so that you read and understand them in this way."[10]

Drawing on the distinction between law and gospel that he had laid down in his preface, Luther placed in his *German New Testament* a fascinating one-page excursus entitled "Which Are the True and Most Noble Books of the New Testament." In effect Luther was telling his readers that not all Scripture was of equal value, since not all taught equally well the proper distinction between law and gospel. The Gospel of John, Paul's epistles (especially the one to the Romans), and Peter's first epistle, he argued, were "the true kernel and marrow among all the books." Every Christian should be advised to read them first and most often, and through daily reading to make them as common as one's daily bread. "For in these you do not find much described about the many works and miracles of Christ, but you do find masterfully depicted how faith in Christ overcomes sin, death, and hell and gives life, righteousness, and salvation, which is the true nature of the Gospel."[11] If he had to choose, Luther wrote, he would rather do without knowledge of the works of Christ than do without his preaching. "For the works do not help me at all but his words give life." The Gospel of John wrote little about Christ's works but very much about his preaching, while the other three Gospels described a great deal about his works but little about his words. Accordingly, the Gospel of John "is the one, tender, true, chief gospel" to be greatly preferred over the other three. Similarly, the letters of Paul and Peter surpassed the other three Gospels. John and the letters of Paul and Peter "are the books that show you Christ and teach you all that is necessary and salvific for you to know even if you never saw nor heard another book or teaching." In contrast to these, the letter of James was "a true letter of straw for it has nothing of a gospel nature about it."[12]

Luther reinforced this contrast in his table of contents, indicating visually and verbally which books of the New Testament should be seen as authoritative (see plate 3). Twenty-three books were numbered and identified as being written by a saint. Set off from this numbered list by a large blank space, four more books were listed but not numbered: "The Letter to the Hebrews," "The Letter of James," "The Letter of Jude," "The Revelation of John." The visual separation, the lack of numbering, and the omission of the designation "saint" made clear to the reader the secondary status of these works. Luther explained this special category in his preface to Hebrews, where he remarked that these four books had a reputation different from the preceding "true, certain, chief books of the New Testament." In challenging the apostolic provenance of the Epistle of James, Luther observed that it "contradicted Paul and all the rest of Scripture in attributing justification to works" and that it failed to mention the suffering, resurrection, and spirit of Christ. "The true touchstone for judging all books is to see whether they promote Christ or not." But all James did was to promote the law and its works.[13] Luther also spoke dismissively of the Book of Revelation because "Christ is neither taught nor known in it, which is the prime responsibility of an apostle to do." He summed up his point of view with the flat observation, "I stick with those books that give me Christ pure and simply."[14]

Luther let his general foreword suffice for an introduction to the Gospels, including John, but in accordance with his judgment of the central importance of Paul's letter to the Romans, he provided an additional eleven-folio-page foreword to this letter. By contrast, his other forewords were quite short, never more than a folio page and often less. He wrote forewords to each of the rest of Paul's letters and to each of Peter's letters, one short foreword to the three letters of John, a foreword to Hebrews, one foreword to James and Judas, and one to Revelation.

Luther began his lengthy preface to Saint Paul's Epistle to the Romans with a ringing declaration: "This epistle is the true, chief part of the New Testament and the purest gospel. It would be right and

Die Bucher des newen testaments.

1. Euangelion Sanct Matthes.
2. Euangelion Sanct Marcus.
3. Euangelion Sanct Lucas.
4. Euangelion Sanct Johannis.
5. Der Apostel geschicht beschrieben von Sanct Lucas
6. Epistel Sanct Paulus zu den Romern.
7. Die erste Epistel Sanct Paulus zu den Corinthern.
8. Die ander Epistel Sanct Paulus zu den Corinthern
9. Epistel Sanct Paulus zu den Balatern.
10. Epistel Sanct Paulus zu den Ephesern.
11. Epistel Sanct Paulus zu den Philippern.
12. Epistel Sanct Paulus zu den Colossern.
13. Die erste Epistel Sanct Paulus zu den Thessalonicern.
14. Die ander Epistel Sanct Paulus zu den Thessalonicern.
15. Die erst Epistel Sanct Paulus an Timotheon.
16. Die ander Epistel Sanct Paulus an Timotheon.
17. Epistel Sanct Paulus an Titon.
18. Epistel Sanct Paulus an Philemon.
19. Die erst Epistel Sanct Peters.
20. Die ander Epistel Sanct Peters.
21. Die erste Epistel Sanct Johannis.
22. Die ander Epistel Sanct Johannis.
23. Die drit Epistel Sanct Johannis.

Die Epistel zu den Ebreern.
Die Epistel Jacobus.
Die Epistel Judas.
Die offinbarung Johannis.

Plate 3. Die Bucher des newen testaments. Table of contents to the first edition ("September Testament") of Luther's *German New Testament* (Wittenberg, 1522).

proper not only for a Christian to know it word for word by heart but also to live it daily as the daily bread of the soul, for it can never be read or thought about too much or too well."[15] Accordingly, Luther explained, he would do his best with God's help "to prepare an entrance into it [Romans] with this preface . . . so that everyone can understand it better, for heretofore it has been wickedly obscured by glosses and all sorts of twaddle, although it itself is a bright light nearly sufficient to illuminate all of Scripture."[16]

Luther's assertion is worth pondering for a moment. Saint Paul's Epistle to the Romans is for Luther the "purest gospel," because it taught more clearly than any other book the right understanding of law and gospel. Together with the Gospel of John and the other letters of Saint Paul and Saint Peter, it formed in effect a canon within the canon. A proper understanding of these "preeminent" books allowed the reader rightly to interpret the rest of Scripture. Scripture interpreted itself, yet as Luther himself remarked, Saint Paul's Epistle to the Romans had been "wickedly obscured by glosses and all sorts of twaddle." Before Scripture could interpret itself, the obscurity had to be lifted from the key to the self-interpretation of Scripture. Printing provided the means, with prefaces and marginalia (not to mention a theologically inspired translation) that opened the "true, chief part of the New Testament" to do its duty. In fact, it was the *printed* text of Scripture that interpreted itself.

In his preface Luther laid out what he understood St. Paul to mean in Romans by terms such as "law," "sin," "grace," "faith," "righteousness," "flesh," "spirit," and the like. In so doing, of course, he was telling his readers how they should understand these words as they read not only the epistle but Scripture generally. He began, for example, with his central concern: the relation between law, works, and grace. "The little word 'law,'" he explained, "you must not understand here in a human fashion as if it were a teaching about what works are to be done or to be omitted as is the case with human laws where one satisfies the law with works even if the heart is not in it."[17] Rather, law was spiritual and could be fulfilled only if God's Spirit fashioned the human heart to desire after it willingly. "So accustom yourself to this way of speaking," Luther directed his readers, "that it is two quite different things to do the works of the law and to fulfill the law."[18] To fulfill the law was to do its works with pleasure and love and without the compulsion of the law. This was only possible as a gift of the Holy Spirit, and the gift of the Holy Spirit came only through faith, and, finally, faith only came through God's Word or Gospel, which preached Christ. "So it happens that only faith justifies and fulfills the law, for it, through Christ's merit, brings the Spirit, which makes the heart happy and free, as the law demands. Thus good works proceed from faith itself."[19] In similar fashion Luther defined the other key terms in the epistle, emphasizing in each case the right and wrong way to understand these crucial concepts.

Although his preface to Romans represented Luther's most elaborate attempt to influence how Scriptures were read, most of the remaining, much shorter prefaces, continued to sound the central themes concerning law and gospel. Specifically, issues of law and gospel are dealt with in the prefaces to 2 Corinthians, Galatians, Ephesians, Philippians, Colossians, 1 Timothy, Titus, 2 Peter, and the three epistles of Saint John (all regarding the first epistle), and in the dismissive preface to Revelation. In the prefaces to Galatians, Philippians, 1 Timothy, Titus, and 2 Peter, Luther equated the "false apostles" or "false teachers" with those who taught that one could be saved through works of the law. For example, in the preface to Galatians, Luther remarked that Paul brought the Galatians "to the true Christian faith, from the law to the Gospel. . . . But after his departure false apostles came, who were disciples of the true apostles and who returned the Galatians to the belief that they must be saved through works of the law and that they sinned when they did not keep the works of the law."[20] But Paul taught that everyone must be justified through Christ alone and without merit, works, or law. Paul, Luther explained, showed that "the law brings more sin and curse than justification, which is promised solely through God's grace and fulfilled by Christ without the law and given to us." Works of love should follow faith.[21]

The contemporary situation was very much in Luther's mind as he wrote these prefaces. In the prefaces to 1 Timothy and Titus, Luther explained that Paul directed bishops to maintain true faith and love and resist the "false preachers of the law" who wished, alongside Christ and the Gospel, to promote the works of the law.[22] Paul taught that a true bishop or pastor should be "one who is pious and learned in preaching the Gospel and in refuting the false teachers of works and human law, who are always fighting against faith and seducing consciences from Christian freedom into the captivity of their own human works, which are in fact useless."[23] Luther clearly did not think that contemporary bishops and pastors were following Paul's teaching. In fact, in the prefaces to 2 Timothy and 2 Peter, Luther insisted that Paul's prophecies regarding the Endtime and Peter's criticism of "avarice, pride, sacrilege, whoring, and hypocrisy" applied to the clergy of his own day.[24]

Readers could, of course, skip the foreword and prefaces. It was more difficult, however, to ignore the glosses that ran down the margins on many of the pages. With this visually unavoidable commentary, Luther further directed readers in their reading of the New Testament. Even a simple cross tabulation can orient us to the overall effort.

What were the issues about which Luther most wanted to influence interpretation? Table 10 offers a tabulation of glosses in the first edi-

TABLE 10   GLOSSES IN THE SEPTEMBER
                        TESTAMENT
              Sorted by glosses per page

	Pages	Glosses	Glosses on Theme	Glosses per Page	% on Theme
Romans	20	50	29	2.50	58%
1 Corinthians	20	45	19	2.25	42%
Ephesians	7	13	6	1.86	46%
Matthew	48	88	33	1.83	38%
Galatians	7	12	9	1.71	75%
2 Corinthians	13	18	6	1.38	33%
1 John	5	4	1	0.80	25%
John	36	20	11	0.56	55%
1 Peter	6	3	0	0.50	0%
Luke	50	23	5	0.46	22%
Colossians	5	2	1	0.40	50%
2 Thessalonians	3	1	1	0.33	100%
Titus	3	1	0	0.33	0%
Mark	30	9	2	0.30	22%
Philippians	5	1	1	0.20	100%
1 Thessalonians	5	1	0	0.20	0%
Hebrews	15	2	1	0.13	50%
Acts	50	4	0	0.08	0%
Revelation	50	1	1	0.02	100%
1 Timothy	6	0	0	0.00	N/A
2 Timothy	4	0	0	0.00	N/A
Philemon	1	0	0	0.00	N/A
2 Peter	4	0	0	0.00	N/A
3 John	1	0	0	0.00	N/A
James	5	0	0	0.00	N/A
Jude	2	0	0	0.00	N/A
Total	401	298	126		

tion (known as the "September Testament" from its September 1522 printing date) sorted by frequency of glosses per page.[25] Although the Gospel According to Saint Matthew has the largest total number of glosses with eighty-eight, three letters of Saint Paul—Romans, 1 Corinthians, and Ephesians—were most heavily glossed, and Romans led with an average of two and a half glosses per page. Of those books that have an average of at least one gloss per page, five of the six are letters of Saint Paul. The Gospel According to Saint Matthew is the only non-Pauline letter to receive comparable attention. Luther devoted more effort—measured at least by glosses per page—to directing the reading of a major part of the Pauline corpus than to any other part of the New Testament.

When examined for content, these glosses reveal even more clearly Luther's central concerns. Table 10 also lists the number of glosses in each book that either dealt with the issues of faith, law, and gospel as defined in our discussion of Luther's prefaces or criticized by name the papacy or monasticism.[26] Just as Luther gave Romans the largest individual preface of any book and devoted to Romans the greatest number of glosses per page, he also devoted over half (58 percent) of his glosses to the issues of law and gospel. Of the six books with more than one gloss per page, only Galatians had a higher percentage with 75 percent. Given the central importance of these two books for Luther's understanding of the gospel, these statistics are hardly surprising, and they illustrate the care with which Luther attempted to direct the reading of these crucial books. Over one-third (38 percent) of the glosses on the one non-Pauline book in this company—the Gospel According to Saint Matthew—also dealt with issues of law and gospel.

Overall, 42 percent of the glosses in the *German New Testament* dealt with issues of law and gospel, faith and works, Christian freedom and promise. Of those glosses that dealt with theological issues generally (as opposed to simple identifications of places, persons, or terms), fully half (50 percent) of the glosses dealt with these issues. These statistics are a stark indication of the effort Luther put into helping his readers understand the New Testament as he himself did.

With the aid of one of the Catholic critics of Luther's translation, we can see in a few examples how both Luther's translation and the accompanying glosses encouraged a reading of the text that differed sharply from a Catholic reading. The critic is Hieronymus Emser, who at the encouragement of his prince, Duke Georg of Albertine Saxony, issued an apology for the duke's recent order to his subjects to turn over copies of Luther's *German New Testament*.[27] In late September 1523, the press of Wolfgang Stöckel at Leipzig issued this lengthy apology, entitled *On What Grounds and for What Reason Luther's Translation of the New Testament Should Properly Be Forbidden To the Common Man*. The treatise's subtitle announced to the reader Emser's intention to explain how and where Luther distorted the text and how he employed glosses and prefaces to mislead readers "from the ancient Christian way."[28]

Emser methodically criticized the whole *German New Testament*. The thrust of his concern can best be illustrated by looking at the crucial book from Luther's perspective, Saint Paul's Epistle to the Romans, specifically at the book's crucial chapter 3, in which Paul argued that all were under the power of sin and all were justified by God's free grace through Christ's sacrificial death (see plate 4). In these examples Emser sought to show that the interpretation that seemed to Luther natural and proper was in fact forced and contrived. Without Luther's glosses and particular translation, Emser maintained, the text yielded a quite different meaning.

Emser objected first to the initial gloss,[29] in which Luther asserted that we should acknowledge our sin. Here is an excerpt from Luther's gloss:

> But the 'works-saints' [*werckheyligē*] quarrel with God over this acknowledgment, and do not wish to allow their works to be sin and so God must be their liar and condemned in his words. For they look at only the crude sinful deeds [*wercksund*] and not the deep, chief original sin, in which nature is conceived, born, and lives, about which, however, David speaks in the verse. This is what Paul means, that sin does not glorify God (otherwise it would be better to sin than to do good) but rather the confession of sin glorifies God and his grace.[30]

Emser found this gloss highly tendentious. "He wishes to convince us," Emser wrote, "to recognize that all our works are sins, since sin also remains in us after baptism, according to his opinion." But that was false and a lie in two respects, for Paul testified in Romans 8 that "all our sin is taken away through faith and baptism." Paul also said that there was "nothing damning" [*nichtzit vordamlichs*] in those who were in Christ Jesus and did not live according to the flesh. "Just as no one may say that he is without sin, thus no one may truly say that all works are sin, for if fasting, giving of alms, praying, doing penance, etc., were sins, then God would have commanded sin and Christ him-

Die Epistel

schneyttung die ym geyst vnd nicht ym buchstaben geschicht/wilchs lob ist nicht aus den menschen/sondern aus got.

Das Dritte Capitel.

WAs haben deñ nu die Juden vorteyls? oder was nu tzet die beschneyttüg? zwar fast viel/zum ersten/yhn ist vertrawet was Got geredt hat/Das aber etlich nicht glewbẽ an das selbige/was ligt dar an? solte yhrer vn glaub gottis glaubẽ auffheben? das sey ferne/Es bleybe viel weger also/das Got sey warhafftig/vñ alle menschen lugenhafftig/wie ge schrieben stehet/Auff das du rechtfertig seyst ynn deynen wortten/vnd vbirwindest/wenn du gerichtet wirdest. psal.1.15 psal.50.

Ists aber also/das vnser vngerechtickeyt/gotis gerechtickeyt prey sset/was wollen wyr sagen? Ist deñ got auch vngerecht/das er dru ber zurnet(Ich rede also auff menschë weyse)Das sey ferne/Wie kund deñ got die welt richten? Deñ so die warheyt gotis durch mey ne lugen herlicher wirt zu seynë preyß/warumb solt ich deñ noch als eyn sunder gerichtet werdë/vñ nicht viel mehr also thun (wie wyr ge lestert werde/vñ wie etlich sprechë/das wyr sagë sollë)Last vns vbel thun/auff das guts draus kome? wilcher verdamnis ist gantz recht?

Was sagen wyr deñ nu? haben wyr eyn vorteyl? gar keynen/deñ wyr haben droben vrkund geben/das beyde Juden vnd kriechen al le vnter der sunden sind/wie deñ geschrieben stehet/De ist nicht der rechtfertig sey/auch nicht eyner/Da ist nicht der verstendig sey/da ist nicht der nach Got frage/Sie sind alle abgewichë/vñ allesampt vntuchtig worden/Da ist nicht der gutis thue/auch nicht eyner. Yhr schlund ist eyn offen grab/mit yhren zungë handeln sie truglich/Ot tern gifft ist vnter yhren lippen/yhrer mund ist voll fluchens vnd bits terkeyt/yhr fuß sind eylend blutt zuuorgissen/yn yhren wegen ist/zu stoung vnd zubrechung/vñ den weg des frides wissen sie nicht/Es ist keyn furcht gotis fur yhren augen. psal.13. psal.5 psal.1.39 psal.10. Prouer.1. Jsaie.59. psal.35.

Wyr wissen aber/das/was das gesetz saget/das sagets denen/die vnter dem gesetz sind/Auff das aller mund verstopfft werde/vñ alle welt sey Gott schuldig/darumb/das keyn fleysch durch des ge setzs werck fur yhm rechtfertig seyn mag/Denn durch das gesetz/kompt nur erkentnis der sund.

Nu aber ist/on zuthun des gesetzs/die gerechtickeyt die fur got gilt/offinbart/betzeuget durch das gesetz vñ die propheten. Ich sage aber von solcher gerechtickeyt fur got/die da kompt/durch den glaw ben an Jhesum Christ/zu allen vnd auff alle/die da glewben.

Denn es ist hie keyn vnterscheyd/sie sind alle zumal sunder/vnnd mangeln des preyses den got an yhn haben solt/vnd werden on ver dienst gerechtfertiget/aus seyner gnad/durch die erlosung/so durch Christo geschehen ist/wilchen gott hat furgestellet zu eynem gnade

stuel/

(herlicher wirt)
Dauid spricht/Jch erkene meyne sünd vor alleyn hab ich gesundigt vñ vbel fur dyr than / auff das du rechtfertig seyst yn deynë worten/vnd vbirwindast/wenn du gerichtet wirdest etc.
Das laut/als solt man sünde thun auff das got rechtfertig sey/wie hie sanct Paulus auch antzeucht/vnnd ist doch nicht also/son dern wir sollen die sund erkennen/ die vns got schuld gibt ynn seynem gesetz/auff dz er also war hafftig vñ recht be tēnet werde. Aber vber disem erkentnis zancke die wer cherligë mit got/vnnd wollen yhe werck nicht sund seyn lassen/vñ mus also gott yhr luge ner/vnd ynn seynen wortenn gericht seyn/Deñ sie sehen nur die grobe werck sund an/vñ nicht die kleffe heubt erb sund/daryn die na tur empfangen/ge porn ist vnd lebet/von wilcher doch Dauid yñ dë verß redet. So nu nu Paulus/dz nit die sunde got preyssen/(sonst weres besser sunde denn guts thun/)sondern der sund bekēnis prey sset gott vnd seyne gnade. Also bleybt got warhafftig vñ alle menschë lugen hafftig die solche nicht bekenne wol lë/vñ yhr vnglaub macht gottis glaw be nicht zu nicht. Deñ er gewynnet doch vnnd bleybet warhafftig.

Plate 4. A Page of Text and Marginalia from the Third Chapter of Romans. From the first edition ("September Testament") of Luther's *German New Testament* (Wittenberg, 1522).

self would have sinned, for he himself also fasted, prayed, preached, and did good works."[31]

Emser also disputed Luther's translation of verses 23–24[32] and their accompanying gloss. Luther's translation reads, "For there is here no distinction: they are all indeed sinners and lack the glory which God should have regarding them, and [they] are justified without merit, out of his grace, through the redemption that has occurred through Christ, which God has put forward as a mercy-seat through faith in his blood."[33] In his gloss to this verse Luther advised the reader that this

> is the main issue and center of this epistle and of the whole Scripture. Namely, that everything is sin that is not redeemed through the blood of Christ and justified through faith. Therefore understand [grasp] this text well, for here all merit of works [werck verdienst] and boasting is laid low.[34]

Emser first objected to the translation itself. "Now of course you dear lords and friends note that Luther wishes to lead and seduce the poor ignorant [people] to his place of lies, for, in the first place, he mistranslates the words of Paul, who does not say, 'they are all sinners,' but rather 'they have all sinned and lack the glory of God.'" It was two different things, Emser insisted, to have committed sin and to be a sinner.[35] It was for this reason, he went on, that Paul said that in this respect there was no distinction between Jews and pagans, for we have all sinned. Paul did not say, however, that all our works were sin or that we all were sinners and remained sinners. In that case, Emser asked, "what use to us would be baptism, confession, and the other sacraments through which our sins are taken away and forgiven?"[36]

Turning to the gloss, Emser stated that it was also not true, as Luther contended, that in this passage all "merit of works" [werck vordinst] was laid low. Rather, the only works that were "laid low" were those which occurred outside of grace and faith. And even these works, Emser contended, were not completely without merit.[37]

There was one more gloss in chapter three in Luther's German New Testament, and Emser did not leave it unremarked upon. To the last phrase of the last verse of the chapter ("Are we rescinding the law through faith? That is far from our intention. Rather we are setting the law up [on its proper footing]"),[38] Luther glossed that "faith fulfills all the law; works fulfill not a tittle of the law."[39] Emser replied, "if Luther had even a faith to topple mountains [but was] without works and love, then his faith would not be worth a tittle, for neither faith nor works nor works without faith fulfill the law but only the two together with divine grace united with each other." For Emser the bottom line was clear. "There must be doing with believing; otherwise nothing comes of it."[40]

Although Emser did not single it out for criticism in this treatise, there was one other verse in the third chapter to which other Catholic critics were to take strong exception. In *The New English Bible* this crucial verse 28 is translated, "For our argument is that a man is justified by faith quite apart from success in keeping the law." In Luther's translation, the choice of words and word order drove home his understanding of "faith alone apart from works of the law." "Thus we maintain that the human being is made righteous not through doing the work of the law, [but] solely through faith [*So halten wyrs nu, das der mensch gerechtfertiget werde, on zuthun der werck des gesetzs, alleyn durch dē glawben*]."[41] To make his theological point emphatic, Luther had added a word not in the Greek or Latin texts, the word "solely" or "*alleyn*": "solely through faith [*alleyn durch dē glawben*]." In his 1530 *Open Letter on Translating and Petitioning the Saints*[42] he replied to his critics that this addition was necessary to translate the Greek into good German.[43] Of course, it also reinforced his theological concerns and assisted readers in reading the text as Luther thought they should.

All of these examples illustrate ways in which Luther attempted to lead the reader into what he believed to be the correct understanding of the New Testament. For our purposes it is beside the point to ask whether Luther or Emser had a better case, either in these few examples or in all the disputed passages and glosses of the whole *German New Testament*. It suffices to note that Luther chose to translate crucial passages in a way not only consistent with his theological program but in a way that tended to reinforce the points he wanted the reader to take away from the text. The two examples from this chapter—to translate "they are all sinners" rather than "they have all sinned," and to add the emphatic "*alleyn*" to verse 28—amply document this point. The glosses made explicit how the text was to be understood and thereby offered additional guidance to the reader. Even the physical layout of the text assisted Luther in making his points. Luther chose to begin new paragraphs with two of the crucial verses we have been considering, 23 and 28, although the conventional paragraphing (that is, the paragraph breaks in the Vulgate edition) came at verses 21 and

31. Even visually, for Luther, these crucial verses stand out on the page. The new paragraphing was but one part of a concerted attempt to direct the reader, but Catholics such as Hieronymus Emser would not go along.

Luther also reinforced the antipapal message of several of his prefaces and glosses in three of the twenty-one large full-page woodcuts depicting matters discussed in the Revelation of John.[44] These three woodcuts provoked considerable outcry since they showed the dragon and the whore of Babylon wearing triple crowns like the papal tiara (see plates 5 and 6). It took little imagination to read the message in this contemporary allusion. The other New Testament books went unillustrated except for woodcut initial letters.

QUESTIONS OF AUDIENCE

We have been examining ways in which Luther attempted to direct the reading of the New Testament. But how successful were these efforts? And how large an audience did this effort reach? Statistics on reprints suggest that the *German New Testament* quickly became a sixteenth-century "best-seller," at least among those who could read.[45] The first edition appeared in September 1522 (the "September Testament") in an unusually large printing of between three and five thousand copies.[46] It sold out immediately and its Wittenberg publisher, Melchior Lotther the Younger, produced another large edition in December of the same year (the "December Testament"). The first complete reprint appeared in Basel in December of 1522, and at least another eleven or twelve complete reprints left the press in 1523, six more in Basel, three in Augsburg, one in Grimma, and one or two in Strasbourg.[47] Another twenty complete reprints appeared in 1524, including three or four in Strasbourg.[48] 1525 saw another eight or so reprints, one of which was issued in Strasbourg. By any measure this indicates a remarkable demand, despite its relatively high price (the September Testament sold for half a gulden for an unbound, undecorated copy, the rough equivalent of the purchase price of about 150 kilograms of wheat, two butchered sheep, 430 eggs, or two weeks' wages for a baker or four months' wages for a serving maid at the city hospital in Vienna).[49]

Approximately forty-three distinct editions appeared in forty months (September 1522 through 1525). Some of these editions were quite large for sixteenth-century printings, and even if a conservative

Plate 5. The Dragon of Revelation Wearing the Papal Tiara. From the first edition ("September Testament") of Luther's *German New Testament* (Wittenberg, 1522).

Plate 6. The Whore of Babylon Wearing the Papal Tiara. From the first edition ("September Testament") of Luther's *German New Testament* (Wittenberg, 1522).

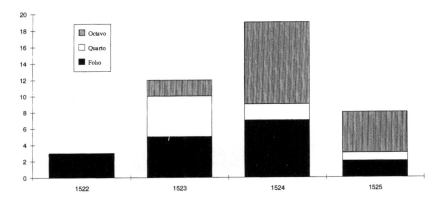

Figure 2. Editions of Luther's *German New Testament* by Publication Format

average of 2,000 copies per printing is assumed, at least 86,000 copies were issued in this short time span. As figure 2 indicates, the expensive folio reprints quickly made way for quarto and octavo editions. These smaller, less expensive editions were likely available to a larger audience than the folio editions.[50] This development suggests that printers were either responding to demand for less expensive and handier editions or at least thought that such editions would be easier to sell. Since there were frequent reprints by the same printer, it seems safe to infer that printers had no difficulty selling the *German New Testament*. For a book as costly as this (undoubtedly an expensive book even in its cheapest and handiest octavo format), these were remarkable sales. No other publication of Luther's came close to this number.

   Six editions were produced in Wittenberg, three of which identified Luther as the translator. The other three gave the place of publication, Wittenberg, and readers would have had no difficulty inferring who the translator was. It is another matter with the other thirty-seven editions printed elsewhere. As best as I can determine only two of these thirty-seven editions named Luther as the translator. Given the highly pointed prefaces and glosses, an alert reader would probably have had no difficulty inferring the provenance of the translation, but this is not a sure thing. Since the early Wittenberg editions did not mention Luther's name, the printers, in typesetting from these editions or from editions based on these early Wittenberg editions,[51] may have simply copied the omission. The printers outside Wittenberg also had an incentive to avoid placing his name on their editions, since the Edict of Worms forbade the publication of Luther's works. By omitting his name, the printers assured a larger market, including readers who remained loyal to the Catholic church, and helped propagate Luther's message to as large an audience as possible.

Most of the reprints also diverged from the September Testament in the significant matter of the woodcuts for the Book of Revelation. In three of the woodcuts in the September Testament the papal tiara graced the brow of the beast or the whore of Babylon. As a result of objection from such worthies as Duke Georg of Albertine Saxony, the upper two crowns were excised already in the second edition published in Wittenberg in December 1522.[52] Most of reprints elsewhere also omitted either the woodcut series in its entirety or offered copies without the offending tiaras. But this was not always the case. The Basel printer Jakob Wolff had the artist Hans Holbein make from the September Testament woodcut copies in a smaller format that included the polemical tiaras. He used these woodcuts in three printings in 1523 and two printings in 1524. The printer Amandus Farkal of Hagenau copied fifteen of Holbein's copies, including the three with the triple crown, for his 1524 edition, and Johann Knobloch of Strasbourg used a subset of the Holbein originals, including the controversial woodcuts, in two of his 1524 editions and in his one 1525 edition. In sum, a little less than a quarter of the editions contained the visual identification of the papacy with the beast or whore of the Book of Revelation.[53] This still means that a significant number of printers (and hence a significant number of readers who purchased their editions of the New Testament) assisted in propagating Luther's conviction, in this case visually expressed, that the papacy was the Antichrist.

Given the importance of the glosses in Luther's effort to supplement Scripture alone, it is worth noting that two of the editions published in Strasbourg did not reproduce in the margins themselves Luther's highly directive marginal glosses. The 1523 edition by Johann Schott reproduced the glosses on twenty-four leaves placed between Acts and Romans.[54] The 1524 Strasbourg edition by Wolfgang Köpfel omitted the glosses entirely. Instead, they were reproduced in a separate booklet.[55] Schott's decision to put the glosses in a special section may have been dictated by considerations of economy, since it was certainly easier to typeset the glosses separately than to typeset them in the margins. Köpfel's separate printing, however, probably reflected the glosses' controversial nature. Just as the text of Luther's speech before the Imperial Diet of Worms may have been modified to blunt the suggestion that Luther was offering new teachings, his marginal glosses may have been separately printed to minimize offense to prospective buyers.[56]

In light of the low literacy rates in sixteenth-century Germany and the expense of even the cheapest *German New Testament*, the purchasers would have made up but a tiny fraction of the German-speaking population. Even so, more people would have had access to a *German New Testament* than at any time in the past. Moreover, Luther did not have to reach everyone, only those in positions of leadership or influence. The statistics suggest that, in fact, he reached a goodly number of such people. But most people would have been influenced by Luther's translation only through preached sermons and oral readings from Scripture. The degree to which glosses and prefaces may have influenced this oral reception is extraordinarily difficult to determine. Bernd Moeller's recent study of preaching has come closest to shedding some light on this question.[57]

Moeller looked at all the publications that he could find that purported to be summaries of sermons that Evangelicals had given in cities and towns—large and small—throughout the Holy Roman Empire. Of the thirty-two sermon summaries that Moeller examined, produced by twenty-six authors, he found four major themes: justification by faith alone apart from works of the law, the church, the Christian life, and, finally, the rapidly approaching Endtime. In each of these treatises can be found the major elements of the doctrine of justification, namely, the totality of human sin, the unconditional reception of salvation promised solely through faith in Christ, and the exclusion of all merit and human accomplishment in regards to salvation. These points are, of course, just the issues of law and gospel that Luther hammered on in his prefaces and marginal glosses.

Vehemently and with regularity these authors rejected their opponents' claim that they so concentrated on grace and faith that they encouraged moral laxity. While these authors characterized the practices of the medieval church as works righteousness and human doctrine, they insisted, nevertheless, that good works necessarily followed from faith. Each treatise repeated the assertion "Where there is faith, there is also love." Christians did good works not for their own sake, but for the sake of the neighbor. Love was the fruit of faith. This was perhaps the most repeated biblical passage in these treatises. All these distinctly Evangelical themes can be found in the apparatus Luther provided for his *German New Testament*. Even the expectation of the imminent Endtime, while left out of the prefaces and marginalia, found visual expression in the woodcuts to Revelation.

The preachers Moeller has studied (and many others who preached in support of the Reformation but did not commit their sermons to print) undoubtedly acquired many of their beliefs from a variety of Luther's publications. But it is also highly likely that these "opinion leaders" were strongly influenced by Luther's *German New Testament*. The extent of this influence, or at least the *likelihood* of the extent of this influence, is made plain by a remarkable study by the historian Holm Zerener. In a 1911 article he showed conclusively that Luther's translation enjoyed incredibly rapid and comprehensive adoption among those publishing both in support of, and (remarkably) in opposition to, the Reformation movement. In this study, he examined a large sample of 681 German pamphlets published between 1522 and 1525. Of those that included citations from the New Testament, 23 percent of those published in 1522 used Luther's translation, 44 percent of those published in 1523, 72 percent of those published in 1524, and 77 percent of those published in 1525.[58] Even a significant number of Catholic controversialists availed themselves of Luther's translation!

The conclusion seems inescapable. The collection even of "proof texts" is not a casual matter, and these authors must have been intensively studying Luther's text and, one would assume, the accompanying glosses and prefaces. Certainly the glosses would be hard to overlook or ignore. If three-quarters of the publicists sampled in Zerener's study were using Luther's translation by 1524–1525, this means that a major fraction of the publicists of the day underwent a thorough and lengthy exposure to Luther's understanding of law and gospel, faith and works. It would be surprising indeed if such an intense exposure would have no influence.

"Scripture alone" was the Evangelical watchword, and "Scripture interprets itself" its theological justification. But Scripture was not disembodied. It took concrete form as typeset letters on a page. As a printed book Scripture had already undergone one interpretation in the choices Luther made to render the Greek into acceptable German. The preface, introductions, and marginalia that Luther added became an integral part of Scripture as published text, adding further interpretation. As a physical artifact, then, that people could pick up and read, Scripture was not alone, but Luther's *German New Testament* certainly interpreted itself.

CHAPTER SIX

Contested Authority in the Strasbourg Press

One of the greater ironies of the early Reformation is that within months of having published a series of blistering attacks on Luther and his teachings on the Lord's Supper, Luther's onetime professorial colleague and fellow reformer, Andreas Bodenstein von Karlstadt, and his family sought and received sanctuary in Luther's own house. Expelled from Electoral Saxony the previous year, Karlstadt had been unable to find a secure refuge, and in the months leading up to his return he had been harried from place to place by the Peasants' War. Luther could provide temporary asylum, but the Saxon princes had to be persuaded to lift their order of expulsion. As their price for his remaining in Electoral Saxony, Karlstadt had to issue an *Explanation of How Karlstadt Regards and Wishes His Teaching On the Highly Revered Sacrament and Other Matters To Be Regarded*, for which Luther provided a foreword.[1]

In the late summer of 1525 this forced recantation arrived in Strasbourg and was quickly reprinted by the presses of Johann Prüß and Johann Knobloch. Both printings started with Luther's uncompromising foreword, which put his own harsh interpretation on Karlstadt's *Explanation*. Accompanying the Prüß edition, however, was a concluding *Admonition to Peace regarding the Indicated Matter*, that is, the quarrel over the Lord's Supper. Its anonymous author—we now know that it was the Strasbourg humanist and reformer Wolfgang Capito—attempted to put an interpretation quite different from Luther's on this document's significance.[2] It is in the odd juxtaposition of these three writings—Luther's foreword, Karlstadt's *Explanation*, and Capito's *Admonition*—that we can see with particular clarity the propagandistic challenge posed by the division in the Evangelical ranks occasioned by the controversy over the Lord's Supper.

It is hard to know what readers in the Strasbourg region would have made of Karlstadt's *Explanation* all by itself. It is unlikely that they would have known it was a forced recantation, and as a result they might well have been puzzled by Karlstadt's carefully hedged statement. The challenge for Karlstadt was stark. How could he recant, as the princes required, without recanting? Or rather, how could he back down honorably when he remained unconvinced of any error (or more strongly put, when he remained convinced that his position was "good, right, true, godly, and wholesome")?

The challenge for Luther, if we can speak of a challenge, since he enjoyed the upper hand as well as the first word in this publication, was to deny that a reconciliation had occurred on anything but his own terms. He sought in his foreword to have the reader interpret the *Explanation* as a vindication of his own understanding of the dispute over the Supper and its import.

For Capito and his fellow Strasbourg reformers, the challenge ran rather in a different direction. Catholics were claiming that the rupture between Luther and Karlstadt proved that the Evangelicals were not of the true church since the Holy Spirit did not produce division. Accordingly, Strasbourg publicists, theologically speaking, had to reassure their own supporters that the Holy Spirit did remain with the Evangelicals, despite this quarrel. Had they simply agreed with Luther's position, this would have been relatively easy. They could have said that Karlstadt had fallen away from the truth. But as it happened, even as the Strasbourg publicists disagreed with Karlstadt's scriptural arguments and deplored his invective, they were inclined to agree with Karlstadt's conclusions or rather with the more convincing reformulations by Huldrych Zwingli, the leading reformer in Zurich, and Johann Oecolampadius, the humanist-reformer in Basel, both of whom had recently offered their own thinking on the matter.[3]

At the same time, the Strasbourg reformers wanted to remain on good terms with Martin Luther. They seemed sincerely to believe that Luther was a specially chosen instrument of God who had revealed the papal Antichrist and had begun the restoration of the true gospel. Accordingly, there were powerful psychological reasons to deny that they in fact *were* in disagreement with him, at least over anything crucial. Luther's extraordinary authority also posed tactical challenges to any Evangelical publicists who chose to disagree with him. How were they going to get a hearing from those convinced that Luther spoke as a contemporary prophet, chosen by God to reveal the papal Antichrist and restore the true gospel of Jesus Christ? For the Strasbourgeois, this intra-Evangelical quarrel was fraught with the very real risk that Luther's authority would prevail.

Both Luther and Capito attempted, therefore, in the jargon of modern media campaigns, to put their own "spin" on Karlstadt's *Explanation*. And of course Karlstadt attempted to put his own interpretation on his recantation. It is these conflicting attempts at "spin control" that makes this joint publication so revealing.

Karlstadt began his *Explanation* saying that he had learned that some readers treated his books on the Lord's Supper as if they contained proven, divine teaching and as if it were certain that the body of Christ could not be bodily in the sacrament. This was a misreading of his works, Karlstadt insisted, since he never claimed certainty and in fact was personally unsure. He had asked in his writings to be instructed if he erred. To be sure, he also knew of no Scripture that compelled him to accept the traditional understanding, that the body of Christ must be bodily in the host.[4] He had written according to the best of his abilities and understanding, but he conceded that many others might well have been given by God greater perception and understanding of Scripture than he. The readers of his books should have considered this and not held anything to be proven and godly without first assuring themselves from Holy Scripture. Until this was done, his readers should consider his teachings as no more than opinion.[5]

This led Karlstadt into an extended attack on the majority of people who paid little attention to what was grounded in the Holy Scriptures but instead extolled people, and who had no other basis for their belief than this or that person had written or taught it.[6] Yet what flesh and blood revealed was satanic and not divine, misleading and not true, to be despised and not to be praised. "Hence it follows," Karlstadt wrote, "that there is nothing good nor can there be anything godly which the flesh and blood of Karlstadt has hit upon, understands, presents, or teaches."[7] Readers should beware in reading his books that they did not mistake something of Karlstadt's for God's. It was repugnant to him, Karlstadt explained, that some people encountered a particular person and adhered to him. "But if you boast according to persons, be they Zwingli or Karlstadt, you will gain nothing, as has just been said, and put yourself in danger, as I have just warned you."[8] Moreover, people should realize that many saints had believed in the bodily presence of Christ in the Sacrament. If one was counting persons, the other side actually had a better case of it.

Karlstadt chose to put the onus of discerning the truth on the readers themselves. "Not only in this article on the highly revered Sacrament," Karlstadt wrote, "but in all matters on which I have written, on the Mass, on idols, and on other articles, I wish the following: no one should think that my teaching is good, right, true, godly, or wholesome, unless he is certain of this on the basis of the wholesome Word of God, for I wish my writing to be judged according to and on the basis of God's Word."[9] Yet many did not separate the "pearls" from the "manure" in his writings. Why? Because they sought novelties and curiosities.[10] In saying this, Karlstadt did not want to discourage the reading of Christian authors or the possibility of Christian revelation. "That which is good and godly is wholesome and true and to be accepted wherever one finds it, be he old or young, man or child, of high or low estate. Also that which is godly in my books I do not recant, nor shall anyone force me to contradict divine truth."[11]

Obviously, this "recantation" was strictly qualified. Karlstadt rejected what did not comport with Scripture and urged his readers to test his writings against Scripture. He characterized his position as "uncertain," but he also stated that he himself continued to be convinced by his reading of Scripture and unconvinced by the opposing position. He strongly criticized those who relied on personal reputation rather than on Scripture, and while he named himself and Zwingli as persons of authority whose writings should be checked against Scripture, this attack on "personal authority" could just as well apply to Luther. His was a "recantation" that recanted very little.

Luther, not surprisingly, put his own construction on Karlstadt's "recantation." In his foreword to the *Explanation*, he interpreted Karlstadt's concessions as not merely an admission that his teachings should not be considered as certain, but as proof that they were false. True instruction by the Holy Spirit produces two virtues, Luther explained: a person so instructed is certain and sure of his position, and he will confess this position "courageously, freely, and confidently" in the face of death and the devil. Since Karlstadt, Zwingli, and others of their persuasion spoke on this matter of the Lord's Supper in terms of opinions and questions, Luther concluded that they certainly did not have the Holy Spirit and therefore spoke from human fancy. Nevertheless, because of Karlstadt's admission of uncertainty Luther could still harbor hope for him and others of his ilk. "We who are certain in this matter have the responsibility," he wrote, "to help such wavering and questioning hearts, to reach out a hand in such dangerous matters, to listen in a friendly fashion to their questions and searchings, reasons and considerations, and to refute with the Scriptures and help them out [of their error]."[12]

If Luther's foreword served to put his particular interpretation on Karlstadt's *Explanation*, Capito's anonymous *Admonition to Peace* attempted to put quite a different interpretation not only on Karlstadt's *Explanation* but also on Luther's foreword and the Supper dispute in general. He had the difficult task of acknowledging Luther's authority while disallowing it, of minimizing the significance of the dispute while respectfully disagreeing with Luther on the substance, of reassuring his readers that they were one with Luther on what really mattered, while potentially disturbing them with the claim that on this point, at least, Luther was in error.

Capito's *Admonition* began with a striking (and given the content of the preceding foreword and *Explanation*, a rather surprising) declaration: "Rejoice, Christian reader, and say thanks to God our Father through our savior Jesus Christ, Dr. M. Luther and Andreas Karlstadt are again one." Since divisions were caused by the flesh (1 Corinthians 3), "truly we should receive with all thankfulness this their unification after such division as a special gift of God and a holy fruit of the Spirit, and we should heartily rejoice in it." And he warned his readers not to "do as some who wish first to dispute a great deal about this pamphlet, [to argue] that this and that [in this pamphlet] is inconsistent with what was read before in both Dr. Luther's and Karlstadt's books."[13] Rather, they should be content with God's gift of this reconciliation.

Capito proceeded to depict the dispute as a product of human weakness. "The ancient holy martyrs and otherwise highly gifted fathers have often shown themselves to be human, how should we expect better in our own times?" We should seek no more of Peter, Paul, or Apollo than that they be true and that they present to us the word of the Lord and not their own opinion. "Therefore we should let fall all respect for persons and hold ourselves to the Scripture alone and through it test and align all things as Dr. Luther himself has so often admonished with complete earnestness."[14] Drawing on passages of

Scripture, Capito urged at some length that his readers could only find unity in following the Word of God, not by respecting people. This was true also in the matter of the Lord's Supper. Unity will come, Capito maintained, "if we allow the good opinion of all men to fall away and seek the correct understanding solely within Scripture." No one should say that this or that person "has not erred in great [matters], [so] he will also not err in this matter, [therefore] I wish to be of his party." Peter, Capito reminded his readers, had not erred in great matters and had freely acknowledged Christ before the high priests in Jerusalem, and had suffered imprisonment and flogging on this account. But in Antioch he erred in a much lesser matter "so that Paul had to chastise him publicly." There was no one, then, who had not shown at some time that he was a human being. "Since God protects His own from erring in the chief matters," he concluded, "is it any wonder that they show themselves to be human beings in lesser matters?"[15] As Capito's subsequent discussion of the issues in question indicates, this admonition was meant more to disabuse people of inordinate deference to Luther than to Karlstadt.

In his discussion of the issues, Capito came down firmly on the side of a spiritual understanding of Christ's presence in the Supper and rejected Luther's insistence on the real presence. At times he seemed clearly to be attacking the Catholic notion of transubstantiation;[16] at most points, however, he seems to have in mind Luther's insistence on the real presence. He was careful, however, not to attack Luther by name. On the contrary, Capito even called on Luther's support for his position. To be sure, Luther had written against Karlstadt and the Waldensians, Capito said. But Luther had also zealously promoted the memory of, and faith in, the death of Christ and had often advocated a spiritual eating. "Though to be sure he is harsh in the books [just] mentioned," Capito observed, "you should remember that he too must show himself to be a human being." Now such weaknesses were much less important in such "accidental matters" than in a "great matter." "You must be faithful to Christ, not to Luther," Capito instructed his readers, "You must pay attention to the word of the Lord, not Luther's or any other word as Dr. Luther himself assiduously teaches you. And therefore you have had after the apostles no author who has not often erred."[17]

Yet even so, Luther and Karlstadt were once more reconciled despite the disagreement on what Capito concluded was a subsidiary and not faith-dividing point. But if a reader believed that the Lord gave

his body to eat bodily in the Supper, a misunderstanding as Capito
saw it, Capito nevertheless urged them to "do as Dr. Luther."

> Do not divide on that account the love and brotherhood with those who
> nevertheless believe all things with you, although they indeed in this point
> believe otherwise. In such fashion Luther treats the Waldensians, and now
> also Dr. Karlstadt who writes in his pamphlet that he still cannot under-
> stand his opinion as other than demonstrable, good, right, godly, and
> wholesome. Still Dr. Luther takes delight in his explanation, which he
> would not do if Karlstadt were a heretic on account of this opinion or was
> in error on a necessary part of the faith.[18]

If this conclusion was not amazing enough, Capito went on to stigma-
tize as "un-Lutheran" those who attacked Zwingli and Oecolampadius
on this matter!

> If, then, Dr. Luther is willing to maintain Christian unity with those who
> do not believe that Christ is bodily in the bread, indeed [with] those who
> regard it as good, right, godly, and wholesome not to believe, how un-
> Lutheran then are those who decry as the greatest masters of error Zwingli
> and Oecolampadius, two so faithful servants of Christ who certainly work
> no less for the honor of Christ [than Karlstadt and the Waldensians do],
> and otherwise belittle them in every way and attempt to destroy them?[19]

Although there would always be disagreements in the interpretation of
Scripture, as long as they were united in the chief issues, why should
disagreement matter on external things that were in themselves not
necessary for salvation?[20] "Without love we are nothing," Capito
asserted, "without faith in the fleshly presence of Christ in the bread,
we may be Christians and Dr. Luther's friend."[21]

In the closing pages of his *Admonition*, Capito offered a "Caution
Regarding Several Points in Dr. Luther's Letter and Karlstadt's Explanation." Here he subjected Luther's foreword to his own particular
reading. For example, he took Luther's statement on how dangerous it
was to waver over articles of faith and effectively argued that Luther
was not serious on this point. "In this regard," Capito wrote, "you
should pay no attention to the fact that Luther regards the presence of
the body of Christ in the bread to be an article of faith, which is to be
believed as necessary for salvation, for otherwise he could not accept
as a brother or friend Dr. Karlstadt, who regards as good, right, godly,
and wholesome just the opposite view, for the Christian should turn
away from such."[22]

To Luther's assertion that true instruction by the Holy Spirit produced the virtues of certainty and courage in confession even in the

face of death or the devil, Capito explained that this should be understood only in regard to the chief issues of the faith. In other lesser points, such as the dispute over the real presence, the Holy Spirit often allows only gradual comprehension. Capito cited as an example errors in Luther's earlier writings that he abandoned only over time. Capito also argued that the Holy Spirit encouraged both a courageous and a humble confession of faith, whichever was best at the time. Luther, too, had first confessed the faith with humble pleas thus better to encourage its acceptance. Bold proclamation did not make a teaching true, nor did questioning presentation make a teaching false. Both must be tested against Scripture.[23]

Capito took issue with Luther's conclusion that Karlstadt's, Zwingli's, and other's uncertainty proved that they did not possess the Spirit. To begin with, he stated, Zwingli, Oecolampadius, and others were not uncertain on this point, although they did not announce their position with such defiance and bravado, having learned from Paul to handle God's word with fear and trembling. Were this principle of Luther's in fact valid, then it would prove that he himself had not originally possessed the Spirit, for although he had written "nothing but the certain Gospel of Jesus Christ," he had at the beginning deferred far more to the pope and "the worst enemies of the truth" than he should have. He had said that he was writing only to inquire into the truth. Although he was "greater in the exegesis of Scripture than anyone we have had in many hundreds of years," he, too, had displayed more deference towards the world and his own weaknesses than perhaps he should have. Truly, Capito concluded, Luther had revealed his humanity in this argument, as in many other places.[24]

Capito closed with the observation that there would always be divisions in the church and disagreements about teachings, so that his readers should not be distressed by such divisions "in our times." Rather they should rejoice that they have the true gospel, learn from this dispute that human beings will be human beings, and commit themselves to Christ alone.[25]

LUTHER'S CHARISMATIC AUTHORITY

To understand Capito's labored attempt to depict Luther as just another human being (while still admitting that he was "greater in the exegesis of Scripture that anyone we have had in many hundreds of years"), it is necessary to recall the authority that Luther had acquired over the last several years and the role it was playing in this dispute over the Supper. For some years the Evangelical press had been portraying him as anything but just another human being.

Chapter 4 explored the public persona that Luther had acquired by 1521–1522. In visual terms, woodcuts such the one that graced two editions of Luther's speech at the Diet of Worms presented Luther as a monk (monastic habit), doctor (doctoral beret), and man of the Bible (held in his hands) who was inspired by God (the dove of the Holy Spirit and the nimbus of a saint).[26] The Strasbourg publicists had given additional content to these signs, describing Luther as everything from a "preacher of truth"[27] to a "light of Christendom," whom God had chosen and sent into the world "to tell us your divine word,"[28] or even a "Christian Angel" sent "to us by God, ordained and raised up in the fervor of the spirit of Elisha."[29] He had been cheered for his attack on the papacy, an attack that for many had apocalyptic overtones, and warmly seconded for his insistence on Scripture alone. His anger and abusiveness had given some people pause, but most of his supporters thought it justified by the enormity of the papal tyranny that he was fighting. His defiant speech at Worms had only confirmed the laudatory picture of him propagated by his supporters.

By the beginnings of the Sacramentarian controversy in 1524–1525 Luther's authority, if anything, had grown. For the past five years his publications had flooded the German-speaking lands in an ever rising tide. In Strasbourg itself well over 150 printings of works by Luther had appeared by the end of 1523.[30] People were purchasing Luther, reading Luther, and purchasing him again. No other author came within publishing even a tenth of Luther's volume. This by itself conveyed massive authority, or rather manifested the authority that alone could account for the demand that such massive printings and reprintings reflected.

To be sure, Luther himself and his fellow publicists pointed insistently to Scripture alone as the sole authority for deciding questions of Christian truth. But Luther had convinced large numbers of people —or at least crucial numbers of significant people, namely, other Evangelical publicists—that his interpretation of Scripture was the "right, true, and godly" reading. As if to bolster this authority as an exegete, Luther had issued his own translation of Scripture along with incisive prefaces and glosses, a translation, as we have seen, that quickly swept the field, coming by 1524 to be cited by almost three-quarters of the other publicists who were explicating Scripture.[31] Even in an argument about the right understanding of "Scripture alone," Martin Luther enjoyed unparalleled authority.

Once Luther's special authority was established, it was only a matter of time before it itself would become an issue even within the Evangelical ranks. With the outbreak of the inter-Evangelical controversy over the presence of Christ in the Lord's Supper, Luther faced novel tactical challenges to the propagation of his understanding of the Gospel. As I have argued at length,[32] it had not been difficult in controversies with Catholics to get the public to see that there were fundamental differences between the Catholic and Evangelical understanding of the Christian message. Since each side based its arguments on different authorities, the reasons for the disagreements were apparent, and each was certain that he was right and his opponent wrong. The various members of the Reformation movement, however, were generally in agreement on the central principles that differentiated their beliefs from Catholicism, and most of them accepted the Scripture as the only authority and source of doctrine. Yet despite their common use of Scripture as the sole basis for their position, each side was, ultimately, unable to convince the other of its error. As we saw in the last chapter, whatever the cogency of the theological principle that Scripture interprets itself, in practice at least among sinful human beings, the "right" understanding of Scripture was not always easily determined. Luther faced the difficult task of convincing people that in this appeal to a common authority, Scripture, his reading was correct. To complicate this task, Luther had to convince his readers that the disagreement was of such significance that it outweighed the widespread perceived agreement on most of the rest of the Evangelical agenda.

Given the confusion that the debate engendered within the Evangelical ranks, Luther had to find a way to help those who were bewildered to see that the disagreement was significant and real, and to make it as likely as possible that they would choose to support his side of the controversy. He could of course rely on whatever force his scriptural and theological arguments carried, and the great bulk of his treatises are devoted to the exegesis of Scripture and debate over theology. But in the confusing context of so internecine a quarrel, this alone was not enough. Luther also needed to sharpen the differences between himself and his Evangelical opponents to make the choice even clearer. He did this by maligning his opponents and thus raising doubts about the validity of doctrine espoused by such evil men. He also delicately claimed special authority for himself, and on this basis attempted to get those who were unsure or who did not fully understand the disagreement or its significance to accept his position.

Before the "reconciliation" announced in Karlstadt's *Explanation,* Luther had issued three blistering attacks on Karlstadt: *Letter to the Christians at Strasbourg Regarding the Fanatic Spirit,* and parts one and two of *Against the Heavenly Prophets.* These attacks drew heavily on biblical images and models that would be widely recognized by Luther's readers. For example, in his *Letter,* he began with a warning that the true gospel was always attacked, persecuted, and tested "from both sides": "Christ must have not only Caiaphas among his enemies, but also Judas among his friends."[33] In this case it was clear that the Judas was Dr. Karlstadt. In his opening lines to the first part of *Against the Heavenly Prophets,* Luther wrote, "Doctor Karlstadt has fallen away from us, [and] has in addition become our worst enemy." And he quickly added, "May Christ grant that we be not afraid and may he give us his mind and courage, that we may not err or despair before the Satan who here purports to rectify the Sacrament but has something quite different in mind, namely, with cunning interpretation of the Scripture to spoil the whole teaching of the gospel, which he has thus far been unable to silence with force."[34] This identification of Karlstadt with Satan runs throughout the treatise, allowing Luther to attack not only Karlstadt's argument but Karlstadt himself.

In fact, the treatise was directed, as its title suggests, at all fanatics and "heavenly prophets," not just Karlstadt. Although much of the treatise dealt directly with Karlstadt, it was actually Karlstadt's *spirit,* which Luther maintained was the same spirit driving Thomas Müntzer, the Zwickau prophets (three men who had visited Luther in 1522, claiming direct inspiration from the Holy Spirit), and the other "heavenly prophets," that bore the brunt of Luther's attack. And Karlstadt was faulted not only for what he had allegedly done but also for what his spirit was allegedly capable of doing, given the opportunity. This "tactic" entailed among other things Luther's charge that Karlstadt was impelled by the "Allstedt spirit," that is, by the same "rebellious, murderous, seditious" spirit that drove Thomas Müntzer and had led to violence in Allstedt and elsewhere. Karlstadt was subsumed under the biblical image of the false prophet. Luther went on at some length to explain and justify this accusation.[35]

Not only did Luther attempt to discredit Karlstadt by identifying him with the biblical false prophets, motivated by the spirit of Satan, he also attempted in a careful way to bolster his own authority as a trustworthy exegete of Scripture and even instrument of God. In his *Letter to the Christians at Strasbourg,* he prefaced his discussion of Karlstadt's contentions with a caveat and an appeal to his personal authority:

> Now my most dear friends, I am not your preacher. No one is obliged to believe me. Each one is responsible for himself. I can warn everyone, I can restrain no one. I hope, too, that you have come thus far to know me through my writings to be one who has dealt so clearly and assuredly with the gospel, the grace of Christ, the law, faith, love, the cross, human law, [and] what one should think of the pope, the monastic estate, and masses, and all the chief matters that a Christian needs to know, so that I am beyond reproach in this regard. And [I hope that it] cannot indeed be denied that I have been an unworthy instrument of God, through whom He has helped many souls.[36]

He advised the Strasbourgeois to hold to the single question: what made a person a Christian? All else was of minor importance, concerned with mere external matters. Those who were unable to take this advice should go slowly and wait for what Luther or others would have to say. "I have thus far dealt rightly and properly with the main points [of faith]," he contended, adding that anyone who claimed otherwise could not be a good spirit. "I hope," he said, "[that] I would not spoil even the external matters on which these prophets devote all their energy."[37]

Luther carefully qualified this appeal to authority with an admonition that accorded fully with his public persona as a "man of the Bible." But all this trading of accusations, Luther maintained, was the devil's trick, diverting men from the proper study of the gospel. They should ask their "Evangelists" to point them "away from Luther and Karlstadt" and towards Christ but not, as Karlstadt did, only to his work, where Christ was an example, which was the least important aspect of Christ and made him comparable to other saints. Rather they should ask to be pointed towards Christ as God's gift or, as Paul said, as "the power, wisdom, righteousness, redemption, and sanctification of God, given to us."[38] Luther had offered similar advice in the past. So long as the debate was with Catholics, this humble appeal to Scriptures served him well. But in this internecine debate over the Supper, Scripture alone proved insufficient to settle the dispute. Other participants would point to such comments in an attempt to minimize Luther's authority in the dispute. And Luther himself would find it necessary to supplement his scriptural arguments with increasing appeals to his own special authority.

THE EVANGELICAL CHALLENGE TO LUTHER'S AUTHORITY

The approaches taken by Karlstadt and Capito illustrate two ways that Evangelical publicists could respond to Luther in the press. Before the Peasants' War had forced him to sue for peace, Karlstadt had seen no need to defer to Luther or to pull his punches. On the contrary, he felt that he had been dealt with shabbily by Luther and wanted the whole world to recognize the hypocrisy and danger in Luther's position. In the fall of 1524, following his expulsion from Saxony, Karlstadt had arranged to have seven treatises published in Basel that attacked both Luther's understanding of the Supper and Luther himself.[39] Johann Schwan's press in Strasbourg subsequently reprinted one of Karlstadt's controversial writings on the Mass and Prüß's establishment another three (as well as a fourth treatise comprising a short statement of faith).[40]

Perhaps as serious as the substance of Karlstadt's attacks on the Catholic and Lutheran understanding of the Supper is his designation of Luther and his fellow supporters as "new papists," for this designation suggested rather forcefully that Luther was continuing the papal oppression, only in a new way.

All Karlstadt's pamphlets contained disparaging references to "papists," "new papists," and "sophists," the later two epithets used by Karlstadt for Luther and his supporters. He made this designation explicit on several occasions. For example, two of the four Strasbourg reprints even announce in their titles that they were directed against the "new papists." *A Beautiful, Brief, and Christian Instruction Concerning the Correct (Against the Old and New Papist) Mass* was reprinted in Strasbourg in 1524,[41] and his *Exegesis of These Words of Christ: This is My Body, Which Will Be Given For You. This is My Blood, Which Will be Poured Out For You. Luke 22. Against the One-Fold [Simple] and Two-Fold Papists Who Use Such Words For the Demolition of Christ's Cross*[42] appeared in 1525.[43]

In his *Instruction* Karlstadt indirectly explained that the term "new papist" fit the Lutherans because they continued a "papistical" understanding of the Lord's Supper. The "new papists" were those who "said and wrote and preached that Christ is no sacrifice and nevertheless carried the word 'Mass' on their lips and called the Lord's Supper a 'Mass.'" This was like saying a person was a pious man and yet calling him a thief or robber, for the word "Mass" meant in Hebrew "a free will sacrifice."[44] "Dr. Martinus" and the "Bishop of Zwickau" [Nicholaus Hausmann], Karlstadt asserted, erred in this regard.[45] He also claimed that whatever they wrote or said to the contrary, the "new papists" in the act of elevating the bread and the cup testified that they thought Christ to be a sacrifice, for that was what elevation meant. All of Wittenberg erred in this fashion, whatever they said they intended by the act. "Thus I say, if they are allowed to elevate the Sacrament, we may speak or write of them that they sacrifice Christ because God dedicated and allotted elevation for sacrificing."[46]

Karlstadt launched his most serious explicit attack on Luther in his *Exegesis*. In the course of his critique of the "old and new papists," Karlstadt labeled his Evangelical opponents "sophists,"[47] "blind guides" and "dizzy spirits" [*schwimmel geister*],[48] "two-fold new papists,"[49] and "double papists,"[50] among other titles of opprobrium. And if there was any doubt to whom these titles referred, Karlstadt's concluding paragraphs removed it. He urged his readers to guard themselves against the "papistic sacraments and idols." They should follow the truth that had been revealed and borne fruit despite the "new sophistic papists' prohibition." "If, however, you were to follow him," he said, obviously referring to Luther, "then God would also allow you to remain stuck in the error in which the sharp sophist is stuck in up to over his ears. And it is possible that you, as he, would remain in your old life and error and would assert that one should judge you only according to your teaching (about which he will suffer no judge in order that he remain learned) and not according to your works." "I fear that he is the Antichrist's late-born [*nachgeborner*] friend," he wrote, "who has scattered precious silver and gold (that is, many good and unreproachable teachings)." Having thus acquired a good reputation for sound doctrine, he "as the devil" sought to lead them "out onto the slippery slope" so that they would now knowingly "hold with the idols and sacraments" and do "all sorts of wicked deeds," things that they had done before out of ignorance and blindness.[51]

Returning to the sore point that Luther's acts belied his words, Karlstadt accused him of treacherously arranging for Karlstadt's banishment without a hearing or an opportunity for debate. "His teaching is that one should overcome those who disagree [*wider-*

sprecher] with wholesome words," Karlstadt wrote. "His work, however, is to chase people from the land without a hearing and without demonstrating their error [die vnuerhôrtē vñ vnüberwundten auß den landen veriagē]." "I had hoped," Karlstadt continued, "that the truth would be revealed without any words of abuse, and he would dispute with me or allow me to write against him without my destruction, which he had offered me with a confirming handshake and promise." But then Luther had stabbed him in the back, forcing his banishment. Those who wished to could sit around and listen "to how the cocky, slippery, and beautiful sophist," whom Karlstadt parenthetically labeled "the malicious assassin [murckler = meuchler?] of the Scripture," "would make his [Eucharistic] host into a food of life and spring of Christian grace." For his part, Karlstadt urged the "god fearing" to avoid the mistake of believing either "D. M. L."—these initials were the only direct identification of who the "sophist" and "new papist" was—or himself. Rather they should inquire after the truth and find out for themselves "which of us is teaching divine truth or not."[52]

This personal invective had a theological meaning. To suggest that Luther was a "new papist," a "malicious assassin of Scripture," a "sophist," and perhaps even the "late-born friend of the Antichrist," was to go beyond simple name-calling and to suggest that Luther's teaching on the Supper was a damnable error and a threat to Christendom. The label "new papist" tapped into the common vocabulary of popular anti-Roman and anticlerical feeling that Luther himself had helped create. By labeling Luther a "new papist," Karlstadt was suggesting to his readers that Luther himself was a defender of clerical abuse, a tyrant in his own right, and perhaps even an associate of the Antichrist, attempting to oppress the laity of the German nation and seduce them into damnable error. This was an argument that had considerable potential appeal to anticlerical sentiment, as the course of the Peasants' War was to show.

As we have seen, Wolfgang Capito took a much less frontal approach to challenging Luther's authority. In both his *Admonition to Peace*, the afterword to Karlstadt's *Explanation*, and in his earlier *What One Should Think and Say About the Schism Between Martin Luther and Andreas Karlstadt* (1524),[53] Capito attempted to walk a fine line, deferring to Luther on the one hand, and pointing out on the other hand that Luther, too, was human and could err, at least on matters of lesser importance. For example, in *What One Should Think and Say*, Capito warned his readers that people were by nature inclined to value men for divine gifts when they should praise God alone for such gifts. This error caused much harm. To avoid this pitfall Paul and Barnabas, when acclaimed as gods in Lystra, bravely resisted and attributed all honor to God. Similarly, Luther warned resolutely "that one not dirty the Gospel with his name," and he was displeased "that some wish to make a sect out of his name and call themselves Lutheran, for he teaches nothing on his own but [only] reports the content of Scripture." Capito added that in his opinion Luther had, to be sure, interpreted Scripture "better and more skillfully than has been done by anyone in several hundred years." "It happens as a result," Capito observed, "that some people put too much [trust] in him and are more astonished with Luther than with God Himself, from whom such gifts come and were given for the good of the Christian community." God had now removed this delusion and shown us, he said, that we did not yet have sufficient faith. That was why, Capito explained, we have gone astray or become faint-hearted on account of a sudden quarrel and schism.[54]

> There is mixed up in this matter all sorts of foolish things [*Ungerathenes*]. In this way the Lord God wishes to inform and instruct you laity how dangerous it is to think more highly of human beings than the Scripture commands, and [it] lets you see that some error will be found in all human beings so that honor remains God's alone. Nevertheless, dear friends, you should not out of heat judge one side [or the other]. Remember that Paul and Barnabas also had a falling out and yet they were both upright apostles.

Capito reminded his readers that they were not commanded to judge persons but rather to check the teaching against sufficient Scripture. "The foundation yet remains; God knows His own."[55]

To take the hard edge off this criticism, Capito attempted in both treatises to minimize the significance of the dispute. In his 1524 treatise, for example, he took pains first to outline the broad agreement among Evangelicals on the "central message of salvation"[56]—that we rely for our salvation on grace and not works—and on a wide range of criticisms of the papal church and its practices, especially regarding the Mass.[57] With surprising nonchalance Capito acknowledged that there was a "misunderstanding" [*Mißverstand*] on whether the word "this" in "this is my body" referred to the body or the bread.[58] "But, dear Friends," he continued, "notice the central point concerning faith and love and consider that Christ is inward and invisible and that he is bound to no external thing, be it a sign or something else, and consider the use of the Lord's Supper, namely the contemplation and remembrance of Christ for the renewal of our hope, through which we are unified in God together with all believers in Christ." That was the reason why the Lord had established the Supper. To inquire further was superfluous. "We should fend off the foolish questions, etc."[59] Hidden under the "etc." was, of course, a wealth of questions that would ultimately split the Evangelical ranks asunder. On the matter of baptism Capito announced almost as casually that "we do not ask ourselves at what time and what age one should baptize children since God grants his grace and gifts supernaturally, and the Lord healed the paralytic on the basis of the faith of those who carried him. Where we have no clear word, we abstain from inquiry; if something further is necessary, God will certainly reveal it."[60] With these few words he disposed of another weighty topic, one that would eventually separate the Anabaptists from the Evangelical ranks.

In seeking to minimize the significance of the dispute, Capito may have been doing several things simultaneously. He was certainly replying to Catholic accusations that the dispute demonstrated the Evangelicals lacked the Holy Spirit. "There is great glee and shouting for joy among the godless, dear pious burghers and Christians," he began his 1524 treatise. "They anticipate victory against the truth because Martin Luther and Andreas Karlstadt are divided on the matter. They say among themselves, 'Every kingdom divided against itself becomes a desert, and house falls on house.'"[61] The Catholic "liars" were even falsely claiming that "we handle the Evangelical matter wrongly and Luther himself already is writing against us."[62] This was no small matter given the reputation Luther enjoyed in the Strasbourg press and, presumably, among Strasbourg Evangelicals.

He may also have been trying to reassure readers who were distressed by the thought that their pastors might be at odds with God's chosen instrument, Martin Luther. He warned his readers not to be influenced by division concerning external things, even if "highly famous men" make much of them, for they did no damage to faith and could bring no offense where one was built on Christ.[63] "If a person is distressed and made anxious," Capito stated, "when he hears that the scholars are questioning themselves concerning sacraments, images, and other external matters, this is a sign that this person does not understand Christ properly." The kingdom of God was internal and was disclosed in the Scripture with sufficient clarity that it could not be hidden from common understanding. "Whatever requires great skill and experience has nothing to do with actual salvation."[64]

Finally, Capito may have been expressing his own sincere conviction. As he remarked, "Without love we are nothing, [but] without faith in the fleshly presence of Christ in the bread, we may be Christians and Dr. Luther's friend."[65] One could argue that this position was disingenuous, that the Strasbourg preachers understood perfectly well what was at stake, and that their claims were feeble attempts to paper over real differences. Certainly a modern historian who reads Capito's *Admonition* might be excused if he or she concluded that Capito has played fast and loose with Luther's foreword and with the issues that divided the two parties. But is this the most reasonable conclusion? Could not this insistence, repeated over and over again by Capito, Bucer, and their colleagues, that the quarrel was over words, and that the issue should not divide true Christians, reflect actual conviction? And if so, would this conviction not influence both how they understood and how they then re-presented Luther's writings on the Supper?

Convinced that the issue of the real presence was of secondary importance and should not separate true believers from "false brethren," Capito attempted as best he could to induce his readers to read Luther's works as he himself in fact did. This misreading became increasingly difficult with time and with Luther's own repeated insistence that the dispute did matter and was crucial for separating true Christians from false. But at least in the early years of the public debate, Capito's position was not implausible. Driven by theological conviction, an irenic temperament, and a heartfelt desire to remain in communion with that "instrument of God," Martin Luther, Capito and his Strasbourg colleagues may have held on as long as possibe to this seductively congenial reading.

CHAPTER SEVEN

Catholics on Luther's Responsibility for the German Peasants' War

"There were many peasants slain in the uprising, many fanatics banished, many false prophets hanged, burned, drowned, or beheaded who perhaps would still all live as good obedient Christians had Luther not written." Such was the conclusion of the Catholic controversialist Johann Cochlaeus. "There are (unfortunately) still many Anabaptists, assailants of the Sacrament, and other mob-spirits awakened by Luther to rebellion and error," he continued. "I'd lay you odds, however, that among all the peasants, fanatics, and mob-spirits not one could be found who has written more obscenely, more disdainfully, and more rebelliously than Luther has."[1] It is a charge that was repeated with variations by almost every Catholic controversialist who touched on the uprising. Luther's writings and teachings, they all insisted, were in large part responsible for the Peasants' War.

Is this defamation or propagandistic exaggeration? Certainly from Luther's perspective, and probably from the perspective of the modern historian who is aware of Luther's many statements before 1525 condemning rebellion, it is.[2] But is it defamation in the specific sense, a deliberate and malicious attempt to ruin Luther's good name by attributing to him responsibility that his critics *knew* was not properly his? I think not. What needs to be understood is how a nonpolemical mindset disposed Catholic apologists to read Luther's writings as they did. To illustrate this process of reception, let us examine why Catholic authors in Leipzig and Dresden, the two leading centers for Catholic controversial literature in the vernacular,[3] could argue on the basis of Luther's own writings that he had incited the Peasants' War of 1525.

EMSER'S ANSWER TO LUTHER'S "ABOMINATION"

Hieronymus Emser's *Answer to Luther's "Abomination" Against the Holy Secret Prayer of the Mass, Also How, Where, and With Which Words Luther Urged, Wrote, and Promoted Rebellion in his Books* (Dresden, 1525) lays out many of the major elements of the Catholic view.[4] In part one of this reply to Luther's *Concerning the Abomination of the Secret Prayer of the Mass, Called the Canon*, Emser offered under five headings or "proofs," multiple excerpts from Luther's writings that demonstrated to Emser's satisfaction that Luther had incited the Peasants' War.

Emser introduced his lists of proof texts with an assertion that was key to at least three of his "proofs." For the last fifteen centuries, he claimed, Christendom was divided into two estates, namely the spiritual and the secular. "This order and differentiation between the two aforementioned estates, namely the priesthood and the laity, is not a human invention as Luther falsely claimed in his book to the German nobility, rather [the two estates] were established by Christ himself."[5] On this foundation Emser then built his case, proof by proof.

Proof one: "How Luther mixed up with each other both estates, the spiritual and the secular, and destroyed the order of Christ and the holy church, and thereby caused all sorts of strife and misfortune and gave the first cause for rebellion."[6] Under this category Emser cited excerpts from Luther that dealt largely with Luther's contention that all baptized Christians were priests and that differences were only ones of office. In rejecting the distinction between clergy and laity, Luther argued that secular authority should exercise its office irrespective of pope, bishop, priest, or ecclesiastical law. Emser also cited several excerpts in which Luther attacked popes, bishops, and priests.

Here are a few of Emser's examples. He excerpted from *To the German Nobility* (1520) from signature "A.4 on the last page"[7] Luther's assertion that "they have cooked up calling the pope, bishop, priests, and the cloistered the spiritual estate and the princes, lords, artisans, and farmers the worldly estate, which is a splendid deceit and hypocrisy, although no one should become timid on this account. For all Christians are truly of the spiritual estate, and there is no difference among them except one of office."[8] Emser reproduced six more excerpts from this pamphlet, including Luther's contention that "Christian secular authority should freely exercise its office without hindrance even though it might affect pope, bishop, [or] priests. That which the spiritual law has said to the contrary is sheer fiction [and] Romanist presumption."[9] Emser also quoted two excerpts from Luther's *A Sermon on the New Testament, That Is, On the Holy Mass* (1520), including one in which Luther asserted that all Christian men were priests and all Christian women, priestesses, "be they young or old, lord or serf, woman or girl, learned or unlearned."[10] Luther's *Answer to the Hyper-Christian, Hyper-Spiritual, and Hyper-Learned Book of Goat Emser at Leipzig* (1521) yielded three more excerpts,[11] his *A Recantation of Dr. Luther of His Error, Forced on Him By the Most Learned Priest of God, Lord Hieronymus Emser, Vicar at Meißen* (1521) four,[12] and his *That a Christian Assembly or Community Has the Right or Power To Judge All Teachings and To Call Teachers* (1523) one.[13] The excerpts from *A Recantation* included some that could be seen as encouraging violence against the clergy, as, for example, Luther's suggestion that it would be best that "we henceforth do not call this peculiar foreign priesthood priests but rather tonsurelings [*blattentreger*] and chase the useless people out of the country. What to us are the tonsured folks, who are neither spiritually nor bodily priests, and what need have we of them since we are all ourselves bodily, spiritually, and in every respect priests."[14]

Although Luther had written similar things in other books, Emser wrote at the end of this list of citations for "proof one," he reckoned that he had provided sufficient citations to prove that Luther "mixed together the spiritual and worldly [estates], incited one against the other, and took it upon himself to make priests out of laity and laity out of priests and to allow them to remain neither priests nor Christians." Luther did all this, Emser alleged, with the goal of "dividing and troubling the general peace, brotherly unity, and the ancient Christian order which . . . has come down to us from Christ and the holy apostles."[15]

Emser obviously was greatly offended by Luther's assertion of the priesthood of all baptized and believing Christians. That which appealed to religiously engaged laity by dignifying their religious stature at the expense of clerical privilege, as seen in earlier chapters, not surprisingly was rejected by some of those such as Emser whose status was reduced or transformed. What is interesting in this is Emser's immediate conclusion that this transformation threatened *all* authority, secular and religious. This conclusion was also reached by Thomas Murner, as seen in chapter 3.[16] I shall return to this point in a moment, but first let us briefly survey Emser's other four collections of "proofs."

Proof two: "How Luther despised, rejected, and condemned the power, government, order, right, and laws of both of the above-mentioned estates, also [how Luther] exhorted their subjects to contempt and disobedience toward the same, made lords serfs and serfs lords and always free, [and] in addition he conceded to them all governmental authority."[17] The excerpts under this head dealt largely with a variety of specific attacks by Luther on human laws in the spiritual realm and on those who promulgated, enforced, and obeyed such laws. Among the laws Luther attacked were those requiring Christians to turn in the Scriptures to Catholic authorities,[18] and those dealing with vows, with the proper mode of receiving the Sacrament, and with mandatory confession. In some of these excerpts Luther advocated the freedom that all Christians had from baptism. This freedom allowed Christians to take the Sacrament as they wished, to confess or not, to judge doctrine, and to select their own pastors. Emser also cited Luther's praise of the Hussites and his rejection of the veneration of the Virgin and the saints. Thirty citations in all make up this "proof," drawn from eleven of Luther's treatises, ten in German and one in Latin.[19]

Proof three: "How Luther attacked with unchristian insults and calumnies the pope, bishops, and the whole spiritual estate, with no exceptions, and incited, angered, and embittered the common people against them."[20] Most of the excerpts under this heading reproduced Luther's highly unfavorable characterizations of the papacy and bishops. After thirty-four citations on this topic Emser quit multiplying examples and simply remarked that "on practically every page" of a whole series of Luther's publications Luther had "most poisonously" reviled and abused "pope, papacy, bishop, bishopric, convent, cloister, and all the clergy from the highest to the lowest." Luther had done this, Emser charged, to awaken "such animosity and hatred among the common people against their spiritual fathers and pastors [seelsorgern] that they no longer want to hear their teaching and preaching." Instead, the common people would run after "Lutheran preachers" even "three miles away," and if they met a monk or priest on the street, they would throw filth or stones and scream at them "like wolves." Finally, they stormed and plundered their houses, foundations, churches, and cloisters and struck them, took them prisoners, ravaged them and drove them into wretched exile. The like had not been seen in Germany before "Luther began his game."[21]

Proof four: "How Luther also especially attacked, insulted, and committed and incurred the crime of lese majesty against secular authorities such as the emperor, king, and princes."[22] Under this heading, Emser presented a series of twenty-three excerpts in which Luther attacked or ridiculed princes and even the emperor when they attempted to exercise their secular authority in the spiritual realm and, from Luther's perspective, overstepped their proper authority. "What of anything good the common man should then take from such horrible abuse, malediction, and injury to majesty and superior authority, to which, as the holy apostles have taught us, every soul is subject," Emser concluded his list, "I shall let the reader be the judge."[23]

Proof five: "How Luther also explicitly counseled rebellion, wrangling, and strife, [and how Luther] defied, scorned, and with the common rabble (whom he also zealously incited to this end) threatened the authorities, both the spiritual and the secular."[24] Under this heading Emser presented some forty-seven excerpts that, on the face, *were* incendiary or which fell under some of the classifications of proofs one through four. To give the most blatant example, he cited an excerpt from Luther's Latin afterword to Sylvester Prierias's *Epitoma responsionis ad M. Lutherum*, in which Luther remarked (albeit in Latin), "Since we punish thieves with the gallows, robbers with the sword, heretics with fire, why do we not even more employ every possible weapon against these teachers of destruction, these cardinals, popes, and all the dregs of the Roman Sodom, who unceasingly lay waste to the church of God, and wash our hands in their blood?"[25] Emser also cited excerpts in which Luther stated that disturbance accompanied the true gospel. For example, Emser cited a passage from Luther's *Answer to the Goat Emser at Leipzig*, in which Luther replied to Emser's charge that his teaching provoked unrest wherever it spread, "that I began in God's name and [that] my teaching is the true word of God has no stronger proof than that it has spread so quickly throughout the world and caused disunity. And if it had not done that, I would have long ago despaired and grown tired."[26] From this long list of examples—and Emser said that for the sake of brevity he had not listed a great number more—Emser concluded that any honest man would recognize that not the papists but rather Luther had lied when he said that he had not awakened or given cause for this uprising.[27]

To summarize, Emser began with the two estates, spiritual and secular. In proof one he rejected Luther's notion of the priesthood of all believers since it involved mixing the divinely established two estates. In proof two he took issue with Luther's notion of the freedom of the Christian since it asserted that all Christians were equal and thereby overturned the proper hierarchy in society and since it further advocated freedom from human laws and thereby encouraged disobedience to proper authority. In proof three he gathered many of Luther's attacks on the papacy and the bishops. In proof four he collected Luther's attacks on and ridicule of secular rulers who overstepped their bounds and attempted to rule in the spiritual realm. In proof five he concluded with what he saw as explicit incitements (and a few could easily be read that way) to rebellion.

Emser's treatise reproduced most of the elements of the Catholic understanding of Luther's responsibility for the Peasants' War. Although it is somewhat arbitrary to do so given the interrelation of the different "proofs," let's look more closely at proof two and bring in some other controversialists to show how they agreed in their reading of Luther.

THE CATHOLIC READING OF CHRISTIAN FREEDOM

Emser read Luther's "Christian freedom" as subversive to social order and as encouraging sin. He argued that Luther had condemned the authority of both estates and turned lords into subjects and subjects into lords and made everyone free.[28] Emser objected, for example, that in his translation of I Corinthians 10, Luther glossed a verse concerning freedom from dietary regulation with the comment "Christ is free and so too are all Christians in all things." And Emser added, "Luther promotes the same thing concerning freedom in many places in his Testament."[29] Emser also objected to Luther's rhetorical question in *To the German Nobility*, why should we become bound by the word of a man since we are all born free in baptism and subject only to the divine word? For Emser, when Luther rejected ordinances or distinctions of rank that limited Christian freedom, when he advocated the freedom to commune in both kinds without all the regulation of the Mass, he was counseling sedition and rejecting legitimate authority.[30]

Johann Cochlaeus agreed. In the 1527 Dresden reprint of his *Answer to Luther's Treatise "Against the Robbing and Murdering Hordes of Peasants,"* he stated that the Lutherans, "under the semblance of Scripture with cunning and deceitful exegesis have so brought the poor unlearned people around to the false freedom of baptism that they believe that since we are all brothers in Christ through baptism, all things should be equal among us, as happens with true brothers." He then addressed Luther directly and cited from Luther's *On the Babylonian Captivity,* "'I tell you truly,' you said, 'that no law can justly be imposed on Christians, neither by human beings nor by angels, no matter how much they wish to, since we are free from them all.'"[31]

The man responsible for the Cochlaeus reprint in Dresden, Petrus Sylvius, summed up the controversialists' position in his 1527 *A Clear Demonstration.* "And in truth had the Christian princes not been so soon awakened against the Lutheran peasants," Sylvius wrote, "then the Lutheran teaching would have turned all lordship and authorities into peasants and there would have not only been no divine service or houses of God but also no castle or noble estate left undestroyed in the German lands." Sylvius was convinced that this contention could be proved from Luther's own writings. One would have had the Lutheran writings and teachings to thank for the overturning of all authority and the destruction of religion, "since Luther has written from the beginning of his publication and especially in the treatise on *Christian Freedom* and the *Babylonian Captivity* that each Christian should be and is free as a matter of right and should be himself a lord, prince, king, bishop, and pope since they were all to a man priests and kings. And each should believe, celebrate, and do whatever he wishes, however he wishes, without regard for anyone."[32] Sylvius buttressed his assertion with reference to Emser's *Against Luther's 'Abomination'* (1525), Cochlaeus's *Answer . . . to Martin Luther's Book* (1525), and the works of "many others."[33]

Underpinning this freedom, as these Catholic authors saw it, was, in Cochlaeus's words, the "false principle that faith alone justifies and sanctifies."[34] Luther knew, Paul Bachmann wrote sarcastically, "that no believer goes to hell even if he is a murderer, thief, a robber, an adulterer and so on. Because no sin condemns a person, only lack of belief."[35] And Johannes Fabri, later bishop of Vienna, remarked with a touch of *Schadenfreude* regarding the lament in the Saxon Visitation Articles that too much was being taught about the forgiveness of sin and too little about repentance, "Yes, dear Luther, not only a few but nearly all your disciples have for more than ten years not said or taught anything else but that only by faith, that faith alone justifies, that mere faith makes one blessed, that one should only believe and that is sufficient. And who, but you, first brought this teaching up?"[36] This indeed was their complaint against Luther and his "disciples" made twelve years ago, "that you forever preached naked faith alone so that the common people, unfortunately, have fallen away from all fear of God, good conscience, love of neighbor, good works, indeed all Christian honesty." Fabri drew a stark conclusion from this: "And who, other than you, is [therefore] responsible for those innocent children who were slain and perished in the Peasants' War?"[37] As he read it, Luther's Christian freedom gave the appearance of teaching improvement and edification but in fact was a "fleshly freedom" that came down to "whatever one wanted to say, one said, and whatever one wished to do, one did."[38]

But the Catholic objection went beyond the reliance on "mere faith." For, as they saw it, Luther said not only that faith without works saved, but that a striving after good works could actually damn. Luther, Sylvius explained in his 1534 *The Last Two Books*, "rejects and slanders good works, even those done as well as possible, as if they were simply horrible sins, and [he] considers as no sins all the vices and wickedness that one can produce, and [he] wishes to deal before God with mere faith alone without any divine love and Christian works."[39] He and his colleagues read Luther to say that "mere, naked faith" would save, apart from works, and that traditional good works such as the Mass were not only unnecessary but positively harmful. As Johannes Mensing put it, "They have promised the people very many freedoms so that they become, indeed, slaves to their flesh . . . so that they would prefer to outrage virgins than to hold mass."[40] Paul Bachmann read Luther much the same way:

> Like the hellish spirits he [Luther] teaches that one should avoid the good and do what is wicked. That is, his teaching is that one should protect oneself from all godly and human laws and commands and from all good works, which God has commanded to do, more than from all sins, and that one should only cling to bare faith, and that he who does all sorts of evil yet relies only on naked faith strengthens faith and is made blessed and holy. But he who does good, what God has commanded to do, has destroyed the faith and is condemned.[41]

Sylvius can be seen to sum up the connection he and his fellow controversialists saw between Christian freedom and equality, "mere" faith, the avoidance of good works, and the Peasants' War. Luther's teachings about Christian freedom and equality made the "Lutheran common people" unable to tolerate authority or be anyone's subject. The "black Lutheran peasants" and "his" Anabaptists had already dared to practice Luther's teaching that in Christendom there could and should be no authority but rather everyone should be equal to every other. Looking towards the future, Sylvius predicted that the "Lutheran common folk"

> will cultivate division, unrest, war, robbery, [and] murder, not only against true Christendom but also against each other. [They will do this] all on account of the many-sided and self-contradictory, wicked Lutheran teaching and their wicked lives, as Luther teaches . . . that one can and may freely practice and commit every vice and wickedness even of the whole world and it would be no sin if one only had mere faith. But one should only protect oneself from good works for although they are done in the best way, they would nevertheless be nothing more than horrible sins.[42]

All the elements of the Catholic view are present in this one summary statement.

THE LOGIC OF THE CATHOLIC VIEW

Are we simply studying various misunderstandings or even deliberate propagandistic distortions of Luther's teachings? To an extent, yes. But that's not all we're doing. To be sure there are misunderstandings and distortions, but such observations miss the point. Readers pick and choose among the ideas introduced to them. Some issues resonate with their life experiences; others do not. And in the dialectic of reader and text, some ideas are invested with new meaning, transposed to a different key, or filled out in ways unintended by their author.

For the most part, Catholic controversialists that I have studied remained wedded to the mind-set or *Erwartungshorizont* (horizon of expectation)[43] of late medieval Christendom, which included belief in divinely established and necessary hierarchy, a distinction between clergy and laity, and the necessity of works in the process of justification. In other words, while Luther and his followers now operated with an *Erwartungshorizont* different from that of late medieval Christendom, the Catholic controversialists continued to work from within the old *Erwartungshorizont*. So their central beliefs and expectations led them to read and understand Luther's text differently than Luther and his partisans did. Of course, the effect of a mind-set or *Erwartungshorizont* is a natural and unavoidable fact of intellectual life. No one approaches a text without presuppositions and commitments, without *Vorverständnisse*; and these presuppositions and commitments necessarily shape one's perception.

Given the Catholic controversialists' commitments, it is hardly surprising that they generally failed to accept or perhaps in some cases even to understand, on the one hand, Luther's distinction between the two realms (*regimente*), spiritual and temporal, and, on the other, Luther's rejection of the distinction between the two estates, spiritual and temporal. So when they read Luther's comments about freedom in the spiritual realm, they did not read or understand them within the context and with the limitations intended by Luther. As a result, they read Luther's insistence on Christian freedom from law and good works *in the spiritual realm* as freedom from law and good works *in general*. This view of things was reinforced by Luther's insistence that justification came through faith apart from works and that works done with an eye toward earning salvation were actually sinful. Catholic controversialists read Luther on this score as encouraging people to think that they could be saved by "mere, naked faith" and discouraging them from performing good works. As the controversialists saw it, statements of this sort were counsels for sin and disobedience. Further, having rejected Luther's distinction between the spiritual and secular realms, they read Luther's comment about equality among Christians *in the spiritual realm* as advocating an end to hierarchy within society generally. This was another encouragement to disobedience.

They were reinforced in this reading of Luther by Luther's many attacks on the governing authorities of the two estates. Since they did not accept or did not understand Luther's distinction between the spiritual and the secular realm, they read Luther's attacks on spiritual and secular authorities who attempted to establish and enforce laws *in the spiritual realm* as *unqualified* attacks on authority, both spiritual and secular. This reading was powerfully reinforced by the rhetoric of Luther's attacks, which could easily overpower his theological qualifications. I shall let Duke Georg of Saxony speak for a number of Catholic polemicists (and rulers—Duke Georg was both) who read Luther's rhetoric as an incitement to violence. For who does not realize that "all his abuse, slander, cursing, scolding, and incitement to disobedience" that was found in Luther's writings, the Duke wrote, was "done with the sole intention that, if the pious princes and lords, which he had attracted to himself, did not wish themselves to instigate war or rebellion, he should nevertheless cause the emperor and other lords [to do so], so that in any case the plans of his lord, the devil, would be successful?" In other words, the force of the rhetoric itself would provoke violence. Were Luther, however, that which he claimed to be, the Duke continued, namely, a true preacher of the gospel, he would undoubtedly do nothing of the sort. Instead, he would chastise the shortcomings and misdeeds of his adversaries "with complete patience and gentleness." He would seek their improvement not destruction. "But since he on the contrary does nothing but scold, curse, rave, and rage, it is to be feared that he will lead to eternal and irreparable destruction not only his adversaries but also his closest adherents."[44] In sum, the disobedience the controversialists expected from Luther's insistence on "mere faith" and "Christian freedom" was confirmed by Luther's attacks and his often inflammatory rhetoric.

The committed Catholic also found ample evidence in events themselves to confirm this reading of Luther. Let me illustrate from the Peasants' War how events could have confirmed Catholics in their view of Luther's writings.

From the early 1520s, Catholic controversialists who disagreed with (or did not understand) Luther's notion of Christian freedom and his distinction between the two realms had been predicting that Luther's message would result in rebellion against secular authority.[45] For example, the Franciscan Thomas Murner put it particularly well in his *The Great Lutheran Fool* (Strasbourg, 1522). In biting verses Murner defined what was required of men and women to become Lutheran. They must despise the papacy, bishops, and clergy; consider the pope the Antichrist; tread under foot all papal pronouncements; give up fasting, confession, and praying; deride all secular authority; hold the mass in contempt and reject its sacrificial character; abandon the other sacraments; destroy churches and cloisters; drive out members of religious orders; abuse the clergy from the pulpit; advocate bloodshed and rebellion; plunder clerical property; and, in short,

Alle ding zu keren vmb,
Dan ist das ewangelium
Gar volkumen mit seim orden.
Also sein wir al lutherisch worden.
[To turn everything upside down fully realizes the gospel arrangement. Thus we have all become Lutheran].

For Murner all these "Lutheran rules" flow from Luther's fleshly Christian freedom, but especially the rejection of authority:

Der cristlich glaub gibt vnss freiheit,
Zü erkennen hie kein oberkeit.

Wir sein im tauff al frei geboren,
Ee keiser, künig, fürsten woren.
[The Christian faith gives us freedom to recognize no earthly authority. We were all born free in baptism before there was an emperor, king, or princes].[46]

Controversialists like Murner believed their prediction confirmed in the most widely circulated peasant manifesto, *The Twelve Articles*.[47] This declaration provided an ideological rationale for religious, economic, and social grievances that united peasant bands throughout southern and central Germany. Composed by Sebastian Lotzer, a journeyman furrier of Memmingen, for the peasants of Upper Swabia, *The Twelve Articles* was reprinted over twenty times in the space of a couple months and became the statement of grievances, either in whole or in part, for peasant bands throughout the area of uprising, excepting only Switzerland and the Alpine region and parts of Franconia and Thuringia.[48] The first and twelfth articles show clearly the influence of the Reformation movement: the first requested that the entire community have the power and authority to choose and appoint a pastor, and the twelfth offered to withdraw any of the previous eleven articles that was shown to be contrary to Scripture. Sandwiched between these two articles, and liberally annotated with references to Scripture, were ten articles dealing with such things as tithing, serfdom, fishing and game laws, wood cutting, feudal services, rents, new laws, communal fields, and the death tax.

Of particular interest to us is its third article, which stated that "it has until now been the custom for the lords to own us as their property." This was "deplorable," the article continued, "for Christ redeemed and bought us all with his precious blood, the lowliest shepherd as well as the greatest lord, with no exceptions." And the article called upon the Bible as its authority:

Thus the Bible proves that we are free and [we] want to be free. Not that we want to be utterly free and subject to no authority at all; God does not teach us that. We ought to live according to the commandments, not according to the lusts of the flesh. But we should love God, recognize him as our Lord in our neighbor, and willingly do all things God commanded us at his Last Supper.[49]

In this demand, together with the first and twelfth articles, Catholic readers such as Cochlaeus and Emser saw Luther's Christian freedom taking its inevitable rebellious form.[50]

We could of course argue, and rightly so, that in their depiction of Luther's notion of Christian freedom both peasants and Catholics misunderstood Luther's position. But the misunderstanding is readily explicable. The historian Peter Blickle has shown that the Reformation changed how the peasants legitimated their long-standing desire to change their relations with their lords. Before 1525 peasants had claimed that their revolts were only to remove innovations that violated traditional law. By 1525, however, appeal to traditional law could not legitimate changes necessary to relieve the tensions that had developed in the last century. Appeal to divine law could, and did. Moreover, appeal to divine law—which could cover any demand that could be deduced from Scripture—allowed the uprising to take on a supraterritorial character.[51] Specifically in the matter of freedom from serfdom, the Reformation allowed the peasants to transcend the traditional law of serfdom and insist that all should be free on principle. If God was lord, the peasants concluded, there could be no seigneurs. "No one but God our creator, father, and lord should have serfs," concluded the villages of Schaffhausen, and in this they were followed by many other peasant articles. The Reformation also allowed the peasants to attack serfdom on the basis of justice and divine law.[52] It proved quite easy, given the peasants' situation and aspirations, to translate into the temporal realm Luther's insistence on the Christian freedom to test all laws against Scripture.

Of course, once the peasants justified their uprising in these terms, it is hardly surprising that Catholics believed their reading of the rebellious potential of Luther's writings had been confirmed by events. So when they charged Luther with responsibility for the Peasants' War, they were only reflecting their honest understanding of his writings.

CONCLUSION

It is a fascinating characteristic of a significant number of the Catholic pamphlets against Luther that in proving a point they often contented themselves with listing excerpts from Luther's works. We looked at this in some detail with Emser's *Answer to Luther's "Abomination,"* but Cochlaeus, for example, also commonly proceeded in the same fashion.[53] Sometimes commentary or exposition followed the list of excerpts, but often not. It is difficult to think of a clearer demonstration that they were reading Luther differently than, say, Evangelically minded readers. The conclusion seems inescapable. If the same text proved one thing to a Catholic and another to an Evangelical, the historic meaning of a text cannot be determined independent of its reader.

Conclusion

A Revised Narrative

What would a narrative look like if it paid primary attention to what the public would have learned about Luther from the local press? Here is one sketch that draws on material from the preceding chapters.

Rumors had been circulating for some months that a monk named Martin Luther had attacked the church's traditional teachings on indulgences. A handful of humanists had in fact read the occasionally cryptic theses that the Augustinian friar and professor had written, but the broader reading public first came to know something about Martin Luther from his *Sermon on Indulgences and Grace*. It swept through the major centers of the empire and was snapped up in large numbers by the curious.[1] In the space of just a few pages, Luther clearly and calmly explained and criticized the scholastic understanding of the sacrament of penance and indulgences, insisting that the associated views and practices were still debatable and lacking adequate scriptural basis. Rather than actually seeking indulgences, it was a thousand times better, Luther taught, that Christians do the good works and suffer the punishment that indulgences were supposed to replace. On the whole, the impression Luther gave was of a morally earnest critic of scholastic theology, concerned that Christians choose good works over indulgences.

This first "best-seller" was quickly followed by a series of short German sermons and devotional works written specifically for the laity. They were issued in a handy format that was cheap to produce, inexpensive to buy, and easily passed from reader to reader. These

163

works seemed to have struck a responsive cord. The reading public sought them out with an avidity that had not been seen before in the short history of printing. Dozens of different pamphlets in multiple editions of hundreds of copies each poured from the presses to meet the demand. Printers competed with each other to see who could quickly rush to market a new work by "Martin Luther, Augustinian" or, as his fame grew, simply "M. L. A."

Two interconnected themes ran through these early works: first, that Christians should acknowledge their own sinfulness and surrender all reliance on their own works, and, second, that they should trust God and God's promise in Christ as their only source of salvation. Addressing topics that directly touched the religious life of the laity, Luther told his readers and hearers that the ordinary lives they lived were far more pleasing to God than clerically prescribed good works so long as they lived their lives in faithful trust of God's forgiveness through Christ. All baptized Christians had to rely solely on God's gracious forgiveness, so that a life dedicated to "good works," even the life of a monk or priest, was in no way superior to the lives of faithful laity and, in fact, could actually be harmful for any who believed that good works, clerically approved or otherwise, counted for anything before God. Clerical claims to mediate salvation through the various sacraments were explicitly questioned. It was the Christian's reliance in faith on God's gracious forgiveness through Christ that made a sacrament efficacious, not anything the priest did or failed to do. In fact, any faithful Christian could, if necessary, do what the priest did. And priestly bans did not necessarily separate Christians from the true church.

Thanks to these largely pastoral and devotional works, Luther became Germany's first best-selling vernacular author, speaking to a far wider audience than, say, the humanists who had used the press before him. Yet in this flood of publications printed and reprinted throughout the German-speaking lands there was almost no mention of his growing estrangement from the papacy. While a few humanists and Latinate readers followed the progress of his appearance before Cajetan in Augsburg, his debate with Eck in Leipzig, and his increasingly trenchant Latin criticism of the papacy and papal claims, this development raised scarcely a ripple in the German-language press. Whatever the readers of Luther's German writings might have heard from their more learned fellow citizens about Luther's conflicts with church authorities and other academics, their own direct encounter with Luther's views suggested a far more edifying than confrontational program.

To be sure, vernacular readers might have caught glimpses of the increasingly acrimonious debate in the writings of a few publicists such as the humanist Ulrich von Hutten, whose name was occasionally linked with Luther's. But it was not until the late summer and fall of 1520 that readers of Luther's vernacular writings learned at first hand what their Latinate fellow citizens had known for some time. In a series of angry yet eloquent treatises, Luther attacked the religious authorities of the day. He claimed that the pope and his supporters had perpetrated a series of frauds on Christendom. He urged his readers to reject the authority of the papacy to interpret Scripture or to call a council. They should liberate themselves from a papal captivity and clerical tyranny that distorted the sacraments and subordinated the laity to a fictitious "clerical estate." All Christians were true priests, and there was no difference among them—be they bishop or priest, prince or commoner, male or female—except one of office. Scripture was the sole authority for determining questions of proper Christian belief and worship.

Vernacular readers in places such as Strasbourg were also treated about this time to the first rebuttals by avowed supporters of the papacy. While disputing this or that point Luther made, they all charged that Luther was upsetting legitimate authority and tradition. These defenders of the papacy argued that the public debate was itself wrong and dangerous, subversive in principle to legitimate hierarchy and authority. While Luther was entreating his readers to make up their own minds on the basis of Scripture alone and not let the papacy and its clerical allies mislead them with fabricated claims to authority, his opponents were issuing treatises that said that the broader public— "the ignorant and rebellious commoners"—should in no way be involved in such disputes. Yet by entering into the vernacular debate, the Catholic publicists were implicitly inviting the commoners to debate the issues and take sides. By refuting Luther's view they actually propagated them. The medium subverted the Catholic message and gave the curious at least a glimpse of Luther's tantalizing ideas. No wonder the Catholic publicists generated such a feeble response to the Evangelical barrage.

The public saw the battle clearly joined when in the summer and fall of 1521 the markets were flooded with copies of the speech Luther had delivered before the emperor and the Imperial Diet assembled in the city of Worms.² Many of these readers surely knew that the pope had excommunicated Luther as a heretic a few months earlier. But for Luther's partisans the Worms speech gave the real reasons for his "persecution" by the papacy. He had issued treatises dealing with "faith and morals so evangelically and simply that even my opponents must confess that they are useful and innocuous and in all respects worthy to be read by Christian people."³ He had attacked the papacy and the papists, who by "their most wicked example" had "devastated, ravaged, and corrupted" the world both "spiritually and bodily."⁴ The "unbelievable papal tyranny" had "devoured" the possessions and property of the German nation and continued to do so through dishonorable means.⁵ He had also attacked others who sought "to protect the Roman tyranny and to destroy the godly service taught by me."⁶ While he sought instruction if he erred, his opponents gave him no hearing but proceeded against him with force. So unless he was "overcome through testimony of Scripture or through evident reasons" (for neither pope nor councils could be relied upon because both had erred repeatedly and contradicted themselves), he was "overcome by the Scripture" that he had cited. His conscience was "captive to the word of God," and he could not recant.⁷

Luther's defiant speech defined the issues at stake for many readers and hearers. Those who opposed the "unbelievable papal tyranny" and insisted on "the testimony of Scripture" would suffer abuse and persecution at the hands of papal hirelings and church authorities. Given all that Luther had accomplished in revealing the "true" meaning of Scripture, many were coming to think of him as not only a learned doctor of the Bible but also as a divinely "chosen light of Christendom," sent to tell of God's divine word and to reveal the sorry state of the present world. For his courageous attacks on the papal "Antichrist," some were even coming to see him in biblical terms, as the prophesied "Angel of the Apocalypse" sent by God and "raised up in the fervor of the spirit of Elias" to begin the final, apocalyptic struggle between the forces of good and evil, Christ and the devil. While Luther took on many of the trappings of a biblical saint or prophet, his opponents were defined in the most negative of terms, as hypocritical, greedy self-seekers and enemies of Christ.

Yet even as his supporters were united with Luther in his insistence on Scripture as the sole authority for deciding doctrine within the church, and even as they shared much if not all of his horror for the papal "tyranny" and its alleged abuses, they did not, or at least many of their leaders did not, see the central issues in the same way that Luther did. For several fateful years, many of Luther's enthusiastic supporters fundamentally misunderstood his theology of justification by faith alone apart from the works of the law. While Luther insisted that a Christian was freed by faith from all laws, human and divine, many of his supporters (at least in southern Germany) agreed that Christians were freed by faith from "man-made" laws not supported by Scripture, but insisted nevertheless that human beings were still required to fulfill the divine law established by Scripture. The Christian's freedom from human laws freed him to serve God's divine commandments. Even as south German Evangelicals came gradually over the succeeding years to understand the full implications of Luther's radical doctrine of justification by faith alone, they continued to put more stress on scriptural example and divine commandment, whether in worship or Christian behavior, than Luther and his "Lutherans" did.

By perhaps an ironic twist of fate, it was this misunderstanding about the right relationship, from Luther's perspective, between gospel and law, be it human or divine, that led Luther by his own admission to fit out "Scripture alone" with a whole panoply of aids to "right" understanding. From highly directive prefaces and forewords, to tendentious glosses and theologically shaped translations of Scripture, Luther attempted mightily to see that readers took away from Scripture the same message that he did. Whatever the cogency to the theological appeal to Scripture alone and to the doctrine that Scripture interpreted itself, in practice Scripture reached the reading public as printed text fitted out with guides to its interpretation. Luther's translation became an "overnight sensation," sweeping all other translations before it. Despite his strenuous efforts, however, he remained unable to dictate the right understanding of Scripture even to his close followers.

This became clear in the fall of 1524, when the reading public was introduced to a dispute among the leaders of the Reformation movement about images in church, the pace of reforms, and, above all, the right understanding of Christ's presence in the Lord's Supper. It seems probable that many readers either did not understand the dispute or found unconvincing or inconclusive the scriptural arguments adduced by either side. To encourage as many people as possible to accept his view of the issues in dispute, Luther began supplementing Scripture with reminders about his own considerable reputation as an "unworthy instrument of God" who had written "with such clarity and certainty" regarding the gospel, the grace of Christ, the law, faith, love, the cross, human ordinances, the papacy, monasticism, the Mass, and the "articles of faith that a Christ should know."

As if to counter this appeal to authority, other authors took to citing Luther himself on the point that faith should not depend upon any human being but stand solely on the word of God. While paying Luther his due as the foremost exegete of Scripture in the last several hundred years, authors tried gently to disagree with him and minimize the significance of the dispute. Readers were assured that the dispute did not touch on the central message of salvation by faith alone, whatever Luther claimed. The important thing was that Evangelicals were united in their opposition to the "papal" understanding of the Mass as sacrifice and all the "unnecessary and damaging additions" that had grown up around its practice. That was all that mattered. Not so, said both Luther and his opponent Karlstadt. Those who failed to properly discern the body of Christ ate to their damnation. The quarrel went on for years without resolving to general satisfaction the meaning of scriptural passages in dispute or the significance of the disagreement for Christianity. This falling out among the Evangelical ranks also contributed to a general trend whereby Luther became increasingly a regional author, writing largely for north and central German audiences.

Also contributing, perhaps, to the rapid fall off in the demand for Luther's works was the German Peasants' War of 1525. Sweeping through large sections of central and southern Germany, this violent movement took the form in the press of a series of articles that gave another twist on Luther's teachings about Christian freedom. "It has until now been the custom for the lords to own us as their property," one article read. This was "deplorable," it continued," "for Christ redeemed and bought us all with his precious blood, the lowliest shepherd as well as the greatest lord, with no exceptions." And the article called upon the Bible as its authority. "Thus the Bible proves that we are free."[8]

While Luther rejected this understanding of Christian freedom and ultimately denounced the peasants in the most ferocious terms, his Catholic critics saw in the peasant uprisings clear confirmation of what they had been saying all along. Luther's attack on the spiritual estate, his insistence that faith alone saves and that good works could in fact damn, his teaching that all Christians were priests and that there was no distinction between pope, bishop, prince, burgher, and peasant, and his violent abuse of popes and princes who defended the traditional faith, had all led the "poor common people" into contempt for legitimate authority, rebellion, and ultimate and disastrous defeat and death. Luther's writings and events themselves confirmed this harsh judgment.

After 1525 or so, large parts of the Reformation movement entered into its institutional phase. The great ideals and principles of the propaganda campaign of the late teens and early twenties were gradually turned into laws, reformed worship services, catechisms, and school orders. The great crescendo of vernacular agitation gradually ebbed, leaving behind an altered landscape and a new, much higher demand for vernacular works than had existed before the Reformation message (or messages) had swept the land.

A COMMENTARY

The omissions in this revised narrative are at least as significant as some of the changes in emphasis and interpretation. There is no mention, for example, of Luther's educational program, since only the humanist elite knew much about it outside Wittenberg. *The Ninety-Five Theses* is only briefly alluded to because, despite its great importance in rallying humanists and other elites to his side, it had relatively limited circulation in vernacular editions and was, in any case, difficult to understand. Instead, it was his *Sermon on Indulgences and Grace* that first introduced Luther to a truly broad public. This sermon made no mention of such topics as justification by faith alone. On the contrary, it advocated good works over indulgences! Given the central position of this work in the biography of the *public* Luther, it is ironic that when American Luther scholars planned the fifty-five volume American edition of Luther's works, they considered it so unimportant, or perhaps so "un-Lutheran," that it was not included. Yet it represented the first widespread introduction of sixteenth-century Germans to Luther.

There is but passing mention of Luther's growing opposition to the papacy in the late teens because this development was reported, if at all, only in Latin publications. His summons to Rome, his appearance before Cajetan, his debate with Eck at Leipzig, his conclusion that popes and councils could both err, his suspicion that the papacy was the Antichrist foretold by Scripture—these milestones in Luther's personal and intellectual biography found little echo in the vernacular press. Luther's ferocious attack on the "papal Antichrist" first made its dramatic appearance in the vernacular in the summer and fall of 1520.

The revised narrative makes no mention at all of Luther's "breakthrough" to justification by faith alone apart from works of the law. Whether one favors the late dating, as I do, or an earlier dating as many other scholars do, it is crucial for our reconstruction of Luther's public career to remember that the first mention Luther made publicly of this "breakthrough" came in his 1545 preface to the collection of his Latin writings. Many of the sources on which scholars base their reconstruction of Luther's early theological development were first published only in the late nineteenth and early twentieth centuries.

Most standard narratives make no mention of the essential confusion that surrounded Luther's teaching in these early years. The "Erasmian" reading of Luther that we saw in the Strasbourg press of 1521 and 1522 may well represent even the majority view among those who followed the debate and cared about the issues. Whether of the majority or minority, those supporting Luther likely did so more because of his appeal to Scripture alone and his attack on papal abuses and traditional observances than because they understood the full implications of justification by faith alone. Scripture alone was the one issue all the supporting publicists agreed upon, and it was the most discussed single issue in all the pamphlet literature, both Evangelical and Catholic. More than that, a rejection of human laws in favor of the divine had its real and obvious attractions, as the Peasants' War was to show a few years later.

This revised narrative also stresses Luther's growing personal authority. The view of Luther as an earnest "man of the Bible" concerned for the spiritual well-being of the laity was well fixed in the public mind months before Luther's great antipapal polemics first appeared in the vernacular press. As people came increasingly to see the contest between Luther and the papacy in apocalyptic terms, Luther's public persona took on many of the attributes of the biblical prophet. For every author who was concerned that his partisans were making an "idol" of Luther, there were many more describing Luther and their own times in apocalyptic terms. In his survey of sermons purportedly preached to urban congregations, Bernd Moeller identified as one of the four most repeated themes the rapidly approaching Endtime.[9] Luther's special, almost prophetic authority fit within this shared vision. It also made it extraordinarily difficult for other Evangelicals to disagree with the Wittenberg reformer.

Without minimizing the importance or cogency of Luther's *theological* conviction that Scripture interpreted itself, this revised narrative also points out that in practice not even Luther was willing to leave Scripture alone. Painful experience taught that people did not read Scripture in the same way, and so Luther devoted extraordinary energy to induce readers to interpret Scripture as he did. Yet disagreements over the right understanding of Scripture only multiplied.

Within a few years of the publication of Luther's *German New Testament*, controversy over the Lord's Supper showed that even Evangelicals who agreed on so much could disagree fundamentally on this point and fail to convince others of their particular reading of Scripture. This is why, the revised narrative claims, the issue of Luther's personal authority became so important both for Luther and for his opponents. When you cannot agree on the basis of the "sole authority," other authorities come into play. In this regard, Luther enjoyed a considerable advantage over his opponents.

Finally, the Catholic claim that Luther was responsible for the Peasants' War takes on new cogency when viewed from the standpoint of publications, and of the message intended versus the message received. Luther could rightly claim that he had written often and powerfully against rebellion, but his Catholic critics could also reasonably argue that whatever Luther said, his writings had the effect of encouraging rebellion. They could point to the Peasant articles and to the tragedy of the Peasants' War itself to document their claim. While understandably rejected by Luther and his supporters, the Catholic charge had its own logic and legitimacy.

I have offered one variation on a revised narrative, a narrative that depends upon the press and its message to a receptive Germany. Scholars may well differ with particulars, but I hope that I have at least persuaded them of my three central concerns. First, the story takes a different form if you structure it around communication and ask what those with an engaged interest would know about Luther and when they would know it. Second, there was frequently a gap between what Luther intended to convey to his readers or hearers and what they understood. This discrepancy makes the narrative more complex and questions of influence and responsibility more difficult. Third, the crisis of authority that was the Reformation owed a great deal to print. Not only did the printing press broadcast the attack on tradi-

tional authorities to a broader audience and with greater rapidity than
had ever been possible before, it itself embodied the subversive message it conveyed.

This book contributes to two lively historiographic debates: the extent to which printing played a crucial role in the German Reformation and the nature of the primary appeal of the early Reformation
movements conveyed by print (and subsequently by preaching) to the
larger population. To be sure, the sharply formulated "Moellerian"
thesis, "without printing, no Reformation," lies in the realm of
metaphysics—there was after all a printing industry and a Reformation, and historians cannot, as it were, replay the tape to see what
would happen without printing.[10] Nevertheless, the more than forty-
fold increase in the number of printed pamphlets that occurred from
1517 through 1524 suggests that critics may need to moderate their
skepticism about the role of print in reaching a large, primarily lay
audience.[11] In fact, given the conservative estimate that in the period
1518 to 1546 the presses of the German-speaking lands produced over
six million vernacular treatises supporting or opposing the Reformation—which works out to one exemplar for every two people in the
empire, literate and illiterate—even the estimates of literacy within
the empire seem improbably low.[12] While undoubtedly only a minority of the population was directly touched and engaged by the propaganda spike of the early German Reformation, their numbers were
not insignificant, their influence often considerable, and their willingness to share their views with others amply demonstrated by events.
The conclusion seems inescapable: the printed word played a crucial
role in the early Reformation, and when multiplied by the effects of
preaching and conversation, can be said to be a major factor in spread-
ing a relatively coherent message throughout the German-speaking
lands.

On the matter of this "relatively coherent" message and its appeal,
the evidence suggests a need for nuance and qualification. While
Luther was the overwhelmingly dominant publicist during these crucial years—the number of printings of works by Luther exceeded, for
example, the combined total of the seventeen other leading Evangelical
publicists—his message was not necessarily the dominant message, at
least in the early years. In the initial years of the Reformation, the message that vernacular readers of Luther were offered was pastoral, not
communal. When picked up by other early publicists, the message was
still more individual than communal but arguably more biblicist and

"Erasmian" than "Lutheran." A significant number of early publicists overheard Luther's doctrine of law and gospel in favor of the idea of the Bible as divine law, a reading of Luther that significantly qualified his insistence on "justification by faith alone apart from the works of the law." The eventual split among Evangelicals over the right understanding of the Eucharist grew out of differences that stretched back to the original spread of the Reformation; it did not arise from "departures" from Luther's doctrine by the urban reformers. Many of these early treatises were as much "prolaity" as "anticlerical," insisting that Christ's death liberated all Christians, both lay and clergy, from both the demands of clerically prescribed late medieval piety and the need for clerical mediation. The principle "Scripture alone" was the most advocated and attacked in the early pamphlet literature, but the principle was supplemented in practice even by its advocates. Luther's notion of Christian freedom was variously understood by different audiences. Their understanding of this concept, as with others, cannot be separated from the context in which they encountered it. In general, the messages sent were not always the messages received, and the historian who seeks to reconstruct the early Reformation message and its appeal must pay at least as much attention to the context of its readers (and hearers) as to the text that they read (or had presented to them).

As Luther's Catholic critics realized, the decision taken by Luther and his fellow Evangelical publicists to use the press to reach as large an audience as possible put the Reformation debate on a whole new footing. The thousands of small, relatively inexpensive vernacular pamphlets circulated rapidly through the German-speaking lands, inviting people to enter into a debate that heretofore would have been the prerogative of a tiny fraction of even the ruling elite. To engage in this ideological contest even the 5 percent of the population thought to be literate at the time was itself a revolution. As people were asked to take sides if only in their own heads as they read or heard the publicist's argument, it was inevitable that opinions would diverge and multiply. Scripture was only the most prominent text that came to be understood so variously as it gained through print a much larger readership. Printing, propaganda, and Martin Luther together ushered in an age that saw the repeated splintering of Western Christianity.

Abbreviations

Aland	Kurt Aland. *Hilfsbuch zum Lutherstudium*. 3d, rev. ed. Witten, 1970.
ARG	*Archiv für Reformationsgeschichte / Archive for Reformation History*
Benzing	Josef Benzing. *Lutherbibliographie*. Bibliotheca Bibliographica Aureliana, vols. 10, 16, and 19. Baden-Baden, 1966.
BenzingStr	Josef Benzing. *Bibliographie Strasbourgeoise*. Baden-Baden, 1981.
Böcking	*Ulrich von Hutten Schriften*. Edited by Eduord Böcking. 4 vols. Leipzig, 1859–1870.
Chrisman	Miriam Usher Chrisman. *Bibliography of Strasbourg Imprints, 1480–1599*. New Haven, 1982.
Clemen	*Flugschriften aus den ersten Jahren der Reformation*. Edited by Otto Clemen. 4 vols. Halle/Saale, 1907–1911. Niewkoop, 1967.
DS	*Martin Bucers Deutsche Schriften*. 7+ vols. Gütersloh, 1960–.
Hertzsch	*Karlstadts Schriften aus den Jahren 1523–1525*. Edited by Erich Hertzsch. 2 vols. Halle, 1957.

Ho   *Flugschriftensammlung Gustav Freitag.* Edited by
              Paul Hohenemser. Frankfurt a.M., 1925. Hil-
              desheim, 1966.

Klaiber   *Katholische Kontroverstheologen und Reformer des
              16. Jahrhunderts.* Edited by Wilbirgis Klaiber. Re-
              formationsgeschichtliche Studien und Texte, no. 116.
              Münster Westfallen, 1978.

Kück   *Die Schriften Hartmuths von Cronberg.* Edited by
              Eduard Kück. Flugschriften aus der Reformations-
              zeit, vol. 14. Halle, 1899.

Laube   *Flugschriften der frühen Reformationsbewegung
              (1518–1524).* Edited by Adolf Laube, Annerose
              Schneider, and Sigrid Looß. 2 vols. Berlin, 1983.

LW   *Luther's Works, American Edition.* Edited by Jaro-
              slav Pelikan and Helmut T. Lehmann. 55 vols. St.
              Louis and Philadelphia, 1955–1986.

Pfeiffer-Belli *Thomas Murner: Kleine Schriften.* Edited by Wolf-
              gang Pfeiffer-Belli. Vols. 6–8 of Thomas Murner's
              Deutsche Schriften, edited by Franz Schultz. Berlin,
              1927–1928.

StA   *Martin Luther: Studienausgabe.* Edited by Hans-
              Ulrich Delius. 4+ vols. Berlin, 1979–.

Tü   *Flugschriften des frühen 16. Jahrhunderts.* Edited by
              H. J. Köhler, H. Hebenstreit, and Chr. Weismann.
              Zug, Switzerland, 1978–1987. The first number
              cited is the fiche number, the second the Flugschrift
              number.

W2   *Martin Luthers sämmtliche Schriften.* 2d ed. Edited
              by Johann Georg Walch. 23 vols. Published in mod-
              ern German. St. Louis, 1880–1910.

WA   *D. Martin Luthers Werke: Kritische Gesamtaus-
              gabe.* 58 vols. Weimar, 1883–.

WABr   *D. Martin Luthers Werke: Briefwechsel.* 15 vols.
              Weimar, 1930–.

WADB   *D. Martin Luthers Werke: Deutsche Bibel.* 12 vols.
            Weimar, 1906–1961.

Zorzin   Alejandro Zorzin. *Karlstadt als Flugschriftenautor.*
            Göttingen, 1990.

Notes

INTRODUCTION

1. The expression is A. G. Dickens's. See A. G. Dickens, *The German Nation and Martin Luther* (London, 1974), 103. Dickens's overview (pp. 102–134) is one of the best in English. See also Louise Holborn, "Printing and the Growth of a Protestant Movement in Germany from 1517 to 1524," *Church History* 11 (1942):123–137; Elizabeth L. Eisenstein, *The Printing Press as an Agent of Change: Communications and Cultural Transformations in Early-Modern Europe* (Cambridge, 1979), 1:303–450; H. Gravier, *Luther et l'opinion publique* (Paris, 1943); and the literature cited in chapter 1.

2. See, for example, Eisenstein, *The Printing Press as an Agent of Change*, 1:303–450.

3. Bernd Moeller, "Stadt und Buch: Bemerkungen zur Struktur der Reformatorischen Bewegung in Deutschland," in Wolfgang J. Mommsen, ed., *Stadtbürgertum und Adel in der Reformation: Studien zur Socialgeschichte der Reformation in England und Deutschland* (Stuttgart, 1979), 25–39. This "Moellerian thesis" is on page 30.

4. See chapter 1, note 29.

5. See, for example, Gerald Strauss, *Luther's House of Learning: Indoctrination of the Young in the German Reformation* (Baltimore, 1978), esp. 247–308.

6. For example, Bernd Moeller, *Imperial Cities and the Reformation: Three Essays* (Philadelphia, 1972).

7. For example, Peter Blickle, *Gemeindereformation: Die Menschen des 16 Jahrhunderts auf dem Weg zum Heil* (Munich, 1985) [*Communal Reformation: The Quest for Salvation in Sixteenth-Century Germany*, trans. Thomas Dunlap (London, 1992)]. For a discussion of Blickle's argument, see my review essay "Die Gemeindereformation als Bindeglied zwischen der mittel-

alterlichen und der neuzeitlichen Welt," *Historische Zeitschrift* 249 (1989): 95–103.

8. For example, Steven E. Ozment, *The Reformation in the Cities: The Appeal of Protestantism to Sixteenth-Century Germany and Switzerland* (New Haven, 1975).

9. For example, Hans-Jürgen Goertz, *Pfaffenhaß und groß Geschrei: Die reformatorischen Bewegungen in Deutschland 1517–1529* (Munich, 1987).

10. Moeller, "Problems of Reformation Research," in *Imperial Cities*, 13.

11. For example, Moeller, *Imperial Cities*, and Blickle, *Gemeindereformation.*

12. For example, he prefaced his 1519 *Sermon on the Estate of Marriage* with the observation that a sermon on this topic had already been published under his name. He was aware that he had preached on the subject, but never put it into writing. He asked his pious readers to disregard the first edition of the sermon. "Further," he continued, "if anybody wants to start writing my sermons for me, let him restrain himself, and let me have a say in the publication of my words as well." And he added a caution that today's scholars of sixteenth-century sermons should take to heart. "There is a great difference," he pointed out, "in making public something with the living voice or dead letters" ["Es ist ein gross unterscheyt, etwas mit lebendiger stymme adder mit todter schrifft an tag zubringenn" (WA 2:166)].

13. See Hans-Joachim Köhler, "The *Flugschriften* and their Importance in Religious Debate: A Quantitative Approach," in Paola Zambelli, ed., '*Astrologi hallucinati': Stars and the End of the World in Luther's Time* (New York, 1986), 153–175; and Hans-Joachim Köhler, "Erste Schritte zu einem Meinungsprofil der frühen Reformationszeit," in Volker Press and Dieter Stievermann, eds., *Martin Luther: Probleme seiner Zeit* (Stuttgart, 1986), 244–281.

14. See the graph on page 23 of my *Luther's Last Battles: Politics and Polemics, 1531–46* (Ithaca, 1983) and the discussion in chapter 1 as well as tables 3 and 4 of this book.

15. Chrisman, and BenzingStr. I have generally found Chrisman to be the more accurate and conservative in its attributions.

In an important article, Hans Christoph Rublack has examined the content of Luther's early "best-sellers" published in Augsburg ("Martin Luther and the Urban Social Experience," in Helga Robinson-Hammerstein, ed., *The Transmission of Ideas in the Lutheran Reformation* [Dublin, 1989]). We characterize the content of Luther's treatises rather differently, demonstrating, if the point needs further demonstration, that the meaning of texts cannot be separated from the perspective of the reader. Briefly, Rublack overstresses Luther's alleged "dualism" and makes him sound like an Erasmian reformer, which he was not. See also Bernd Moeller, "Das Berühmtwerden Luthers," *Zeitschrift für Historische Forschung* 15 (1988):65–92, with whom I am in substantially greater agreement.

16. New Haven, 1982.

CHAPTER 1: EVANGELICAL AND CATHOLIC PROPAGANDA IN THE EARLY DECADES OF THE REFORMATION

1. Felician Gess, ed., *Akten und Briefe zur Kirchenpolitik Herzog Georgs von Sachsen* (Leipzig, 1905), 1:641.

2. According to Hans-Joachim Köhler, between 1517 and 1518 there was a 530 percent increase in pamphlet production. Although Köhler gives percentages rather than exact figures, his tables suggest that there was nearly an additional eight-fold (7.8) increase from 1518 to 1524. From these two figures I calculate an increase of more than forty-fold over the eight-year period. As Köhler points out, this rapid increase in production yielded for the years 1520 through 1526 an annual production 55 times higher than the average annual production before 1518. See Hans-Joachim Köhler, "The *Flugschriften* and their Importance in Religious Debate: A Quantitative Approach," in Paola Zambelli, ed., '*Astrologi hallucinati': Stars and the End of the World in Luther's Time* (New York, 1986), 153–175; and "Erste Schritte zu einem Meinungsprofil der frühen Reformationszeit," in Volker Press and Dieter Stievermann, eds., *Martin Luther: Probleme seiner Zeit* (Stuttgart, 1986), 244–281; and the discussion below.

3. In the period 1518 to 1520, Leipzig produced 29 percent of all the printings of Luther's works: 41 treatises by Luther in 1518, 65 treatises in 1519, 49 treatises in 1520, then 5 in 1521, and none in 1522. See table 3.

4. For the following description, I am indebted to Hans-Joachim Köhler, "Die Flugschriften der frühen Neuzeit," in W. Arnold et al., eds., *Die Erforschung der Buch- und Bibliotheksgeschichte in Deutschland* (Wiesbaden, 1987), 307–345, esp. 310–314.

5. Ibid., 312.

6. Ibid., 325. More on the likely purchasers in the next section.

7. Köhler, "A Quantitative Approach," 156, who cites Heiko A. Oberman, "Zwischen Agitation und Reformation: Die Flugschriften als 'Judenspiegel'," in *Flugschriften als Massenmedium der Reformationszeit: Beiträge zum Tübinger Symposium 1980*, Spätmittelalter und Frühe Neuzeit, vol. 13 (Stuttgart, 1981), 269–289, esp. 287; and Johannes Schwitalla, "Deutsche Flugschriften im ersten Viertel des 16. Jahrhunderts," *Freiburger Universitätsblätter* 76 (1982):37–58.

8. See John W. Bohnstedt, *The Infidel Scourge of God: The Turkish Menace as Seen by German Pamphleteers of the Reformation Era*, Transactions of the American Philosophical Society, vol. 58, part 9 (Philadelphia, 1968), and his bibliography.

9. See Köhler, "A Quantitative Approach," and "Meinungsprofil," 244–281.

10. Köhler, "A Quantitative Approach," 155. For this same material presented in greater detail, see his "Meinungsprofil."

11. Ibid., 156.

12. From 28 percent German and 72 percent Latin to 74 percent German and barely 26 percent Latin. In the following year the Latin proportion fell to

9.5 percent, marking a 72 percent decline in just three years (Köhler, "Die Flugschriften der frühen Neuzeit," 331).

13. In 1518, 47 percent of the printings of Luther's works are in German. This rises to 63 percent in 1519, 85 percent in 1520, 78 percent in 1521, 95 percent in 1522, and then hovers in the high eighties and low nineties for the rest of the decade. See table 1.

14. Zorzin, 19–83. Zorzin's work also contains a fine bibliography of the relevent literature on pamphlets and publicists during this period.

15. For this figure I have rearranged Zorzin's statistics (Zorzin, 24). There is a discrepancy of 59 editions between my count of the German printings through 1525 (1524 editions) and Zorzin's (1465 editions). I cannot account for this discrepancy except to hypothesize that the difference may be due to the ways in which the two of us dated what were in fact undated editions. For a discussion of my methodology, see the appendix in my *Luther's Last Battles: Politics and Polemics, 1531–46* (Ithaca, 1983), 209–211.

16. Köhler, "Die Flugschriften der frühen Neuzeit," 317.

17. We do not have a study for all Evangelical publications comparable to my study of the Catholic controversial theologians ("Catholic Controversial Literature, 1518–1555: Some Statistics," *ARG* [1988]:189–205). Given that we currently lack a complete bibliography of sixteenth-century imprints, this would be a difficult undertaking. Köhler's bibliography of pamphlet literature and the Munich-Wolfenbüttel bibliographies are currently in progress. When completed they may provide a basis for such a project.

18. See figure 1 and tables 1 to 4. Parts of the following statistics were discussed from another perspective in my *Luther's Last Battles*, esp. 6–14, 20–23. Bernd Moeller, "Das Berühmtwerden Luthers," *Zeitschrift für Historische Forschung* 15 (1988):65–92, esp. 82–92, persuasively shows using publication statistics for Luther's works through 1519 that Luther had become an incredibly successful auther well before the famous treatises of late 1520. I strongly agree with Moeller's conclusions on this and other points and wish only that we had been aware of each other's research earlier on.

19. The exact ratios are 5.94 to 1 for the period 1516 through 1525, and 3.36 to 1 for the subsequent period.

20. For the logic of this assumption, see the discussion in the introduction.

21. David V. N. Bagchi, *Luther's Earliest Opponents: Catholic Controversialists, 1518–1525* (Minneapolis, 1991), is the authoritative source on Catholic controversialists during the period under study. Bagchi's chapters 7 and 8 deal in detail with a number of the issues raised in this section.

22. Although we are relatively well supplied with bibliographies of publications for the initial decades of the Reformation, there can be no pretense of completeness in any statistics on Reformation printing. For my survey, I used Klaiber, supplemented and on occasion corrected by other bibliographies, especially Tü. For a critical evaluation of Klaiber, see Jean-François Gilmont, "La bibliographie de la controverse catholique au 16e siècle; quelques suggestions methodologiques," *Revue d'histoire ecclésiastique* 74 (1979):362–371. For Cochlaeus, I used Martin Spahn, *Johannes Cochläus: Ein Lebensbild* (Berlin, 1898); and for Eck, J. Metzler, ed., "Verzeichnis der Schriften Ecks," in

Tres orationes funebres, Corpus Catholicorum, 16 (Münster, 1930), lxxii–cxxxii. For a discussion of the Tübingen Flugschriften project and other bibliography, see Hans-Joachim Köhler, ed., *Flugschriften als Massenmedium der Reformationszeit* (Stuttgart, 1981). Although I am primarily interested in Catholic vernacular publications, I included in my statistical survey all Latin and vernacular treatises published in the Holy Roman Empire. Klaiber's bibliography, and hence my survey, is restricted largely to major publicists and hence overlooks many of the small pamphlets published anonymously or by some otherwise obscure individual. Nevertheless, I believe that it represents accurately the general extent and complexion of the Catholic published response to the Reformation. In a recent article based on the *Short-title Catalogue of Books Printed in the German-speaking Countries* (London, 1962), Richard A. Crofts also examines the printing of Catholic and Protestant works ("Printing, Reform, and the Catholic Reformation in Germany [1521–1545]," *The Sixteenth Century Journal* 16 [1985]:369–381). I discuss our two pieces in my contribution to the *Festschrift* in honor of Miriam Chrisman ("Statistics on Sixteenth-Century Printing," in *The Process of Change in Early Modern Europe: Essays in Honor of Miriam Usher Chrisman,* ed. Sherrin Marshall [Athens, Ohio, 1988]). I want to thank Miriam Usher Chrisman for her assistance in thinking about the implications of these statistics.

23. See especially Hans Becker, "Herzog Georg von Sachsen als kirchlicher und theologischer Schriftsteller," *ARG* 24 (1927):161–269. For additional bibliography and a discussion of several of his polemical efforts, see my *Luther's Last Battles,* 20–67, and Bagchi, *Luther's Earliest Opponents,* 230–236.

24. See Spahn, *Cochläus,* esp. 166–229.

25. A. G. Dickens, *The German Nation and Martin Luther* (London, 1974), 182.

26. See esp. Peter Blickle, *Gemeindereformation: Die Menschen des 16. Jahrhunderts auf dem Weg zum Heil* (Munich, 1985; London, 1992), and my review of this book and the associated literature ("Die Gemeindereformation als Bindeglied zwischen der mittelalterlichen und der neuzeitlichen Welt," *Historische Zeitschrift* 249 [1989]:95–103).

27. See Köhler, "A Quantitative Approach" and "Meinungsprofil."

28. Or at least their understanding of the message. I discuss this problem of reception in subsequent chapters.

29. For an exchange on the issue of literacy, audience, and "effectiveness" of pamphlet literature, see the articles by Moeller, Scribner, and Ozment in Wolfgang J. Mommsen, ed., *Stadtbürgertum und Adel in der Reformation: Studien zur Socialgeschichte der Reformation in England und Deutschland* (Stuttgart, 1979). See also the essays by Ozment, Moeller, and Scribner in Hans-Joachim Köhler, ed., *Flugschriften als Massenmedium.* Ozment originally laid out his position in *The Reformation in the Cities: The Appeal of Protestantism to Sixteenth-Century Germany and Switzerland* (New Haven, 1975). Scribner continues the discussion in "Oral Culture and the Diffusion of Reformation Ideas," *History of European Ideas* 5 (1984):237–256. The best work on publication statistics has been done by Hans-Joachim Köhler in "A

Quantitative Approach" and "Meinungsprofil." See also Scribner's *For the Sake of Simple Folk: Popular Propaganda for the German Reformation* (Cambridge, 1981). Richard Gawthrop and Gerald Strauss, "Protestantism and Literacy in Germany," *Past & Present* 104 (1984):31–55; Gerald Strauss, *Luther's House of Learning: Indoctrination of the Young in the German Reformation* (Baltimore, 1978); Gerald Strauss, "Lutheranism and Literacy: A Reassessment," in Kaspar von Greyerz, ed., *Religion and Society in Early Modern Europe, 1500–1800* (London, 1984). On the issue of literacy in general, see, especially, Rolf Engelsing, *Analphabetentum und Lektüre: Zur Sozialgeschichte des Lesens in Deutschland zwischen feudaler und industrieller Gesellschaft* (Stuttgart, 1973).

30. Köhler, "Die Flugschriften der frühen Neuzeit," 338, offers a similar analysis.

31. See, for example, Scribner, *For the Sake of Simple Folk.*

32. Otto Clemen, ed., *Flugschriften aus den ersten Jahren der Reformation* (Nieuwkoop, 1984) 4:88–90, 94–96. For another example from the early Strasbourg press, note the extended title to . . . *mancherley büchlin vnnd tractetlin . . .* that speaks of those who "read these books or have them read" to them: *Martini Luthers der waren götlichen schrifft Doctors, Augustiner zů Wittenbergk, mancherley büchlin vnnd tractetlin. In wölchē ein yegklicher auch einfaltiger Lay, vil heylsamer Christlicher lere vnd vnderweysung findet, so not seindt zů wissenn, einem yegklichen Christen menschen, der nach Christlicher ordnung (als wir alle söllen) leben will. Deren biechlin namen findest du am andern blatt, mit zale der blättern, in wölchem yegklichs eygentlich anfahet, vnd ein epistel zů denen die söllich büchlin lesen, oder hören lesen von D. Martini Luther außgangen. Item Apologia: das ist ein schirmred vnd antwort gegen etlicher einrede, so geschehen wider D. Martinū Luthern vnd seine Ewangelische lere, mit fast schönen wollgegrünten bewerungen, das sein leere, als warhafftig, Christlich, vnnd göttlich anzůnemen sey.* (Strasbourg: Schürer Erben, 1520). This collection was first published by Andreas Cratander in Basel in May 1520.

33. Matheus Zell, *Christeliche Verātwortūg M. Matthes Zell von Keyserßberg Pfarrherrs vnd predigers im Münster zů Straßburg, vber Artickel jm vom Bischöfflichem Fiscal daselbs entgegen gesetzt, vnnd im rechten vbergeben.* (Strasbourg: Köpfel, 1523), b; Tü 217/613.

34. Köhler, "Die Flugschriften der frühen Neuzeit," 318.

35. See my "Catholic Controversial Literature" and "Statistics on Sixteenth-Century Printing."

36. Although the point hangs on exactly what Rublack means by "lutherischer Überzeugungen," I am inclined with Bernd Moeller to feel that the very volume of the printing and reprinting of Luther's works allows the historian to make defensible inferences about the interests and perhaps even the convictions of the reading public. See Hans-Christoph Rublack, "Martin Luther und die Städtische soziale Erfahrung," in V. Press and D. Stievermann, eds., *Martin Luther: Probleme seiner Zeit* (Stuttgart, 1988), 88–123: "Niemand dürfte die Quantität von Lutherdrucken für Indikatoren von Intensität und Verbreitung von Überzeugungen halten. Der Indikator Ausgabenzahl weist lediglich auf

erhöhte Bereitschaft, das von Luther Angebotene zu lesen. Man kann also nicht die Massenhaftigkeit von Druckschriften, deren Autor Luther war, zugunsten einer adaequaten Massenhaftigkeit lutherischer Überzeugungen überbuchen" (p. 105). Cited in Moeller, "Das Berühmtwerden Luthers," 86, n. 128.

CHAPTER 2: FIRST IMPRESSIONS IN THE STRASBOURG PRESS

1. *Martini Luthers der waren götlichen schrifft Doctors, Augustiner zů Wittenbergk, mancherley büchlin vnnd tractetlin. In wölchē ein yegklicher auch einfaltiger Lay, vil heylsamer Christlicher lere vnd vnderweysung findet, so not seindt zů wissenn, einem yegklichen Christen menschen, der nach Christlicher ordnung (als wir alle söllen) leben will. Deren biechlin namen findest du am andern blatt, mit zale der blättern, in wölchem yegklichs eygentlich anfahet, vnd ein epistel zů denen de söllich büchlin lesen, oder hören lesen von D. Martini Luther außgangen. Item Apologia: das ist ein schirmred vnd antwort gegen etlicher einrede, so geschehen wider D. Martinū Luthern vnd seine Ewangelische lere, mit fast schönen wollgegrünten bewerungen, das sein leere, als warhafftig, Christlich, vnnd göttlich anzůnemen sey.* (Strasbourg: Schürer Erben, 1520). This collection was first published by Andreas Cratander in Basel in May 1520. See Laube 1:512.

2. Laube 1:501.

3. See also Bernd Moeller's "Das Berühmtwerden Luthers," *Zeitschrift für Historische Forschung* 15 (1988):65–92. My focus on the publications of Strasbourg yields many of the same conclusions that his broader survey of both German and Latin works in the period through 1519 does.

4. I have used Georg Buchwald, *Luther Calendarium* (Leipzig, 1929), for the dates of publications.

5. Although some of the sermons and treatises that I shall discuss in the following pages may have appeared at the same time as the controversial writings of late 1520, most probably preceded the major polemics of the last quarter of the year. In any case, there is sufficient repetition of themes in these works to sketch an outline of Luther's earliest message and the impression it likely conveyed.

6. One (or three) sermon(s): (a) *Ein Sermon von dem Elichen standt,* (b) *Ein Sermon uon der Betrachtung des heyligen leidens Christi* [Benzing, but not Chrisman, who shows 2 editions in 1520], and (c) *Ein Sermon von dem gebeet vnd procession yn der Creutzwochen* [Chrisman, 1 edition in 1520; Benzing, 1 in 1519 attributed to a different publisher].

7. One sermon collection: *Die syben Bůsz psalmē;* one polemic: *Vnderrichtung, vff etlich Artickel, die jm vō seinen mißgünnern vffgelegt vnd zugemessen werden;* and one devotional treatise: *Theologia teütsch.*

8. (a) *Ein Sermon uon der Betrachtung des heyligen leidens Christi* [2 Chrisman; 0 Benzing, who has 1 in 1519], (b) *Ein Sermon von dem gebeet vnd procession yn der Creutzwochen* [Chrisman, 1 edition in 1520; Benzing, 1 in 1519], (c) *Ein Sermon von dē Hochwurdigē sacramēt des heiligen waren lychnams Christi, vnd von den Brüderschaffen,* (d) *Ein Sermon von dem Heiligen*

hochwirdigen Sacramēt der Tauffe, (e) *Ein Sermon uon dem wůcher,* (f) *(E)yn Sermon von dē nüuwen Testament: das ist vō der heiligē Mesz,* (g) *Ein Sermon von dem Sacrament der Büß* [2 editions], (h) *(E)In sermō von dem Bann Doctor Martini Luthers,* and (i) *Ein nützlich predig . . . wie sich ein Christenmensch . . . bereiten sol zu sterben.*

9. See note 1 above.

10. The collection contains the following (with the appropriate number from Aland:

Aland 742: *Auslegung deutsche des Vaterunsers für die einfältigen Laien . . . Nicht für die Gelehrten,* 1519. WA 2(74):80–130; LW 42(15):19–81.

Aland 557: *Ein kurze Form, das Paternoster zu verstehen vnd zu beten (für die jungen Kinder im Christenglauben),* 1519. WA 6(9):11–19; W2 10:166–175.

Aland 115: *Ein Sermon vom Sakrament der Buß,* 1519. WA 2(709):713–723; LW 35(3):9–22.

Aland 408: *Ein Sermon von der Betrachtung des heiligen Leidens Christi,* 1519. WA 2(131):136–142; LW 42(3):7–14.

Aland 209: *Sermon de digna praeparatione cordis pro suscipiendo sacramento eucharistiae,* 1518. In German translation. WA 1(325):329–334; W2 12:1342–1352.

Aland 556: *Duo sermones de passione Christi,* 1518. In German translation. WA 1(335):336–345; W2 10:1176–1193.

Aland 5: *Ein Sermon von Ablaß und Gnade,* 1517 (1518). WA 1(239):243–246; W2 18:270–275.

Aland 738: *Luthers Unterricht auf etliche Artikel, die ihm von seinen Abgönnern aufgelegt vnd zugemessen werden,* 1519. WA 2(66):69–93, 759; W2 15:699–705.

Aland 177: *Ein Sermon von dem ehelichen Stand (verändert und korrigiert),* 1519. WA 2(162):166–171; LW 44(3):7–14.

Aland 698: *Ein Sermon von der Bereitung zum Sterben,* 1519. WA 2(680):685–697, 759; LW 42(95):99–115.

Aland 779: *[Großer] Sermon von dem Wucher,* 1520. WA 6(33):36–60, 630; LW 45(231):345–410.

Aland 60: *Ein Sermon von dem Bann,* 1520. WA 6(61):63–75, 630; LW 39(3):7–22.

Aland 392: *Ein Sermon von dem Gebet und Prozession in der Kreuzwoche,* 1519. WA 2(172):175–179; LW 42(83):87–93.

Aland 714: *Ein Sermon von dem heiligen hochwürdigen Sakrament der Taufe,* 1519. WA 2(724):727–737; LW 35(23):29–43.

Aland 655: *Ein Sermon von dem hochwürdigen Sakrament des heiligen wahren Leichnams Christi vnd von den Bruderschaften,* 1519. WA 2(738):742–758; LW 35(45):49–73.

Aland 656: *Verklärung D.M. Luthers etlicher Artikel in seinem Sermon von dem heiligen Sakrament,* 1520. WA 6(76):78–83 (82Z.10ff. Kurzer Lebenslauf Luthers), 630; W2 19:452–459.

Aland 476: *Ein Sermon gepredigt zu Leipzig auf dem Schloß am Tage Petri und Pauli Matth. 16, 13–19,* 1519. WA 2(241):244–249; LW 51(53):54–60.

Aland 615: *Auslegung des 109. (110.) Psalms,* 1518. WA 1(687):690–710; W2 5:888–921.

Aland 761: *Von den guten Werken,* 1520. WA 6(196):202–204*, 204–276 (Druck), 631; LW 44(15):21–114.

Spengler's *Schutzrede* is the only piece in the collection not by Luther. Published anonymously, the full title of the piece when originally published was *Schutzred vnnd christēliche antwurt ains erbern liebhabers gotlicher warhayt. der heyligen schrifft. auff etlicher vermaint widersprechen. mit anzaygūg warumb Doctor Martini Luthers leer nit als vnchristenlich verworffen. sonder mer fur christenlich gehalten werdē sol. yetz widerumb corrigirt vñ mit ainem newen Dyalogo gebessert.*

11. (a) *Theologia teütsch* [1 (Benzing 2) edition, published after 1 August 1520]; (b) *Ein heilsams Büchlein von Doctor Martinus Luther August. von der Beycht gemacht* [German translation, in 1520]; (c) *(E)In kurtze vnderwisung Wie man beichtē sol*; and (d) *(E)In kurtze Form das Pater noster zů verston, vnd zů betten.*

12. Chrisman lists 12, Benzing 9.

13. *Von der Freyhayt Aines Christenmenschen* [Chrisman 2 editions in 1520, Benzing 1 in 1520, after 16 November 1520].

14. *Doctoris Martini Luther Appelation oð berüfung an eyn Christlich frey conciliū* [2 editions, after 17 November 1520].

15. *Von dē Bapstum zů Rom Wider den Hochberümpten Romanistē zu Leiptzck* [after 26 June 1520, reprinted in *Drey Biechlin* in 1521 or 1522].

16. *Teütscher Adel. (A)N den Christēlichen Adel teütscher Nation.* [Benzing 2, Chrisman 4 editions, after 18 August 1520].

17. *Von der Babylonischen gefengknuß der Kirchen* [Benzing 3, Chrisman 2 editions, after 6 October 1520].

18. *Doctor Martinus Luthers antwort Auf die zedel, so vnð des Officials zů Stolpē sigel ist außgangen* [after 11 Feb 1520, date of first Wittenberg publication].

19. Probably came in the second half of the year, following the treatise to which it objected.

20. In fact, two of the treatises indicate on their title pages that they were intended "For the Laity" (*Ein Sermon von dem hochwürdigen Sakrament des heiligen wahren Leichnams Christi vnd von den Bruderschaften,* 1519; WA 2:739) and "For the simple laity . . . not for the learned" (*Auslegung deutsche des Vaterunsers für die einfältigen Laien . . . Nicht für die Gelehrten,* 1519; WA 2:77). I owe this observation to Bernd Moeller, "Das Berühmtwerden Luthers," 72.

21. See the listing of treatises above.

22. See for example, the comments of Matthias Zell, discussed in the last chapter.

23. WA 1:165.

24. WA 1:212–213.

25. WA 2:175.

26. WA 2:175–176. Points two and three.

27. WA 2:176.

28. StA 1:264.

29. WA 2:59.

30. This point is also made by Hans-Christoph Rublack, "Martin Luther and the Urban Social Experience," in Helga Robinson-Hammerstein, ed., *The Transmission of Ideas in the Lutheran Reformation* (Dublin, 1989), 67–70. I would, however, place Rublack in the camp of those who see the Reformation's appeal more in political and social terms than in religious.

31. To call this message anticlerical, as some scholars have, is to put a

positive program in negative terms. Certainly, the message had the effect of
reducing clerical power, but that was not its goal or even its primary attraction. That attraction was in offering the laity a religious vision that dignified
their status, responded to their situation as laity, and urged that they make up
their own minds by reading Scripture. Anticlericalism certainly offered fuel to
the later fire, but the early vernacular message was constructive rather than
critical, an attempt to build a new piety, not to exploit lay resentment of clerical power and abuse.

32. WA 2:169–170.

33. WA 2:139.

34. StA 1:267–268. Luther did concede that there were higher estates,
such as that of a priest or bishop. But he insisted that such estates should be
distinguished by greater suffering and more speedy preparation for death.

35. StA 1:244–257.

36. StA 1:247.

37. StA 1:248.

38. StA 1:249.

39. StA 1:249.

40. StA 1:249–250.

41. StA 1:250.

42. StA 1:250.

43. StA 1:253.

44. StA 1:253–254.

45. StA 1:251–252, 254.

46. StA 1:256.

47. StA 1:256.

48. In his treatise *How One Should Confess*, Luther offered advice that
must have been comforting to lay Christians who dreaded the late medieval
practice of confession. The Christian reader was told that before he confessed
his sins to a priest, he should first confess his misdeeds and sins to God as if
speaking with his closest friend (WA 2:59). Then, in confession itself, the
Christian should not worry about confessing all of his deadly sins because it
was impossible to remember them all and, in any case, all our good works,
when judged by God in earnest rather than in mercy, are deadly and damnable
sins. Luther also urged the Christian to dispense with the extensive and complicated set of distinctions in late medieval confessional practice between sins
and circumstances in which the sins were committed (WA 2:60). He further
insisted that the Christian should make a large distinction between sins against
the commandments of God and sins against the commandments and laws of
human beings. "For no one can be saved without the commandments of God,"
Luther explained, "but one can well be saved without the commandments
of human beings" (WA 2:60). We should, Luther advised, accustom our consciences firmly to trust in God's mercy (WA 2:64). This advice, if followed,
would greatly simplify the process of confession for the laity and would likely
relieve some of the anxiety associated with the sacrament even as it reduced
the authority of the priest.

49. WA 6:63–75.

50. WA 6:64.

51. WA 6:64. Luther identifies this as the "small ban" and contrasts it with the "large ban" (WA 6:64). To those spiritual authorities that attempt to go beyond the "large ban" to coerce the banned individual with the sword, Luther remarked that the secular sword belonged to temporal rulers and not to the spiritual estate, who possessed only a spiritual sword, namely, the word and commandments of God (WA 6:64). This is obviously a point of considerable interest to laity who had fallen afoul of a clerical ban enforced by the secular authorities. Luther also censured clerics who used the ban to collect money and to redress injuries done to them (WA 6:65).

52. WA 6:65.

53. Some of them were, as a result, more deserving of the ban than those on whom they imposed the ban (WA 6:66–67). Some were "tyrants who seek no more than their power, fear, and profit" in the ban. In so doing they do horrible damage to themselves "because they pervert the ban and its work, and make a poison out of a medicine, and seek only to terrify fearful human beings and think nothing about their improvement. They will be held to account for this" (WA 6:68). Much of the latter half of the sermon was devoted to a detailed criticism of spiritual authorities who misused the ban or otherwise failed properly to exercise their spiritual authority. Luther concludes, however, that wicked spiritual rulers, of which the age had many, were God's punishment for the people's sins and, therefore, should not be resisted (WA 6:66–75, passim). Given the impassioned description of clerical abuses, this ultimate counsel of submission may have lacked persuasion.

54. WA 2:742–743. Incidentally, a reply to this treatise prompted Luther to write one of the only two polemics that were published in Strasbourg during this early period, *Doctor Martin Luther's Answer to the Notice That Was Published Under the Seal of the Official at Stolpen*. In this brief treatise, Luther sarcastically defended his suggestion that a general council of the church decree that laity as well as clergy should commune in both kinds (WA 6:137–141). In this treatise Luther verbally attacked those who used the ban and other "underhanded" means to silence critics, including burning them. He compared his treatment with the treatment metted out to Reuchlin (WA 6:140–141).

55. WA 6:7.

56. For Hutten's treatises, I have used Böcking.

57. Hutten, *Clag vnd Vormanüg gegē den übermåssigen vnchristlichen gewalt des Bapstes zů Rom, vnd der vngeislichen geistlichen. Durch herrn Vlrichen vō Hutten, Poeten, vnd Orator der gantzē Christenheit, vnd zůruoan dem Vatterland Teütscher Nation zů nutz vnd gůt, Von wegen gemeiner beschwernüß, vnd auch seiner eigenen notdurfft, Jn reimens weise beschriben. Iacta est alea. Jch habs gewagt.* Strasbourg: Knobloch, 1520 (late) (Chrisman P3.2.1.; Böcking 3:473–526); *Ein Clagschrift des Hochberůmten vnd Eernuestē herrn Vlrichs vō Hutten gekrőneten Poeten vñ Orator an alle stend Deüscher nation, Wie vnformlicher weise vñ gātz geschwind, vnersůcht oder erfordert einiges rechtēs. Er mit eignem tyrañischē gewalt, vō dem Romanistē, an leib, eer vnd gůt beschwert vñ benőtiget werde . . . Ein grosses dingk ist die*

warheit, vnd starck über alle. iij. Esdre .iiij. Strasbourg: Flach, 1520 (Chrisman P3.2.3.; Böcking 1:405–419); *Herr Ulrichs von Hutten anzöig Wie allwegen sich die Römischen Bischöff, oð Bǎpst gegen den teütschen Kayßeren gehalten haben, vff dz kürtzst vß Chronicken vnd Historien gezogen, K. maiestǎt fürzǔbringen. Jch habs gewogt.* Strasbourg: Schott, 1520 (Chrisman P3.2.5.; Böcking 5:364–384).

58. Böcking 3:508.

59. Böcking 5:383–384.

60. The first treatise, *A Christian and Fraternal Admonition,* left the press of the Strasbourg printer, Johannes Grüninger, on 11 November 1520. It is a reply in large part to Luther's *Sermon on the New Testament, That is, the Holy Mass,* his *To the Christian Nobility of the German Nation,* and *Concerning the Papacy in Rome Against the Highly Famous Romanist at Leipzig.* A second edition, with some changes, appeared on 21 January 1521. The next treatise followed just fourteen days later. *Concerning Doctor Martin Luther's Teaching and Preaching,* published on 24 November 1520, dealt less with Luther personally and more with his influence. It also responded to Lazarus Spengler's *Defense and Christian Reply of an honorable lover of the divine truth of Holy Scripture.* As we shall see in a moment, Spengler's treatise had been published in Strasbourg in October 1520 in a reprinted collection of Luther's writings. Murner's third treatise, *Concerning the Papacy, that is, the highest authority of Christian Faith,* issued from Grüninger's press on 13 December 1520. It is a reply to Luther's *Resolutiones Lutheriana de potestate Papae* of 1519, his *To the German Nobility,* and his *Concerning the Papacy in Rome Against the Highly Famous Romanist at Leipzig.* This dry treatise became a special target of *Karsthans.* Murner's fourth and final treatise of 1520, *To the Most Mighty and Enlightened Nobility of the German Nation,* appeared around Christmas. The last treatise of this series appeared on 17 February 1521, when Murner issued *How Doctor M. Luther, Moved by the Wrong Reasons, Has Burnt the Canon Law,* attacking Luther's justification for this act of defiance. See Pfeiffer-Belli, and chapter 3 of this book.

61. For example, in his earliest treatise he criticizes Luther's "priesthood of all believers" (e.g., Pfeiffer-Belli 6:43, 6:58–59, 6:64–65), his suggested reform of the Mass (e.g., Pfeiffer-Belli 6:51–54, 6:64–65), and his understanding of a "spiritual" church (e.g., Pfeiffer-Belli 6:75), and he specifically accuses Luther of turning too much over to the common people (Pfeiffer-Belli 6:84). We examine Murner's attack in some detail in the next chapter.

62. Laux Gemigger, *Zü lob dem Luther vnd eeren der gantzen Christenhait,* Strasbourg, 1520. The title verse reads: "Wölt yemant wissen wie der hieß | Der disen spruch außgon liess | Das hat gethon Laux Gemigger student | Auß vrsach, dz man des Luthers bücher hat verprent" (Laube 1:548–557).

63. Chrisman identifies two 1520 editions. By way of contrast, Laube, while also identifying two Strasbourg and one Augsburg edition, dates the first edition, the Augsburg edition, as 1521, but with some uncertainty. Internal evidence suggests that the treatise was written at the earliest about the end of November 1520, and at the latest by March 1521.

64. Laube 1:548.

65. Laube 1:550–551.
66. Laube 1:552–553.
67. Laube 1:548–549.
68. Laube 1:549–550.
69. Laube 1:554.
70. For example, Laube 1:554.
71. Laube 1:557.
72. For Spengler, see Harold Grimm, *Lazarus Spengler: A Lay Leader of the Reformation* (Columbus, Ohio 1978), and Bernd Hamm, "Lazarus Spengler und Martin Luthers Theologie," in V. Press and D. Stievermann, eds., *Martin Luther: Probleme seiner Zeit* (Stuttgart, 1986), 124–136. On the importance of this treatise as the first German defense written by a lay person, see Bernd Moeller, "Das Berühmtwerden Luthers," 80–81.
73. Laube 1:512. The title of the revised second edition runs: *Schutzred vnnd christēliche antwurt ains erbern liebhabers gotlicher warhayt. der heyligen schrifft. auff etlicher vermaint widersprechen. mit anzaygūg warumb Doctor Martini Luthers leer nit als vnchristenlich verworffen. sonder mer fur christenlich gehalten werdē sol. yetz widerumb corrigirt vn̄ mit ainem newen Dyalogo gebessert.* It was published in Nuremberg by Jobst Gutknecht in 1520. The Strasbourg collection reproduced the first edition. I have not been able to determine the exact title used in the Strasbourg edition.
74. See note 1 above.
75. Laube 1:501.
76. Laube 1:502.
77. Laube 1:504–505.
78. Laube 1:505.
79. Laube 1:507.
80. Laube 1:507.
81. Laube 1:509–510.
82. Laube 1:510.
83. Laube 1:505.
84. Laube 1:505–506.
85. Laube 1:506.
86. Laube 1:506–507.
87. Laube 1:507–508.
88. In this I side with Bernd Moeller against a more skeptical Hans-Christoph Rublack. See chapter 1, note 36.
89. See, among others, Lorna Jane Abbray, *The People's Reformation: Magistrates, Clergy, and Commons in Strasbourg, 1500–1598* (Ithaca, 1985); René Bornert, *La Réforme Protestante du Culte à Strasbourg au XVIe Siècle (1523–1598)* (Leiden, 1981); Thomas A. Brady, Jr., *Ruling Class, Regime and Reformation at Strasbourg, 1520–1555* (Leiden, 1978); Miriam Usher Chrisman, *Strasbourg and the Reform: A Study in the Process of Change* (New Haven, 1967); Marc Lienhard and Jakob Willer, *Straßburg und die Reformation* (Basel, 1982); and William S. Stafford, *Domesticating the Clergy: The Inception of the Reformation in Strasbourg, 1552–1524* (Missoula, 1976).

CHAPTER 3:   THE CATHOLIC DILEMMA

1. The full title read, *To the Most Mighty and Enlightened Nobility of the German Nation, That they Protect the Christian Faith Against the Destroyer of the Faith of Christ, Martin Luther, a Seducer of Simple Christians.* Its author, as we shall see in a moment, was Thomas Murner.

2. *Ein Christenliche vnd briederliche ermanung zů dem hoch gelerten doctor Martino luther Augustiner order zů Wittemburg (Das er etlichen reden von dem newen testament der heillgen messen gethon) abstande, vnd wider mit gemeiner christenheit sich vereinige* (Strasbourg: Grüninger, 1520).

3. *Von Doctor Martinus luters leren vnd predigen. Das sie argwenig seint, vnd nit gentzlich glaubwirdig zů halten.* (Strasbourg: Grüninger, 1520).

4. *Martini Luthers der waren götlichen schrifft Doctors, Augustiner zů Wittebergk, mancherley büchlin vnnd tractetlin . . .* (Strasbourg: Schürer Erben, 1520). This collection was first published by Andreas Cratander in Basel in May 1520. See Laube 1:512. The title of the revised second edition runs: *Schutzred vnnd christēliche antwurt ains erbern liebhabers gotlicher warhayt. der heyligen schrifft. auff etlicher vermaint widersprechen. mit anzaygůg warumb Doctor Martini Luthers leer nit als vnchristenlich verworffen. sonder mer fur christenlich gehalten werdē sol. yetz widerumb corrigirt vñ mit ainem newen Dyalogo gebessert.* It was published in Nuremberg by Jobst Gutknecht in 1520. The Strasbourg collection reproduced the first edition. I have not been able to determine the exact title used in the Strasbourg edition.

5. *Von dem Babstenthum das ist von der höchsten oberkeyt Christlichs glauben wyder doctor Martinum Luther* (Strasbourg: Grüninger, 1520). According to Pfeiffer-Belli, this treatise left Grüninger's press on 13 December 1520. The first half was a reply to Luther's *Resolutiones Lutheriana de potestate Papae* (1519) with a brief digression concerning Luther's *To the Christian Nobility.* The second half deals with Luther's invective against Alveldt, *Von dem Bapstum zu Rom widder den hochberumpten Romanisten zu Leiptzk.* It is the "driest" of Murner's treatises and does not go beyond glossing Luther. In the first half, Murner plays Luther's rapidly evolving position on the papacy against itself, quoting from Luther's earlier *Resolutiones,* in which Luther gives arguments (although Murner considers them weak and designed to enfeeble the true scriptural basis for papal authority), against Luther's later highly critical remarks about the papacy. Murner's central claim or accusation is that Luther is taking this position to promote rebellion and that there are certain matters of belief that should not be discussed because even opening the question promotes rebellion. Luther's position, according to Murner, is designed to create favorable attitudes among the common people to error and falsehood that is contrary to Christian faith. Murner particularly wants to attack the notion of communal authority (or congregational authority) within the church.

6. *An den Großmechtigsten vnd Durchlüchtigsten adel tütscher nation das sye den christlichen glauben beschirmen, wyder den zerstörer des glaubens christi, Martinum luther einen verfierer der einfeltigen christen* (Strasbourg: Grüninger, 1520).

7. *Wie doctor M. Luter vß falschen vrsachen bewegt Das geistlich recht verbrennet hat* (Strasbourg: Grüninger, 1521).

8. *Eyn sermoñ von dem newen Testament, das ist von der heyligen Messe D M L A* [after the end of April 1520]. According to Benzing, the one Strasbourg reprint was done by Martin Flach and appeared in 1520. It was also published in *Drey Biechlin*, mentioned below.

9. See the discussion in chapter 2.

10. *Von dē Bapstum zů Rom Wider den Hochberümpten Romanistē zu Leiptzck* [after 26 June 1520, reprinted in *Drey Biechlin* in 1521 or 1522].

11. *(A)N den Christēlichen Adel teütscher Nation* [Benzing 2, Chrisman 4 editions, after 18 August 1520).

12. *Von der Babylonischen gefengknuß der Kirchen* [Benzing 3, Chrisman 2 editions, after 6 October 1520].

13. Sometime in the late fall there also appeared two Strasbourg printings of *Doctor Martin Luther's Renewed Appeal or Petition to a Free Christian Council [Doctoris Martini Luther Appelation oð berüfung an eyn Christlich frey conciliū]* [2 editions, after 17 November 1520].

14. *Drey Biechlin zůletst von dem Hochberůmbtenn vnnd Ewangelischen Lerer Doctor Martin Luther außgangenn. Nemlich von dem Deütschen Adel. der heiligē Mess dem Babstumb zů Rom.* (Strasbourg: Schürer Erben, 1520 or 1521–1522). Chrisman has 1520, Benzing has 1521–1522.

15. *Von der Freyhayt Aines Christenmenschen* [Chrisman 2 editions in 1520, Benzing 1 in 1520; after 16 November 1520]. I discuss this treatise in the next chapter.

16. Pfeiffer-Belli 6:31.

17. Pfeiffer-Belli 6:91.

18. Karsthans ["Hans Hoe," *Karst* = hoe] was Murner's derogatory designation for the typical peasant. This name would later be taken up by Murner's opponents and turned against him, as we shall see in the next chapter.

19. Pfeiffer-Belli 6:91; cf. Pfeiffer-Belli 6:31.

20. Pfeiffer-Belli 6:92.

21. Pfeiffer-Belli 6:40–41.

22. Pfeiffer-Belli 6:113.

23. Pfeiffer-Belli 6:114.

24. Pfeiffer-Belli 6:114–115.

25. Pfeiffer-Belli 6:42.

26. See the discussion of Catholic publicists in chapter 1 and the fuller discussion in David V. N. Bagchi, *Luther's Earliest Opponents: Catholic Controversialists, 1518–1525* (Minneapolis, 1991).

27. In concluding each treatise Murner informed Luther and his readers that he had given his name to the bishop of Strasbourg so that his treatise could not be stigmatized as an anonymous libel (Pfeiffer-Belli 6:87). In the earlier treatises he also announced that he was not giving his name to show that he was not seeking fame in responding to Luther (Pfeiffer-Belli 6:31–32). He claimed, for example, that it was only the truth of the gospel that he sought to secure when he defended the papacy against Luther's attack. He neither received nor did he expect to receive payment from the papacy for such defense,

nor had the papacy commanded him to answer Luther (Pfeiffer-Belli 7:53).
The impression of himself that he wished to convey, it seems clear, was of one
concerned only for the truth of Christianity.

  28. *Ein christliche vnd briederliche ermanung zů dem hoch gelerten doctor
Martino luter Augustiner ordē zů Wittemburg (Dz er etlichē reden von dem
newē testamēt der heillgē messen gethō abstande, vñ wiϑ mit gemeiner christenheit sich vereinige* (Strasbourg: Grüninger, 11 November 1520). A second
edition, with some changes, appeared on 21 January 1521. Scholars now recognize that this treatise was a reply in large part to Luther's *Sermon on the
New Testament, That is, the Holy Mass,* his *To the Christian Nobility of the
German Nation,* and his *Concerning the Papacy in Rome Against the Famous
Romanist at Leipzig.* Contemporaries would not necessarily be aware of the
treatises to which this was a reply. In fact, this treatise may have provided the
first orientation to the dispute.

  29. Pfeiffer-Belli 6:31–33.
  30. Pfeiffer-Belli 6:31.
  31. Pfeiffer-Belli 6:31–32.
  32. Pfeiffer-Belli 6:34–36.
  33. Pfeiffer-Belli 6:39.
  34. Pfeiffer-Belli 6:40.
  35. Pfeiffer-Belli 6:43.
  36. Pfeiffer-Belli 6:48; cf. Pfeiffer-Belli 6:49–50.
  37. Pfeiffer-Belli 6:51.
  38. Pfeiffer-Belli 6:54.
  39. Pfeiffer-Belli 6:54.
  40. Pfeiffer-Belli 6:58–59.
  41. Pfeiffer-Belli 6:64–65.
  42. Pfeiffer-Belli 6:71.
  43. Pfeiffer-Belli 6:75, 80.
  44. Luther summarized his position as follows:

There is, first, the testator who makes the testament, [namely] Christ. Second, the
heirs to whom the testament is assigned, which are we Christians. Third, the testament itself, which is the words of Christ when he says, 'This is my body which is
given for you. This is my blood which is shed for you, a new eternal testament,' etc.
Fourth, the seal or sign of authenticity [*wartzeychen*] is the sacrament [of] the bread
and wine, under which are his true body and blood. . . . Fifth, there is the assigned
good that the words signify, namely, remission [*ablas*] of sins and eternal life. Sixth,
the duty, remembrance, or memorial, which we should do for Christ; that is, that we
should preach his love and grace, hear and contemplate it, so that we are incited and
maintained in love and hope in him (WA 6:359; StA 1:294; LW 35:86–87).

  45. WA 6:369; StA 1:303; LW 35:99.
  46. WA 6:370; StA 1:304; LW 35:100–101.
  47. Pfeiffer-Bell 6:59–60.
  48. WA 6:370; StA 1:304; LW 35:101.
  49. WA 6:407; StA 2:99; LW 44:127.
  50. WA 6:408; StA 2:101; LW 44:129.
  51. Pfeiffer-Belli 7:61.
  52. Pfeiffer-Belli 7:115–116.

53. WA 6:292; W2 18:1013; LW 39:65.
54. WA 6:296; W2 18:1017; LW 39:69.
55. WA 6:297; W2 18:1017; LW 39:70.
56. WA 6:296; LW 39:69–70.
57. Pfeiffer-Belli 6:80.
58. WA 6:288; W2 18:1007; LW 39:59.
59. For example, WA 6:288–289; LW 39:59–61.
60. WA 6:288; W2 18:1008; LW 39:60.
61. WA 6:307–308, 309–313; LW 39:84, 91.
62. WA 6:316; W2 18:1044; LW 39:95.
63. WA 6:407; StA 2:99; LW 44:127.
64. WA 6:411–412; StA 2:104–105; LW 44:134–135.
65. WA 6:413; StA 2:106; LW 44:136.
66. WA 6:414; StA 2:107; LW 44:138.
67. WA 6:414–415; StA 2:108; LW 44:138–139.
68. In this recitation he touched on such matters as various reforms of the papacy, cardinals, and curial officials; on reforms of the mendicant orders and monasticism, which he suggested should be abolished; on clerical celibacy, which he also opposed; on endowed masses for the dead, which should be curtailed or eliminated; on what he saw as an overly complicated system regulating marriage within prohibited degrees; on miracles and pilgrimages; on begging, brotherhoods, and indulgences; and so on. This was a potentially revolutionary set of reforms that would fatally compromise the papacy and institutional church as it currently existed. Note also his comment about the Strasbourg bishop in StA 2:115, esp. note 164.
69. WA 6:427; StA 2:121; LW 44:156. Having achieved a head of steam on reforms of the papacy, Luther listed a veriety of abuses and appropriate reforms for the institutional church generally. Among the more drastic were suggestions that all pilgrimages be dropped, that monasticism and especially the mendicants be curbed and monastic life be made voluntary, that clerical celibacy be ended and priests allowed to marry, that endowed masses for dead be abolished, and that restrictions on marriage within prohibited degrees be relaxed. Among other things, he also made important suggestions about the reform of poor relief.
70. Pfeiffer-Belli 6:91.
71. Pfeiffer-Belli 6:92.
72. Pfeiffer-Belli 7:5.
73. Pfeiffer-Belli 6:43–44.
74. Pfeiffer-Belli 6:83.
75. Pfeiffer-Belli 6:40, 47, 83–87.
76. WA 6:322; W2 1051; LW 39:102. See also his prediction that if the German princes and nobles did not do something soon about papal exploitation of Germany, Germany would be desolated (WA 6:289; LW 39:60).
77. WA 6:404; StA 2:96; LW 44:123.
78. WA 6:413; StA 2:106–107; LW 44:137.
79. Pfeiffer-Belli 6:31.
80. For Luther's charge, see WA 10/2:227; Murner's admission and

Stifel's accusation are reproduced in WA 6:488. I consulted several printings reproduced in the Tübingen collection. The quotations are from Tü 1679–1680/4341, which, from the evidence of the woodcut, appears to be the edition published by J. Schott. I have identified the woodcut from the list in R. W. Scribner, *For the Sake of Simple Folk: Popular Propaganda for the German Reformation* (Cambridge, 1981), 251–256. Both Chrisman and Benzing give the publication date as 1520, but it seems more likely that it was first printed in 1521, since Murner makes no reference to the treatise in his own 1520 publications, or at least no reference that I identified.

81. Ibid.

82. *Babilonischen*, Tü 1679–1680/4341, Div(v).

83. *Babilonischen*, E.

84. *Babilonischen*, E(v).

85. *Babilonischen*, Fiii(v).

86. See, for example, Vadian's *Karsthans*, discussed in the next chapter.

87. The following summary is taken from Hubert Jedin, "Die geschichtliche Bedeutung der katholischen Kontroversliteratur im Zeitalter der Glaubensspaltung," *Historiches Jahrbuch* 53 (1933):70–97, esp. 73–76. See also Bagchi, *Luther's Earliest Opponents*, chapter 8, which does a fine job of exploring the difficulties the Catholic publicists faced when seeking assistance from the Catholic establishment.

88. Johannes von Döllinger, ed., *Beiträge zur Politischen, Kirchlichen und Cultur-Geschichte der Sechs Letzten Jahrhunderte* (Vienna, 1892), 3:275.

89. Jedin, "Die geschichtliche Bedeutung," 73–74.

90. Döllinger, *Beiträge*, 3:247.

91. Jedin, "Die geschichtliche Bedeutung," 74–75.

92. *Nuntiaturberichte aus Deutschland nebst ergänzenden Aktenstücken* (Gotha, 1892–1912), 1:319.

93. *Nuntiaturberichte*, 4:174, 2:178–179, 2:196.

94. *Nuntiaturberichte*, 2:63.

95. Ludwig Cardauns, ed., *Zur Geschichte der Kirchlichen Unions- und Reformbestrebungen von 1538 bis 1542* (Rome, 1910), 144. Note that, as Fabri indicated, the Catholic controversialists generally had to *pay* to have their works printed, while the Evangelical publicists were largely printed for free because their works generally sold well. See the discussion in chapter 1.

96. Martin Spahn, *Johannes Cochläus: Ein Lebensbild* (Berlin, 1898), 188–190, 258.

97. Bachmann, *Wider die Natterzungen . . . Antwort auff Constantini Donation* (Dresden, 1538), Ai(v).

98. This summary is drawn from Jedin, "Die geschichtliche Bedeutung," 73.

99. On the replies by Catholic publicists to Pope Adrian's inquiry and the Pope's own efforts to support a Catholic counterattack, see Bagchi, *Luther's Earliest Opponents*, 222–227.

100. On this point see Bagchi, *Luther's Earliest Opponents*, 202–207, 211–214, 221.

101. Johannes Mensing, *Von dem Opffer Christi yn der Messe* (n.p., 1526), Aij(v).

102. Bachmann, *Ein sermon . . . yn auffnhemung der Reliquien Sancti Bennonis* (Dresden, 1527), Ai(v).

103. To those who reply that the Protestants do everything in German, Bachmann replies that "es ist nicht gut das mann alles in deutscher sprache handelt, zumal was die Sacrament vnd geheimnisse betrifft der heiligen Mess." In support of this view, he offered an example of shepherds who blasphemously went through a mock Mass (Paul Bachmann, *Vonn Ceremonien der Kirchen . . . von Priesterlichem Celibat* [Leipzig, 1537], C3). Johannes Mensing explained that "es haben auch, die heyligen tzwölff boten die worte, der wandelunge, heymlich haben wollen, als die dem gemeynen volcke nicht nöttig tzuwissen gewesen. Solten auch noch pillich den heyden vnd Juden vorporgen sein. . . . Jha es were gut, das sie auch etlichen Christen, als nemlich, der vnuorstendigen, thollen vnd thummen Jugent vorporgen gebliebn weren, auff das sie nicht, missbraucht wurden" (Johannes Mensing, *Von dem Opfer Christi in der Messe* [n.p., 1527], Dij(v)).

104. Bachmann, *Von Ceremonienn der Kirchen*, C3(v)–Cv.

CHAPTER 4: LUTHER'S EARLIEST SUPPORTERS IN THE STRASBOURG PRESS

1. R. W. Scribner, *For the Sake of Simple Folk: Popular Propaganda for the German Reformation* (Cambridge, 1981), 14–36.

2. Ibid., 17–19.

3. *ACTA ET RES GESTAE, D. MARTINI LVTHERi, in Comitijs Principu̅ Vuormaciae, Anno M.D.XXI.* (Strasbourg: Johann Schott, 1521).

4. *Handlung so mit doctor Martin Luther Vff dem Keyßerlichen Reichs tag zů Worms ergangen ist, vom anfang zům end, vff das kürtzest begriffen* (Strasbourg: Johann Schott, 1522).

5. In 1521 and 1522 a number of other authors entered the fray, either to criticize the traditional faith or to support Luther or in many cases to do both. By Miriam Chrisman's count there were thirty-two such polemical writings in 1521 and twenty-five polemics in 1522. Of these, twenty were by Luther—he continued to dominate the press—but only nine by Ulrich von Hutten. Effectively half the output—another twenty-eight treatises—were published by other authors. (For tables see Miriam U. Chrisman, *Lay Culture, Learned Culture: Books and Social Change in Strasbourg, 1480–1599* [New Haven, 1982], 156–158). These figures are approximate—dating pamphlets is an uncertain undertaking—but the rough proportions likely reflect the actual publication pattern of these years. It is within this growing literature of criticism of the traditional church and support for Luther that we begin to see the variety in the ways in which people understood Luther and his message. Of course, not all of this literature is relevant to our concerns; some devote their whole treatise to an attack on the papacy and on traditional practices with hardly a mention of Luther. But at least thirteen of these treatises (by ten or eleven different authors) explicitly deal with Luther and his message and can therefore further our understanding of his image in the popular press of his day. With few exceptions these publications deal largely with Luther's treatises through 1520 and neither mention explicitly nor engage with Luther's

treatises of 1521 and 1522. In other words, even as Luther flooded the market with new works, the other publicists appearing in the Strasbourg press in 1521 and 1522 were still assimilating and reacting to his earlier writings.

6. Joachim Vadian, *Karsthans* (Strasbourg: Prüß, 1521); Clemen 4:83.

7. *Ain schôner dialogus Und gesprech zwischen aim Pfarrer und aim Schulthayß, betreffend allen übel Stand der gaystlichen. Und bôß handlung der weltlichen. Alles mit geytzigkayt belanden. etc.* (Strasbourg: M. Schürer Erben, 1521). See DS 1:396–399. References to the "pious Luther" are found on pages DS 1:407, 459, and 469–470.

8. Clemen 4:90–91.

9. DS 1:469–470.

10. *Uerkündungs Brieff der hochberüemptē Uniuersitet Erdfürt, zů schütz schirm vñ handhabung des Christlichē gots diener vñ lerers. D. Martin Luthers. Durch Wolffgang Rüßen verteütschet* (Strasbourg: J. Prüß, 1521); Tü 1258/3223.

11. *Uerkündungs Brieff der Uniuersitet*, i(v).

12. *Uerkündungs Brieff der Uniuersitet*, ii, ii(v), iii.

13. The text is as follows:

> Die worheit ligt am tag fürwor,
> Würt nit zerspaltet vmb ein hor.
> Ist Luther den ein ketzer ye,
> Wer schreyb dann recht vff erden hye?
> Ist dan die gschrifft falsch, vngerecht,
> So bstot wol irer feynd gebrecht. [= Lärm, Geschrei]
> Die schrifft ist aber wor, stât, vest,
> Durch Christum selbs schôn überglest, [= glänzend gemacht]
> So [= Dagegen] lugen seind all menschen tand,
> On schrifft, vom teüfel hâr gesandt.
> Schrifft, schrifft, schreyt Luther über lut,
> Vnd stellt ir zů kopff, hals vnd hut.
> Wilt Luther stillen [= zum Schweigen bringen?] fûr jn geschrifft,
> Sunst ist dein leeren eytel gifft.
>> *Von der Christfôrmigen, rechtgegrundten leer Doctoris Martini Luthers, ein überuß schôn kunstlich Lyed, sampt seiner neben vßlegung* (Strasbourg: unknown, ca. 1522); Clemen 3:342.

14. Clemen 4:85–86.

15. Clemen 4:110.

16. DS 1:445.

17. *Ein hübsch christenliche vnd gôtliche erinnerung vnd warnung, so Kayserlicher Maiestat vô eynem iren Kayserlichen Maiestat armen Reüterlyn, vnd underthenigem diener beschicht* (Strasbourg: Prüß, 1522); Kück, 5.

18. *Hüpsch argument red fragen vnd antwurt Dreyer personen Nemlichen ains Curtisanen aines Edelmans vñ aines Burgers Nit allain kürtzweylig Sunder vast nutzlich zu lesen vnd zů heren Alles D.M.L. leer betreffent.* (Strasbourg: Reinhart Beck, 1522); Ho 3922.

19. For example, *Hüpsch* Aij(v), B(v)–Bij, Bij(v)–Biij, Cij(v)–Ciij, Ciij(v)–Civ.

20. *Hüpsch* Civ.

21. *Wider Doctor Murnars falsch erdycht Lyed: von dem vndergang christlichs Glaubens. Bruoder Michael Styfels von Esszlingen vßleg vnnd Christliche gloß darüber.* (Strasbourg: Prüß, 1522), Eiij(v), Ciij(v).

22. Stifel, *Wider Doctor Murnars falsch erdycht Lyed*, Dij(v).

23. Kück, 3.

24. *Ableynung des vermeinlichen unglimpffs so dem Andechtigen Hochgelerten vnd Cristenlichen vatter Doctor Martin Luther Augustiner orders. u(sw) von vielen zůgelegt, jn dem das er vnsern vatter den Babst ein Vicari des Teüfels vnd Antecrists u(sw) genant hat.* (Strasbourg: Prüß, 1522); Tü 1889/4824; Kück, 18–31.

25. Kück, 26.

26. *Zü lob dem Luther vnd eeren der gantzen Christenhait.* The verse on the title page reads "Wőlt yemant wissen wie der hieß | Der disen spruch außgon liess | Das hat gethon Laux Gemigger student | Auß vrsach, dz man des Luthers bůcher hat verprent" (Laube 1:548). The Hohenemser (Ho 4329) is identified as a Nuremberg printing done in 1522. Laube gives an uncertain date of 1521, printed in Augsburg by Erhard Öglin Erben. Chrisman dates the work to 1520 and has identified two editions printed in Strasbourg. From the internal evidence, the treatise was written earliest by the end of November 1520 and latest by March 1521. The 1520 dating is probably too early. Laube identifies two Strasbourg editions and one Augsburg edition (Laube 1:555).

27. Laube 1:548.

28. *Passion D. Martins Luthers, oder seyn leydung durch Marcellum beschriben* (Strasbourg: Prüß, 1521), a3; Ho 3908; Tü 1566/4061.

29. *Brüder Michael Stifel Augustiner von Esszlingen. Von der Christförmigen, rechtgegründten leer Doctoris Martini Luthers, ein uberuss schön kunstlich Lyed, sampt seiner neben vsslegung* (Strasbourg, 1522). Reprinted twice, once shortly after 1522 and the second time before 1525. See Chrisman, *Bibliography* P.3.9.7; Clemen 3, no. 7.

30. Clemen 3:282.

31. Clemen 3:283.

32. Clemen 3:286.

33. For example, Marcellus, a2(v)–a3.

34. *Hüpsch*, Ai(v)–Aii.

35. *Hüpsch*, Cij(v)–Ciij; cf. *Hüpsch*, Aiij(v).

36. *Hüpsch*, Aiij(v), Civ–Civ(v).

37. Clemen 3:282.

38. Scribner, *For the Sake of Simple Folk*, 21.

39. Clemen 3:283.

40. Even for those who did not, at least at this point, accept Luther's characterization of the papacy as the Antichrist, his opposition to the papacy was often welcomed and elicited a feeling of solidarity in a common struggle to reform the church of serious abuses. For example, our moderate, the anonymous author of *A Pleasant Argument* simply mentioned that Luther believed that the pope was a bishop like any other bishop (*Hüpsch*, Aii(v)). Yet the anonymous author strongly supported Luther's scripturally based reforms.

The author of *A Good Coarse Dialogue* had one of his characters point out that, although Luther attacked the pope for abuses, he did not say that there should be no pope or papal assistants, so long as the pope did not introduce a new faith or allow heresy to grow. Yet this comment was placed within a long attack on the practice of indulgences [*Ain gůtter grober dyalogus Teüsch, zwyschen zwayen gůten gesellen, mit namen Hans Schőpfer, Peter Schabēhůt, bayd von Basel die auh nit nőttiger gschåfft sunst außzů richten habent angericht vō eim wirt.* (Strasbourg: Beck, 1521); Ho 3904, Biij].

41. See note 24 above.
42. Kück, 18.
43. Kück, 20.
44. Kück, 4–5.
45. Marcellus, a2(v).
46. Clemen 4:94–95.
47. DS 1:418–419.
48. DS 1:441. In the pamphlet's closing list of thirty articles adopted by "Noble Helferich, Knight Heintz, and Karsthans and all their adherents," article five called the pope the "Endchrist," the Antichrist of the Endtimes, and article six labeled the "cardinals, protonotories, officials, bishops, auditors, and others at Rome" the "devil's apostles" (DS 1:443).
49. See chapter 3.
50. Clemen 4:108–109.
51. DS 1:446.
52. See, for example, *Karsthans, New Karsthans,* Stifel's *Against Murnar's . . . Song.*
53. *Uerkündungs Brieff der Uniuersitet,* i(v).
54. *Uerkündungs Brieff der Uniuersitet,* ii–iii.
55. *Ain gůtter grober dyalogus Teütsch,* Aiv(v).
56. DS 1:469–470.
57. *Ain gůtter grober dyalogus Teütsch,* Aiv(v).
58. *Ain gůtter grober dyalogus Teütsch,* Aiij(v).
59. DS 1:459.
60. *Uerkündungs Brieff der Uniuersitet,* iij(v). Eck and the bull of excommunication are also severely criticized by the author of *Ain schőner dialogus,* DS 1:468–469.
61. Laube 1:548–557.
62. Clemen 4:89.
63. Clemen 4:90–91.
64. Clemen 3:289.
65. DS 1:468.
66. Clemen 4:83.
67. Kück, 26.
68. Kück, 26–27.
69. *Hüpsch,* Aii(v).
70. *Hüpsch,* Aiv(v).
71. Murner's name is deliberately misspelled to pun on the word for clown [*Narr*].

72. *Wider Doctor Murnars falsch erdycht Lyed: von dem vndergang Christliche glaubens. Bruoder Michael Stifels von Esszlingen vßleg vnnd Christliche gloß darüber* (Strasbourg, 1522).

73. *Wider Doctor Murnars falsch erdycht Lyed*, F(v).

74. Clemen 4:76.

75. Marcellus, a4–a4(v).

76. Clemen 4:91.

77. DS 1:417.

78. *Hüpsch*, Aij(v)–Aiij.

79. Another distinctive teaching, dealt with by only a few of the pamphleteers is Luther's view of the sacraments. *A Pleasant Argument* explains that Luther taught that the Mass was a testament (B–B(v)), that there was a purgatory and masses did help souls (Biv(v)–C), and that there were no more than three sacraments (Eij). Stifel, in *Wider Doctor Murnars falsch erdycht Lyed*, informed its readers that Luther taught that the Mass was an admonition and a certain sign to all believers of the remission of all sins. It was not a sacrifice that we offer but rather a pledge that we should receive (Bij–Bij(v)). As with the case of the priesthood of all baptized Christians, some of the characterization in *A Pleasant Argument* would likely have been disputed by Luther himself.

80. Clemen 4:116–117.

81. *Hüpsch*, Bij.

82. *Hüpsch*, Bij–Bii(v).

83. *Hüpsch*, Bij(v)–Biij.

84. Although I interpret the evidence somewhat differently, I am indebted to Gottfried Blochwitz, "Die antirömischen deutschen Flugschriften der frühen Reformationszeit (bis 1522) in ihrer religiös-sittlichen Eigenart," *ARG* 27 (1930):145–254, for alerting me to this division.

85. Chrisman P1.1.3.

86. StA 2:265; WA 7:21. For a translation from the Latin version, see LW 31:344.

87. StA 2:273; WA 7:24–25. For a translation from the Latin version, see LW 31:349.

88. StA 2:271.

89. StA 2:271, 273.

90. DS 1:415.

91. DS 1:425.

92. DS 1:433–434.

93. DS 1:429.

94. DS 1:427.

95. DS 1:419.

96. For example, DS 1:436.

97. DS 1:423–424.

98. DS 1:445.

99. DS 1:446.

100. Laube 1:552–553.

101. Kück, 19–20.

102. Kück, 28.
103. Kück, 22.
104. Clemen 3:49.
105. Clemen 3:340.
106. Clemen 3:316.
107. *Hüpsch*, Biij(v)– Bɪᴠ.
108. *Hüpsch*, Biv.
109. *Hüpsch*, Biv.
110. *Hüpsch*, Biv–Biv(v).
111. Hans-Joachim Köhler, "The *Flugschriften* and their Importance in Religious Debate: A Quantitative Approach," in Paola Zambelli, ed., *'Astrologi hallucinati': Stars and the End of the World in Luther's Time* (New York, 1986), 159.
112. Ibid., 161.
113. It is worth noting that Luther's Catholic critics did not overlook this theme!

CHAPTER 5: SCRIPTURE AS PRINTED TEXT

1. Except perhaps a few fringe spiritualists such as the Zwickau prophets.
2. *UF das Fürhaltē so durch Keyserliche Maiestat Vnd des heiligen Reichs versamleten Churfürsten, vnd stånde, Dem Hochgelertē Doctori Martino Luther. etc. durch des Reich Redner zů Wormbs erzelt. Ist diß sein personlich (Zům kürtzistenn) begriffen antwort* . . . (Strasbourg: Knobloch, 1521), iiij(v)–iiiij.
3. See, for example, Walter Mostert, "Scriptura sacra sui ipsius interpres: Bemerkungen zum Verständnis der Heiligen Schrift durch Luther," *Lutherjahrbuch* 46 (1979):60–96, and the wealth of literature cited there.
4. The literature on the German Luther Bible is immense. For the best scholarly treatment and an extensive bibliography, see Hans Volz, *Martin Luthers deutsche Bibel: Entstehung und Geschichte der Lutherbibel* (Henning Wendland, ed.; Hamburg, 1978; Berlin, 1981). For subsequent bibliography, see editions of *Vestigia Biblia: Jahrbuch des Deutschen Bibel-Archivs Hamburg*. For a stimulating yet different (and occasionally flawed) treatment of the topic of this chapter, see Jane O. Newman, "The Word Made Print: Luther's 1522 *New Testament* in an Age of Mechanical Reproduction," *Representations* 1 (1985):95–133.
5. WADB 6:2; LW 35:357.
6. WADB 6:4; LW 35:358.
7. WADB 6:8.
8. WADB 6:8; LW 35:360–361.
9. WADB 6:8; LW 35:361.
10. WADB 6:9.
11. WADB 6:9; LW 35:362.
12. WADB 6:10; LW 35:362.
13. WADB 7:384; LW 35:396–397.
14. WADB 7:404; LW 35:399.

15. WADB 7:2; LW 35:365.
16. WADB 7:2; LW 35:365–366.
17. WADB 7:2, 4; LW 35:366.
18. WADB 7:6; LW 35:366.
19. WADB 7:6; LW 35:368–369.
20. WADB 7:172.
21. WADB 7:172; LW 35:384.
22. WADB 7:258; LW 35:388.
23. WADB 7:284; LW 35:389.
24. WADB 7:272, 314; LW 35:389, 392.
25. I have not counted as glosses the many cross-references to other parts of Scripture found in the pages of the *German New Testament*. These cross-references also perform a certain function in directing the reader's understanding of the text, but Luther's cross-references do not appear to differ significantly from cross-references in previous vulgate editions.
26. Only five glosses explicitly criticized the papacy or monasticism. Three are found in 1 Corinthians and one in 2 Corinthians and one in Matthew. The rest of the glosses tabulated as "on Theme" deal with issues of faith, promise, law, works, and Christian freedom.
27. For a brief overview of Emser's efforts and their background, see Kenneth A. Strand, *Reformation Bibles in the Crossfire* (Ann Arbor, 1960).
28. Hieronymus Emser, *Auß was grůnd vnd ursach Luthers dolmatschung vber das nawe testament dem gemeinē man billich vorbotten worden sey. Mit scheynbarlicher anzeygung, wie, wo, vnd an wölchen stellen, Luther den text vorkert, vnd vngetrewlich gehandelt, oder mit falschen glosen vnd vorreden auß der alten Christlichen ban, auff seyn vorteyl vnd whan gefurt hab.* (Leipzig: Stöckel, 1523); Tü 318– 321/905.
29. This gloss refers to verse 7 (in today's versification; Luther's *German New Testament* did not have verse numbers). In Luther's translation this verse reads, "For if in such fashion the truth of God becomes through my lies more wonderful to His glory, why should I still be condemned as a sinner?" [Deñ so die warheyt gotis durch meyne lugen herlicher wirt zu seynē preysz, warumb solt ich deñ noch als eyn synder gerichtet werdē? (WADB 7:36)].
30. WADB 7:36.
31. Emser, *Auß was grůnd,* xij.
32. *The New Jerusalem Bible* translates these verses: "No distinction is made: all have sinned and lack God's glory, and all are justified by the free gift of his grace through being set free in Christ Jesus. God appointed him as a sacrifice for reconciliation, through faith, by the shedding of his blood."
33. WADB 7:38.
34. WADB 7:38.
35. Emser, *Auß was grůnd,* xij(v).
36. Emser, *Auß was grůnd,* xij(v).
37. Emser, *Auß was grůnd,* xij(v).
38. WADB 7:40.
39. WADB 7:40.
40. Emser, *Auß was grůnd,* xiij.

41. WADB 7:38. Note that Luther emphasized this verse by having it begin a paragraph. The same is true with the verse singled out by the second gloss.

42. WA 30/2:632–646.

43. WA 30/2:640–643.

44. The literature on this and other sixteenth-century biblical illustrations is extensive. See the bibliography in Volz, *Martin Luthers deutsche Bibel*. See also Philipp Schmidt, *Die Illustration der Lutherbibel 1522–1700* (Basel, 1962), and Hermann Oertel, "Das Bild in Bibeldrucken vom 15. bis zum 18. Jahrhundert," *Jahrbuch der Gesellschaft für Niedersächsische Kirchengeschichte* 75 (1977):9–37. For the woodcuts in Revelation, see Peter Martin, *Martin Luther und die Bilder zur Apokalypse: Die Ikonographie der Illustrationen zur Offenbarung des Johannes in der Lutherbibel 1522–1546* (Hamburg, 1983).

45. The following discussion is based on the bibliographic descriptions in WADB 2. Unfortunately, the description of each edition is not consistent, and for a few editions the description in the WADB seems incomplete. For example, the WADB does not explicitly indicate that Luther's name was omitted in two editions, yet the title as cited for each edition does not mention Luther's name. Is this an oversight by WADB or is Luther's name mentioned elsewhere in the edition, say, in a preface? I was unable to examine the specific editions myself. Although the WADB indicates that there were twenty printings issued in 1524, one of these editions, printed in Leipzig, was seized and destroyed at the insistence of the staunchly Catholic Duke Georg of Albertine Saxony. As a result, we do not know its format or whether it gave Luther's name or reproduced the offending woodcuts in Revelation.

46. M. Reu, *Luther's German Bible* (Columbus, Ohio, 1934), 164 and 355, n. 46. See also WABr 2:581, n.9.

47. This is the count I get from WADB 2. Hans Volz, in his introduction to *Die gantze Heilige Schrifft Deudsch* (Munich, 1972), 61*, identified three from Augsburg, seven from Basel, and one in Grimma and one in Leipzig. WADB identifies two Strasbourg editions. One [number 243] by "Hans" Schott was probably published in 1523. Chrisman dates this Schott edition to 1522, which WADB allows as possible but unlikely. The second Strasbourg edition, produced by Johann Schott in 1523, is number 248. Where Chrisman identifies only one edition, WADB has two.

48. Based on my count of editions in WADB 2. Chrisman lists only one Knobloch edition in 1524 (while WADB has three). The only Köpfel edition she lists is for 1538, while WADB lists this for 1524 [number 52]. I assume this is Chrisman's mistake, since the Köpfel edition is dated. This Köpfel edition is also interesting since in it Luther's glosses have been removed from the margins and published in a separate pamplet (WADB 2:326–327). See the discussion below.

49. The recorded price for the September Testament ranges from one-half to one and one-half guldens. The difference probably depends on whether the New Testament was bound or unbound and whether it had specially hand-decorated initials (Martin Brecht, *Martin Luther: Shaping and Defining the*

Reformation, 1521–1532 [Minneapolis, 1990], 53). The price equivalents come from Walter Krieg, *Materialien zu einer Entwicklungsgeschichte der Bücher-Preise und des Autoren-Honorars 15. bis zum 20. Jahrhundert* (Vienna, Bad Bocklet, Zurich, 1953), 19–22. For those interested in further equivalents, Krieg's list of equivalents for one and one-half guldens goes on for two pages. It should be noted, however, that the price for Luther's *German New Testament* was but a sixteenth or less of the price paid for a printed German Bible (Old and New Testaments) just fifty years earlier. Printing costs had come down considerably, making material such as the *German New Testament* accessible to much larger numbers of people.

50. Over half of the editions of 1523 (seven of twelve, or 58 percent) were the handier and less expensive quarto and octavo format. In 1524 almost two-thirds of the editions (twelve of nineteen, or 63 percent) were quarto or octavo, and in 1525 three-quarters of the editions (six of eight, or 75 percent) were quarto or octavo. If we consider only the handiest (and likely least expensive) octavo editions, their percentage of the total rises from a sixth in 1523 (two of twelve, or about 17 percent) to slightly more than half of all editions in 1524 (ten of nineteen, or about 53 percent) to five-eighths of all editions in 1525 (five of eight, or about 63 percent). Note that although there were twenty editions in 1524, we know the format for only nineteen, since the twentieth, printed in Leipzig, was seized and destroyed.

51. See the "genealogy" of these editions in WADB 2:201–727.

52. See Peter Martin, *Martin Luther und die Bilder zur Apokalypse.*

53. These figures are based on the bibliographic descriptions in WADB 2.

54. WADB 2:698–699, no. 243.

55. WADB 2:326–327, no. 52.

56. See chapter 4.

57. Bernd Moeller, "Was wurde in der Frühzeit der Reformation in den deutschen Städten gepredigt?" *ARG* 75 (1984):176–193.

58. Holm Zerener, *Studien über das beginnende Eindringen der Lutherischen Bibelübersetzung in die deutsche Literatur nebst einem Verzeichnis über 681 Drucke—hauptsächlich Flugschriften—der Jahre 1522–1525,* Archiv für Reformationsgeschichte Texte und Untersuchungen, Ergänzungsband IV (Leipzig: M. Heinsius Nachfolger, 1911).

CHAPTER 6: CONTESTED AUTHORITY IN THE STRASBOURG PRESS

1. *Erklerung Wie Karlstat sein ler von dem hochwirdigen Sacrament, vnd andere achtet vnnd geachtet haben wil. Mit eyner Epistel M. Lutheri.* (Strasbourg: Johann Knobloch, 1525). For the attributions, see Zorzin, nos. 77E and 77F.

2. The *Admonition* was separately reprinted the following year under the title *The Rejoicing of a Christian Brother Concerning the Union Undertaken Between Dr. M. Luther and Dr. Andreas Karlstadt. With an Indication What Is To Be Maintained Concerning the Articles on the Body and Blood of Christ (As One Calls Them).* [*Frolockūg eins christlichē bruders von wegen der*

veregynigung, Zwische D. M. Luther vnd D. Andres Carlostat sich begeben. Mit annzeyg was von dem artickel des leybs vnnd bluts cristi (as mans nent) sey zu halten. (Strasbourg, 1526)].

3. For their involvement see Walter Köhler, *Zwingli und Luther: Ihr Streit über das Abendmahl nach seinen politischen und religiösen Beziehungen,* 2 vols. (Leipzig, 1924; Gütersloh, 1953); Ernst Bizer, *Studien zur Geschichte des Abendmahlsstreits im 16. Jahrhundert* (Gütersloh, 1940; Darmstadt, 1962); Thomas Kaufmann, *Die Abendmahlstheologie der Straßburger Reformatoren bis 1528* (Tübingen, 1992); and my *Luther's Last Battles: Politics and Polemics, 1531–46* (Ithaca, 1983), esp. chapter 4.

4. W2 20:312.

5. W2 20:312–313.

6. W2 20:313. The attack goes on for several paragraphs.

7. W2 20:314.

8. W2 20:314.

9. W2 20:314.

10. W2 20:314–315.

11. W2 20:315.

12. WA 18:454.

13. *Frolockūg,* Aij. All citations are taken from *Frolockūg* but have been checked against the original printing in the Prüß edition of the *Explanation.*

14. *Frolockūg,* Aij.

15. *Frolockūg,* Aij(v)–Aiij.

16. For example, *Frolockūg,* B–B(v).

17. *Frolockūg,* B(v).

18. *Frolockūg,* B(v)–Bij.

19. *Frolockūg,* Bij.

20. *Frolockūg,* Bij–Bij(v).

21. *Frolockūg,* Bij(v).

22. *Frolockūg,* Biij–Biij(v).

23. *Frolockūg,* Biij(v)–Biv.

24. *Frolockūg,* Biv.

25. *Frolockūg,* Biv(v).

26. *ACTA ET RES GESTAE, D. MARTINI LVTHERi, in Comitijs Principū Vuormaciae, Anno M.D.XXI.* (Strasbourg: Johann Schott, 1521).

27. *Passion D. Martins Luthers, oder seyn leydung durch Marcellum beschriben* (Strasbourg: Prüß, 1521), a3; Ho 3908; Tü 1566/4061.

28. Laube 1:548.

29. *Brüder Michael Styfel Augustiner von Esszlingen. Von der Christförmigen, rechtgegründten leer Doctoris Martini Luthers, ein uberuss schön kunstlich Lyed, sampt seiner neben vsslegung.* (Strasbourg, 1522), Aii.

30. By my tally 166 printings had occurred through 1523, not counting editions of the *German New Testament.* Another 25 printings were issued in 1524. These figures may differ from Chrisman's since, as has been remarked upon, identification and dating of printed works is at best an inexact science.

31. See chapter 5.

32. *Luther and the False Brethren* (Stanford, 1975).

33. WA 15:392; LW 40:66.
34. WA 18:62; cf. WA 18:136.
35. See my *Luther and the False Brethren*, 52–53.
36. WA 15:393.
37. WA 15:394.
38. WA 15:396–397. We see here several characteristics of Luther's tactics with intra-Evangelical polemics. As I have argued at length in *Luther and the False Brethren*, Luther found it polemically effective and necessary in intra-Evangelical disputes to enhance his own authority with special claims and denegrate the authority of his opponents with *ad hominem* attacks. I do not claim that either tactic was disingenuous, only that they helped distinguish the positions when agreement was large and disagreement relatively small. We see both these tactics at work in this letter.

39. In the middle of October 1524, Karlstadt paid a short, four-day visit to Strasbourg. Shortly after Karlstadt left Strasbourg, the city council issued on 31 October a mandate to the preachers that they preach "only the clear Gospel" and that they refrain from topics that might promote unrest. They were also urged in their sermons to their congregations to turn away from direct action [von tätlichem Zugriff abzuweissen] and themselves not to induce any substantial innovations. This mandate was probably prompted by Karlstadt's visit (Hermann Barge, *Andreas Bodenstein von Karlstadt* [Leipzig, 1905], 2:213–214). Prior to this visit, eleven of his treatises had been reprinted in Strasbourg, thanks largely to the efforts of the printers Johann Prüß and Johann Schwan. During his brief stay, he arranged to have two more sermons published. Somewhat later, on 6 November 1524, the Prüß press issued *Reasons Why Andreas Karlstadt Was Driven Out of the Lands of Saxony*, a collection of letters Karlstadt had left behind to document his allegedly unjustified expulsion from Electoral Saxony. The list is from Erich Freys and Hermann Barge, "Verzeichnis der gedruckten Schriften des Andreas Bodenstein von Karlstadt," *Zentralblatt für Bibliothekswesen* 21 (1904):153–179, 209–243, 305–331.

Ad Leonem X. Pontificem Maximvm. Resolutiones disputationum de uirtute indulgentiaru . . . Contra D. Joannem Eckium Ingoldstadiensem Sophisti cum argutatorem, Apologetice propositiones D. Andreae Bodenstein Archidiaconi Vuttenbergesis . . . (Strasbourg: Matthias Schürer, 1519).
Uon vermügē des Ablas: wider Brůder Franciscus Seyler Barfusser ordēs Anders Carolstatt Doctor. (Strasbourg: Martin Flach, 1520).
Uon geweychtem Wasser vnd Saltz: Do. Andreas Carlstat Wider den vnuerdienten Gardian Franciscus Seyler. (Strasbourg: Martin Flach, 1520).
Von den Empfahern: zeichen: vnd zůsag des heyligē Sacraments, fleysch vnnd blůts Christi. (Strasbourg: Johann Prüß).
Von den empfahern: zeichen: vnd zůsag des heiligē Sacraments, fleisch vnd blůts Christi. Auch von anbettůg vnd eer erbietůg der zeichen des Neüwen Testaments. (Strasbourg?, 1521).
Von anbettung vnd eer erbietung der zeychen des neüwen Testaments. (Strasbourg, 1521?).
Von beyden gestalten der heylige Messze. Von zeichen in gemeyn was sie wircken vnd deüten. Sie seind nit Behemen od' ketzer, die beyde gestalt namen, sond' Euangelische Christen. (Strasbourg: Johann Pruß, 1522).

*Sendtbrif. D. Andree Boden. von Caralstat meldende seinner wirtschaat. Nůuwe
geschicht von pfaffen vnd mũnchē zů Wittenberg.* (Strasbourg: Johann Prüß,
1522).

*Uon manigfeltigkeit des eynfeltigen eynigen willen gottes. was sundt sey. Andres
Bodensteyn von Carolstat eyn newer Ley.* (Strasbourg?, 1523).

Uō dē Sabbat vnnd gebotten feyrtagen. (Strasbourg: Johann Schwan, 1524).

*Von den zweyen hōchsten gebotten der lieb Gottes, und des nechsten, Matheı. 22.
wie die rechte lieb zů dem nechsten nıcht menschlich, sonder gōtlich sein, vnd
auß Gottes willen fliessen.* (Strasbourg: Johann Prüß, 1524). Preached in 1523
but probably printed in October, when Karlstadt visited Strasbourg.

Von Engelen vnd Teüffelen ein Sermon. (Strasbourg: Johann Prüß, [October] 1524).
Preached in 1523 but not published ın Strasbourg until Karlstadt's vısıt.

Vrsachen der halben Andres Carolstatt auß den landen Zů Sachsen vertryben. (Strasbourg: Johann Prüß, [6 November] 1524). Reprınted ın Hertzsch 2:50–58.

40. *Ob man mit heyliger schrifft erweysen mūge, das Christus mıt leyb, blũt vnd
    seele im Sacrmament sey.* (Strasbourg: Prüß, 1525); Tü 1127/2883. See Zorzin,
    no. 66B, n. 56, for the attribution.

*Dialogus oder ein gesprech büchlin. Von dem grewlıchen vnd abgöttischen miß-
brauch, des hochwirdigsten Sacraments Jesu Christı. Andreas Carolstatt.* (Strasbourg: Prüß, 1525). Reprinted in Hertzsch 2:5–49; W2 20:2313–2359.

*Auszlegung dieser wort Christi. Das ist mein leyb, welcher für euch gegebē würt.
Das ist mein Blůt, welches für euch vergossen würt. Luce am. 22. Wider die einfeltige vnd zwyfeltige papisten, welche soliche wort, zů einē abbruch des kreützes
Christi brauchen.* (Strasbourg: Prüß, 1525). The Basel first edıtion is found in Tü
1446/3833.

*EIn schone kurcze vñ Christliche vnterrichtũg der rechten (widder die alte vnnd
neüwe papistische) meß.* (Strasbourg: Johann Schwan, 1524). The Basel first edıtion is found in Tü 95/256. Reprinted in W2 20:2306–2313.

*Wie sich der glaub vnd vnglaub gegen dem lıecht vñ finsternus, gegen warheyt vnd
lügen, gegen Gott vnd dem Teüffel halten. Was der frey will vermōge. Ob man
als bald glaub, als man Gottes warheyt gehōrt. Von dem eınsprechen Gottes.
Wer Augen hat der wirt mercken, was die sünd in den heyligen geyst. Item, Wenn
man tauffen. Item, Wie ein erleüchtes, vnd hohes leben des Christen ist. Die
rouhen Christen seind in dem kleynen vngetrew vnnd vngelassen, wie mōchten
sye in dem grossen gelassen vnd getrew sein?* (Strasbourg: Prüß, 1525); Tü 1128/
2884. For the attribution see Zorzin, no. 71B, n. 56.

41. *Ein schone kurcze vñ Christliche vnterrichtũg der rechten (wider die
alte vnnd neüwe papistische) mess* (Strasbourg: Johann Schwan, 1524). Reprinted in W2 20:2306–2313.

42. *Auszlegung dieser wort Christi. Das ist mein leyb, welcher für euch
gegebē würt. Das ist mein Blůt, welches für euch vergossen würt. Luce am.
22. Wider die einfeltige vnd zwyfeltige papisten, welche soliche wort, zů einē
abbruch des kreützes Christi brauchen* (Strasbourg: Prüß, 1525). The Basel
first edition is found in Tü 1446/3833. There is a pun in the "einfeltige vnd
zwyfeltige papisten" that I was unable to render into Englısh. "Einfeltige" also
means "simple." This is a variation on Karlstadt's "old and new papists," that
is, followers of the Roman Church and followers of Luther.

43. Of the two other reprints, *Whether One May Prove With the Holy
Scripture That Christ With Body, Blood, and Soul Is In the Sacrament*, and
*Dialogue or Conversational Pamphlet Concerning the Horrible and Idolatrous
Misuse of the Most Highly Revered Sacrament of Jesus Christ*, both reprinted

in 1525, the former was the least polemical of the lot, while the latter presented in dialogue form several of the arguments advanced in the other treatises, along with a good deal of ridicule for the opposing position. *Ob man mit heyliger schrifft erweysen müge, das Christus mit leyb, blůt vnd seele im Sacrament sey*. Andres Carolstatt. M.DXXV. (Strasbourg: Prüß, 1525); Tü 1127/2883. See Zorzin, no. 66B, n. 56, for the attribution. *Dialogus oder ein gesprechbüchlin. Von dem grewlichen vnd abôttischen mißbrauch, des hochwirdigsten Sacrament Jesu Christi*. Andres Carolstatt M.D.XXV. (Strasbourg: Prüß, 1525); Tü 136/369. Reprinted in Hertzsch 2:5–49; W2 20:2313–2359. Citations from Hertzsch.

44. W2 20:2308.
45. W2 20:2309.
46. W2 20:2310.
47. For example, *Auszlegung*, aij.
48. *Auszlegung*, aij(v).
49. *Auszlegung*, aiij.
50. *Auszlegung*, b.
51. *Auszlegung*, dv(v)–dvi.
52. *Auszlegung*, dv(v)–dvi.
53. Wolfgang Capito, *(W)Aß man halten, vnnd antwurten soll, von der spaltung zwischen Martin Luther vnd Andres Carolstadt* (Strasbourg: Köpfel, 1524); Tü 79/213; W2 20:340–351.
54. W2 20:346.
55. W2 20:346–347.
56. W2 20:347.
57. W2 20:347–349.
58. W2 20:349.
59. W2 20:349–350.
60. W2 20:350–351.
61. W2 20:340.
62. W2 20:341–342.
63. W2 20:351.
64. W2 20:351.
65. *Frolockūg*, Bij(v).

CHAPTER 7: CATHOLICS ON LUTHER'S RESPONSIBILITY FOR THE GERMAN PEASANTS' WAR

1. Johann Cochlaeus, *Sieben kopffe Martin Luthers, von sieben sachen des Christlichen glaubens* (Dresden: W. Stöckel, 1529), bij(v).
2. The literature on Luther and the Peasants' War is extensive. See the discussion and cited literature in Bernhard Lohse, *Martin Luther: Eine Einführung in sein Leben und sein Werk* (München, 1981).
3. See the discussion in chapter 1 and especially figures 7 to 10, and my article "Catholic Controversial Literature, 1518–1555: Some Statistics," *ARG* 79 (1988):189–205.
4. Hieronymus Emser, *Auff Luthers grewel wider die heiligen Stillmess*

Antwort Item wie, wo und mit wolchen wortten Luther yhn seyn büchern tzur auffrur ermandt, geschriben und getriben hat (Dresden, 1525); Tü 242/667 and Theobald Freudenberger, ed., *Hieronymus Emser: Schriften zur Verteidigung der Messe* (Münster: Aschendorf, 1959).

5. Emser, *Auff Luthers grewel*, Aiv(v).

6. Emser, *Auff Luthers grewel*, B.

7. The Catholic publicists were careful to cite accurately and identify the location of the citation. They used the printer's marks to locate the quote since pagination was seldom practiced at this point. Although the citations were accurate, they were often taken out of context, a practice that could easily distort their meaning.

8. WA 6:407.

9. WA 6:409.

10. WA 6:370.

11. WA 7:630, 10; 631, 19–20, and 32–33.

12. WA 8:251, 36; 252, 5, 17–19, and 24–27.

13. WA 11:408, 22–23.

14. WA 8:251.

15. Adolf Laube, ed., *Flugschriften der Bauernkriegszeit* (Berlin, 1978), 362.

16. David V. N. Bagchi, in his *Luther's Earliest Opponents: Catholic Controversialists, 1518–1525* (Minneapolis, 1991), does a superb job showing how the issue of authority is at the center of the Catholic response to Martin Luther.

17. Emser, *Auff Luthers grewel*, Bij(v).

18. Luther was referring particularly to Duke Georg's demand that his subjects turn in Luther's translation of the New Testament. The Duke's objection was not to a vernacular New Testament per se but to Luther's specific translation. The Duke later sponsored Emser's revision of Luther's translation. See, among others, Hans Becker, "Herzog Georg von Sachsen als kirchlicher und theologischer Schriftsteller," *ARG* 24 (1927):161–269, and my *Luther's Last Battles: Politics and Polemics, 1531–46* (Ithaca, 1983), chapter 3, esp. 41–42.

19. Luther's *To the Christian Nobility; German New Testament; Answer to the Hyper-Christian . . . Book; On Taking Both Kinds of the Sacrament; On Secular Authority, To What Extent It Should Be Obeyed; That A Christian Assembly Has the Right to Judge Teachings; A Faithful Admonition to All Christians To Guard Themselves From Rebellion; On Confession and Whether the Pope Has the Power To Command It; A Sermon on the New Testament, That Is, The Holy Mass;* and *On the Adoration of the Sacrament of the Holy Body of Christ.* The one Latin work was Luther's *Confitendi ratio* of 1520.

20. Emser, *Auff Luthers grewel*, C.

21. Laube, *Bauernkriegszeit*, 367–368.

22. Emser, *Auff Luthers grewel*, Ciij.

23. Laube, *Bauernkriegszeit*, 370.

24. Emser, *Auff Luthers grewel*, D.

25. "Si fures furca, si latrones gladio, si haereticos igne plectimus, Cur non magis hos Magistros perditionis, hoc Cardinales, hos Papas et totam istam Romanae Zodomae colluviem, quae Ecclesiam dei sine fine corrumpit, omnibus armis impetimus et manus nostras in sanquine istorum lavamus." (WA 6:347, 22–26). For obvious reasons, this is a favorite in the Catholic arsenal. Here is Emser's comment: "In dem buchlin wider Sylvestrum Prieratem. In disem buchlin ermanet Luter den adel abermaln, dass sie die hend yn der geistlichen blut waschen sollen, wölchs er in dem buchlin: Auff das uberchristlich etc. D am letzten bletlin also dewtet, er hab es per contentionem geschriben. Dann wo der bapst die ketzer verbrennen woll, sey es billich, dass man yn mit all seyn secten auffs allerschentlichst erwurge" (Emser, *Auff Luthers grewel*, D(v)).

26. "G.iij. Dz ich yn Gotes namen angefangen, vnd meyn leer das rechte wort Gotes sey, Hab ich keyn stercker beweysung, Dann dz sie so geschwind yn alle welt vermhert worden, vnd vneynikeit anricht, vnd wan sie das nit thet, wer ich langst vertzagt vnd mat worden" (Emser, *Auff Luthers grewel*, D(v)). Although I checked two different editions of Luther's treatise, I was unable to find this exact wording. Emser appears to have used ellipses to good polemical effect and also added a few words. The WA and the two editions I checked in the Tübingen collection read: "ich hab meyner hoffnung, das ich in gottis namen angefangen und das recht wort gottis lere, keyne sterker beweysung und wundertzeychen, denn das sie sso schwindt yn alle welt on meyn treyben und suchen, dartzu durch untzehlich widderstend und vorfolgung aller geweltigen und gelereten vormehret worden ist und uneynickeit anricht, Und wenn sie das nit thet, were ich lengst vortzagt und mat worden" (WA 7:280, 25–31). This passage does *not* occur on Giij in either edition. In fact, the treatise is too short to even have a Giij. Given the page reference, Emser may be working from a collection that I have not identified.

27. Laube, *Bauernkriegszeit*, 373.

28. Emser, *Auff Luthers grewel*, Bij(v).

29. Emser, *Auff Luthers grewel*, Biij. This was picked up and used by Petrus Sylvius: "Das er aber auch fürnympt mit seynem anhang Gotte gleych zu seyn ynn der herschafft vnd freyheyt, bezeuget seyn eygen schrysst, so er bey der Epistel j. Cori. x. am rande also schreybet. Christus ist Herre vnd frey, also auch alle Christen ynn allen dingen uzw" (Sylvius, *Die letzten zwey beschlisslich . . . büchleyn . . . so das Lutherisch thun an seyner person . . . schrifftlich entplossen* [Leipzig: M. Blum, 1534], E; Ho 3430).

30. Emser, *Auff Luthers grewel*, Biij(v).

31. Johann Cochlaeus, *Antwort Joannis Cochlei zu Martin Luthers buch, genant Wider die Stürmenden Bawern Jetzt auffs nawe mit einer sonderlichen Schlussrede M. Pe. Sylvii in Druck gebracht* (Dresden: W. Stöckel, 1527). I have not been able to find this edition, so I am using the 1525 Cologne edition reprinted in Laube, *Bauernkriegszeit*, 376–412. The quotation is on page 378, 31–40.

32. Petrus Sylvius, *Eyn klare beweisung wie Luther würde seyn eyn*

vrsache, des steten eynzuges des Türcken, des vnchristlichen yrthums, zwi-tracht, auffruhr, vnd empörung des gemeynen volckes . . . (Leipzig: J. Thanner, 1527), B(v)–Bij; Tü 1183/2965.

33. Sylvius, *Eyn klare beweisung*, Bij. I found a quite similar quote in a 1525 treatise that may have been published in Leipzig or Dresden. In this trea-tise Petrus Sylvius identified Luther's notion of Christian freedom with the priesthood of all believers and saw both as subversive since they destroyed the two estates and undercut all hierarchy and authority:

> Darumber hat er ouch offentlich geschrieben vnd geleret, Das eynitzlicher Christen von rechtswegen sall seyn vnd ist frey, vnd syn selbest eyn Herre, Furste, Konig, Bob-ist [sic] vnd Bischoff uzw. Syntmall die Christen wern alle zu gleych Priestern vnd Konigen, vnnd ein yeder magk glawben halten vnd thun was er wil vnd darff nyemand ansehen. Sall ym ouch nymand etwas widdersprechen, Wie er dann tzum ersten yn seynem Tractat von der Christlichen freyheit vnd Babilonischen gefengknis angetzeygt vnd nachmals yn viel Tractat, Als von beyden gestalt des Sacrament zu entpfahen. Item ym Tractat wyder den falsch genant geystlichen stand, Vnd sonder-lich ym Tractat von weltlicher öberkeyt klerlich aus gedruck hat Darynne er die geistliche vnnd weltliche herschafft gantz verkleynet vnd vernichtet, Sprechend, Das die Fursten vnd Hern seyn gemeynigklich dy grosten buben vnd narren tzu welchen man sich nichts guts versehen sall, Dann sie seyn Gots stockmeyster vnd hencker vnd büttel, Vnd das vnder den Christen sal vnd kan keyn öberkeyt seyn, sonder ein itzlicher ist dem ander zu gleych vnderthan uzw (Petrus Sylvius, *Eyn Mssive* [sic] *ader Sendbriff an die Christliche versamlunge und szonderlich an die oberkeit Deutz-scher Nation zu wegern den untthergang irer herschafft, vnd das iemmerlich verterb-nis der Christenheit,* [Dresden? Leipzig? 1525]; Tü 996/2528).

34. Johann Cochlaeus, *Sieben kopffe Martin Luthers, von acht hohen sachen des Christlichen glaubens* (Dresden: W. Stöckel, 1529), Aiv(v)–Bi; Tü 136/370.

35. Paulus Bachmann, *Luthers widerruf vom Fegefewer mit farbe ausz ge-strichen durch den Abbt zur alden Zcellen* (Dresden, 1530), Eij; Tü 691/1789.

36. Johannes Fabri, *Christenliche vnderrichtung Doctor Johann Fabri, vber ettliche Puncten der Visitation* (Dresden: W. Stöckel, 1528), Bij–Bij(v); Tü 520/1342.

37. Fabri, *Christenliche vnderrichtung*, Bi.

38. Johannes Fabri, *Christenliche vnderrichtung*, Eiij(v).

39. Sylvius, *Die letzten zwey* . . . *büchleyn*, C–C(v).

40. Johannes Mensing, *Von dem Opffer Christi in der Messe: Allen Christ-glaubigen / Teutscher Nation not tzuwissen Denen zu Magdeburgk in son-derheyt / tzu gut geschriben vnd auszgangen. Beweret mit Götlicher schriffte.* (Leipzig: N. Schmidt, 1526), Aiv(v).

41. Paulus Bachmann, *Ein sermon des Abts zur Cellen yn auffnhemung der Reliquien Sancti Bennonis, gehabt am .xxi. tag des Monats Julij. Geteylt in drey artickel* (Dresden, 1527), Dij(v); Tü 1183/2966.

42. Sylvius, *Die letzten zwey* . . . *büchleyn*, Giv–Giv(v).

43. This effect of a "mind-set" or *Erwartungshorizon* is well known in psychology of perception and in literary theory. For a discussion of the *Erwar-tungshorizont*, see Hans Robert Jauss, *Toward an Aesthetic of Reception*

(Minneapolis, 1982), and Robert C. Holub, *Reception Theory: A Critical Introduction* (London, 1984).

44. Duke Georg of Saxony, *Widder des Luthers warnung an die Tewtschen, das sie dem Kaiser nicht sollen gehorsam sein, Ein ander Warnung, das sie sich dar durch nicht verführen, noch zu vngehorsam bewegen lassen, durch einen gehorsamen vnparteischen* (Dresden: W. Stöckel, 1531); WA 30/3:421. This particular passage is found only in the two reprints, one in Dresden, the other in Leipzig. For a full discussion of this treatise and the Catholic reading of Luther's rhetoric, see my *Luther's Last Battles*, especially chapter 3.

45. See, for example, Wolfgang Wulffer, *Wider die unselige Aufruhre Merten Luthers* (Leipzig: M. Landsberg, 1522), and Emser's and Alfeld's many early treatises.

46. *Deutsche Nationale Literatur*, J. Kürschner, ed. (Stuttgart, 1884–1893), 18, 17, 2, 163, 160.

47. Subtitled "The just and fundamental articles of all the peasantry and tenants of spirtual and temporal powers by whom they think themselves oppressed."

48. Peter Blickle, *Die Revolution von 1525* (2d rev. ed.; Munich, 1983) [*The Revolution of 1525: The German Peasants' War from a New Perspective*, trans. Thomas A. Brady, Jr., and H. C. Erik Midelfort (Baltimore, 1981)], chapter 3.

49. From the translation in the English version of Blickle, *The Revolution of 1525*, 197–198.

50. See the discussion above.

51. Peter Blickle, *Die Revolution von 1525*.

52. Peter Blickle, *Gemeindereformation: Die Menschen des 16. Jahrhunderts auf dem Weg zum Heil* (Munich, 1985), 69–71.

53. See, for example, Cochlaeus's *Sieben kopffe Martin Luthers, von sieben sachen des Christlichen glaubens*, with which we began the chapter. The other books in Cochlaeus's "Seven Heads" series were compiled in the same way.

CONCLUSION: A REVISED NARRATIVE

1. WA 1:239–246; Benzing, nos. 90–114. This little sermon went through twenty-five editions in three years and was published all over Germany, from Wittenberg and Leipzig to Augsburg and Basel.

2. There were at least thirty-three reprints of the speech itself [Benzing, nos. 905–937].

3. *Uf das fürhaltē*, ij(v).

4. *Uf das fürhaltē*, ij(v). Interestingly, although the manuscript speaks of "their most wicked teaching and example," the Strasbourg first edition dropped "and teaching." See WA 7:870, notes to line 11. Whether this was an oversight or a deliberate omission is hard to say.

5. *Uf das fürhaltē*, iij.

6. *Uf das fürhaltē*, iij.

7. *Uf das fürhaltē*, iiij(v)–iiiij.

8. From the translation in the English version of Peter Blickle, *The Revolution of 1525: The German Peasants' War from a New Perspective*, trans. Thomas A. Brady, Jr., and H. C. Erik Midelfort (Baltimore, 1981), 197–198.

9. Bernd Moeller, "Was wurde in der Frühzeit der Reformation in den deutschen Städten gepredigt?" *ARG* 75 (1984):176–193.

10. Bernd Moeller, "Stadt und Buch: Bemerkungen zur Struktur der Reformatorischen Bewegung in Deutschland," in Wolfgang J. Mommsen, ed., *Stadtbürgertum und Adel in der Reformation: Studien zur Socialgeschichte der Reformation in England und Deutschland* (Stuttgart, 1979), 25–39. The thesis is on page 30.

11. This statistic does not take into account the likelihood that the size of print runs also increased in this period, a fact that makes this upsurge even more dramatic.

12. It may be that more Germans were able to read than were able to write and that literacy figures need to uncouple the two skills.

Bibliography of Primary Works Discussed or Cited in the Text

Bachmann, Paul [Amnicola]. *Luthers widerruf vom Fegefewer mit farbe ausz gestrichen durch den Abbt zur alden Zcellen.* Dresden, 1530. Klaiber no. 185;Tü 691/1789.

———. *Ein sermon des Abts zur Cellen yn auffnhemung der Reliquien Sancti Bennonis, gehabt am .xxj. tag des Monats Julij. Geteylt ın drey artickel.* Dresden, Stöckel, 1527. Klaiber no. 183; Tü 1183/2966.

———. *Vonn Ceremonien̄ der Kirchen, das is, von eusserlichem dıenste Gottes, oder von Leiblıcher vbunge Göttlicher Ampter. Appendix von Priesterlichem Celibat oder Keuscheit.* Leipzig: Wolrab, 1537. Klaiber no. 192; British Library 3832.cc.3b.

———. *Wider die Natterzungen, Honsprecher vnd Lestermeuler, so sich itzo ein zeitlang haben herfür gethan on allen schawen yeden Standt vnd Grad zuuerlestern, Ein gemeine wortstraff in der Schrifft gegründet. Dobey ein Antwort auff Constantini Donatıon, welche der Luther spöttlich nennet den Hohen Artickel des aller heyligisten Bebstlichen glaubens.* Dresden: Stöckel, 1538. Klaiber no. 193; Ho 3448.

[Bucer, Martin]. *Gesprech biechlin neüw Karsthans.* Strasbourg: Schürer Erben, 1521. Chrisman P3.11.1; Tü 172/475; DS 1:406–444.

———. *Ain schöner dialogus vn̄ gesprech zwischen aim Pfarrer vnd aim schulthayß, betreffend allen übel Stand der geystlichen. Vnd bȯß handlūg der weltlichen. Alles mit geytzigkayt beladen &c.* Strasbourg: Prüß, 1521. Chrisman P3.11.2; Tü 1661/4282; DS 1:445–495.

Capito, Wolfgang. *Frolockūg eins christlichē bruders von wegen der vereynigung, Zwischē D. M. Luther vnd D. Andres Carlostat sich begeben̄. Mit annzeyg was von dem artıckel des leybs vnnd bluts crıstı (as mans nent) sey zu halten.* Strasbourg, 1526. Tü 1185/2975. For the attribution, see Zorzin, 104, n. 45.

————. (W)Aß man halten, vnnd antwurten soll, von der spaltung zwischen Martin Luther vnd Andres Carolstadtt. Strasbourg: Köpfel, 1524. Köhler 500; Tü 79/213; W2 20:340–351.

Cochlaeus, Johannes. Antwort Joannis Cochlei zu Martin Luthers buch, genant Wider die Stürmenden Bawern Jetzt auffs nawe mit einer sonderlichen Schlussrede M. Pe. Sylvii in Druck gebracht . . . Dresden: W. Stöckel, 1527. Spahn no. 32d; the 1525 Cologne edition is reprinted in Adolf Laube, ed., Flugschriften der Bauernkriegszeit (Berlin, 1978), 376–412.

————. Sieben kopffe Martin Luthers, von acht hohen sachen des Christlichen glaubens. Dresden: Stöckel, 1529. Spahn no. 63; Tü 136/370.

————. Sieben kopffe Martin Luthers, von sieben sachen des Christlichen glaubens. Dresden: Stöckel, 1529. Spahn no. 64; Tü 12/50.

Cronberg, Hartmuth von. Ableynung des vermeinlichen unglimpffs so dem Andechtigen Hochgelerten vnd Cristenlichen vatter Doctor Martin Luther Augustiner orders. u(sw) von vielen zůgelegt, jn dem das er vnsern vatter den Babst ein Vicari des Teüfels vnd Antecrists u(sw) genant hat. Strasbourg: Prüß, 1522. Chrisman P3.3.8; Tü 1889/4824; Kück, 18–31.

————. Ein hübsch christenliche vnd gőtliche erinnerung vnd warnung, so Kayserlicher Maiestat vō eynem iren Kayserlichen Maiestat armen Reüterlyn, vnd underthenigem diener beschicht. Strasbourg: Prüß, 1522. Köhler 626; Tü 3/8; Kück (xiv–xix) 1–8.

Emser, Hieronymus. Auff Luthers grewel wider die heiligen Stillmess Antwort Item wie, wo und mit wolchen wortten Luther yhn seyn büchern tzur auffrur ermandt, geschriben und getriben hat. Dresden, 1525. Klaiber no. 998; Tü 242/667.

————. Auß was gründ vnd ursach Luthers dolmatschung vber das nawe testament dem gemeinē man billich vorbotten worden sey. Mit scheynbarlicher anzeygung, wie, wo, vnd an wōlchen stellen, Luther den text vorkert, vnd vngetrewlich gehandelt, oder mit falschen glosen vnd vorreden auß der alten Christlichen ban, auff seyn vorteyl vnd whan gefurt hab. Leipzig: Stöckel, 1523. Klaiber no. 989; Tü 318–321/905.

Fabri, Johannes. Christenliche vnnderrichtung Doctor Johann Fabri, vber ettliche Puncten der Visitatıon, sso jm Churfürstenthumb Sachssen gehalten, vnd durch Luther beschriben, Welche antzunehmen vnd zuuerwerffen seyend. Dresden, 1528. Klaiber no. 1087; Tü 520/1342.

Gemigger von Heinfelt, Laux. Zů lob dem Luther vnd eeren der gantzen Christenhait. Strasbourg: Prüß, 1520, and ca. 1520. Chrisman P3.3.1.; Ho 4329 [Nuremberg version]; Laube 1:548–557.

Georg, Duke of Saxony. Widder des Luthers warnung an die Tewtschen, das sie dem Kaiser nicht sollen gehorsam sein, Ein ander Warnung, das sie sich dar durch nicht verführen, noch zu vngehorsam bewegen lassen, durch einen gehorsamen vnparteischen. Dresden: Stöckel, 1531. WA 30/3:416–423.

Ain gůtter grober dyalogus Teütsch, zwyschen zwayen gůten gesellen, mit namen Hans Schőpfer, Peter Schabēhůt, bayd von Basel die auh nit nőttiger gschäfft sunst auß zů richten habent angericht vō aim wirt. Strasbourg: Beck, 1521. Chrisman 3.3.2; Ho 3904.

Hüpsch argument red Fragen vnd antwurt Dreyer personen Nemlichen ains Curtisanen aines Edelmans vñ aines Burgers Nit allain kürtzweylig Sunder vast nutzlich zů lesen vnd zů heren Alles D.M.L. leer betreffent. Strasbourg: Beck, 1522. Chrisman P3.9.5; Ho 3922.

Hutten, Ulrich von. *Ein Clagschrift des Hochberůmten vnd Eernuestē herrn Vlrichs vō Hutten gekrôneten Poeten vñ Orator an alle stend Deütscher nation, Wie vnformlicher weise vñ gātz geschwind, vnersůcht oder erfordert einiges rechtēs. Er mit eignem tyrañischē gewalt, vō dem Romanistē, an leib, eer vnd gůt beschwert vñ benôtiget werde . . . . Ein grosses dingk ist die warheit, vnd starck über alle. iij. Esdre .iiij.* Strasbourg: Flach, 1520. Chrisman P3.2.3.; *Deutsche Schriften,* 176–186; Böcking I:405–419; Tü 115/308.

————. *Clag vnd Vormanūg gegē den übermãssigen vnchristlichen gewalt des Bapstes zů Rom, vnd der vngeislichen geistlichen. Durch herrn Vlrichen vō Hutten, Poeten, vnd Orator der gantzē Christenheit, vnd zůuoran dem Vatterland Teütscher Nation zů nutz vnd gůt, Von wegen gemeiner beschwernüß, vnd auch seiner eigenen notdurfft, Jn reimens weise beschriben. Iacta est alea. Jch habs gewagt.* Strasbourg: Knobloch, 1520 (late); Schott, 1520 (Oct.-Nov.); Schott, 1520 (Nov.-Dec.). Chrisman P3.2.1.;Tü 594/1542, 115/307; *Deutsche Schriften,* 200–243; Böcking 3:473–526.

————. *Herr Ulrichs von Hutten anzôig Wie allwegen sich die Rômischen Bischôff, od Bãpst gegen den teütschen Kayßeren gehalten haben, vff dz kürtzst vß Chronicken vnd Historien gezogen, K. maiestãt fürzůbringen. Jch habs gewogt.* Strasbourg: Schott, 1520 and 1521. Chrisman P3.2.5; Böcking 5:364–384.

Karlstadt, Andreas Bodenstein von. *Auszlegung dieser wort Christi. Das ist mein leyb, welcher für euch gegebē würt. Das ist mein Blůt, welches für euch vergossen würt. Luce am. 22. Wider die einfeltige vnd zwyfeltige papisten, welche soliche wort, zů einē abbruch des kreützes Christi brauchen.* Strasbourg: Johann Prüß, 1525. Zorzin no. 69B; Chrisman P4.1.16; the Basel first edition is found in Tü 1446/3833.

————. *Dialogus oder ein gesprechbüchlin. Von dem grewlichen vnd abgôttischen mißbrauch, des hochwirdigsten Sacrament Jesu Christi.* Strasbourg: Prüß, 1525. Zorzin no. 67C; Chrisman P4.1.15; Tü 136/369; reprinted in Hertzsch 2:5–49 and W2 20:2313–2359.

————. *Erklerung Wie Karlstat sein ler von dem hochwirdigen Sacrament, vnd andere achtet vnnd geachtet haben wil. Mit eyner Epistel M. Lutheri.* Strasbourg: Knobloch, 1525; Prüß, 1525. Zorzin, nos. 77E and 77F; Tü 1936/4939; 206/585; W2 20:312–323.

————. *Ob man mit heyliger schrifft erweysen müge, das Christus mit leyb, blůt vnd seele im Sacrament sey.* Strasbourg: Prüß, 1525. See Zorzin no. 66B, n. 56, for the attribution; Tü 1127/2883.

————. *Ein schone kurcze vñ Christliche vnterrichtůg der rechten (wider die alte vnnd neüwe papistische) mess.* Strasbourg: Schwan, 1524. Zorzin no. 68B; reprinted in W2 20:2306–2313.

Luther, Martin. *ACTA ET RES GESTAE, D. MARTINI LVTHERi. In Com-*

itijs Principū Vuormaciae, Anno M.D.XXI. Strasbourg: Schott, 1521. Aland 775; Chrisman P3.1.16; Benzing, 909; WA 7:815–887.

———. *Auslegung des 109. (110.) Psalms.* In *mancherley büchlin.* Strasbourg: Schürer Erben, 1520. Aland 615; WA 1:690–710; W2 5:888–921.

———. *Auslegung deutsch des Vaterunsers für die einfältigen Laien . . . Nicht für die Gelehrten.* In *mancherley büchlin.* Strasbourg: Schürer Erben, 1520. Aland 742; WA 2:80–130.

———. *Doctoris Martini Luther Appelation oð berüfung an eyn Christlich frey conciliū.* Strasbourg: Prüß, 1520; Schürer Erben, 1520. Chrisman P3.1.5; Benzing 778; WA 7 (83):85–90, 889–890; W2 15:1602–1607; Aland 134B lists only Prüß; after 17 Nov. 1520.

———. *Doctor Martinus Luthers antwort Auf die zedel, so vnð des Officials zů Stolpē sigel ist außgangen.* Strasbourg: Flach, 1520. Chrisman P3.1.8; Benzing 613; WA 6 (135):137–141; W2 19:462–469; Aland 702; after 11 Feb. 1520.

———. *Drey Biechlin zůletst von dem Hochberůmbtenn vnnd Ewangelischen Lerer Doctor Martin Luther außgangenn. Nemlich von dem Deütschen Adel. der heiligē Mess dem Babstumb zů Rom.* Strasbourg: Schürer Erben, 1520, (1521–1522). Benzing 12; Chrisman P3.1.10; Aland 7, 502, 548; Tü 402–403/1094; Chrisman has 1520, Benzing has 1521–1522.

———. *[Großer] Sermon von dem Wucher.* In *mancherley büchlin.* Strasbourg: Schürer Erben, 1520. Aland 779; WA 6:36–60, 630.

———. *Ein heilsams Büchlein von Doctor Martinus Luther August. von der Beycht gemacht, Durch Georgium Spalatinū geteütscht.* Strasbourg: Knobloch, 1520. Chrisman P1.1.2; Benzing 626; WA 6:157–169 [Latin]; W2 19:786–807, W2 21a:248–249.; Phil. ed. 1 (73) 81–101; Aland 142; Tü 1630/4198; Spalatin's preface is dated 8 May 1520.

———. *(E)In kurtze Form das Pater noster zů verston, vnd zů betten. Für die iungen Kinder im Christen Glauben.* Strasbourg: Flach (Knobloch), 1520. Chrisman P5.1.1; Benzing 547; WA 6 (9):11–19; W2 10:166–175; Aland 557 Chrisman has Flach, Benzing Knobloch; after 1519; also in *mancherley büchlin* (Strasbourg: Schürer Erben, 1520).

———. *(E)In kurtze vnderwisung Wie man beichtē sol . . .* Strasbourg: Flach (Knobloch), 1520. Chrisman P5.1.2; Benzing 292; WA 2 (57):59–65; W2 10:2158–2165; Lenker 24:328–334; Aland 71; Chrisman has Flach, Benzing Knobloch; after 1519.

———. *Martini Luthers der waren götlichen schrifft Doctors, Augustiner zů Wittenbergk, mancherley büchlin vnnd tractetlin. In wölchē ein yegklicher auch einfaltiger Lay, vil heylsamer Christlicher lere vnd vnderweysung findet, so not seindt zů wissenn, einem yegklichen Christen menschen, der nach Christlicher ordnung (als wir alle söllen) leben will. Deren biechlin namen findest du am andern blatt, mit zale der blättern, in wölchem yegklichs eygentlich anfahet, vnd ein epistel zů denen die söllich büchlin lesen, oder hören lesen von D. Martini Luther außgangen. Item Apologia: das ist ein schirmred vnd antwort gegen etlicher einrede, so geschehen wider D. Martinū Luthern vnd seine Ewangelische lere, mit fast schönen wollgegrünten bewerungen, das sein leere, als warhafftig, Christlich, vnnd göttlich anzůnemen sey*. Strasbourg: Schürer Erben, 1520 (Oct.). Benzing 8; Chrisman P3.1.9 contains Aland 742, 557, 115, 408, 209, 556, 5, 738, 177, 698, 779, 60, 392, 714, 655, 656, 476, 615, 761; also L. Spengler's Schutzrede.

――――. *Ein nützlich vnd fast tröstlich predig oder vnderrichtung wie sich ein Christenmensch mit frewden bereiten sol zů sterbenn*. Strasbourg: Flach, 1520; Schürer Erben, 1523. Chrisman P2.1.7; Benzing 452, 453; Aland 698; WA 2(680):685–697, 759; LW 42(95):99–115; W2 10. Benzing does not have the 1520 Flach, but does have two Schürers for 1523, one of them flagged with a question mark; after 1519; also in *mancherley büchlin*. (Strasbourg: Schürer Erben, 1520).

――――. *Sermon de digna praeparatione cordis pro suscipiendo sacramento eucharistiae*. In German translation in *mancherley büchlin*. Strasbourg: Schürer Erben, 1520. Aland 209; WA 1 (325):329–334; W2 12:1342–1352.

――――. *Ein Sermon gepredigt zu Leipzig auf dem Schloß am Tage Petri und Pauli Matth. 16, 13–19*. In *mancherley büchlin*. Strasbourg: Schürer Erben, 1520. Aland 476; WA 2:244–249.

――――. *Ein Sermon uon dem wůcher. D.M.L.* Strasbourg: Flach, 1520. Chrisman P2.1.2; Benzing 538; WA 6(1):3–8, 630; W2 10:856–861; Aland 778; after 1 Nov. 1519.

――――. *Ein Sermon uon der Betrachtung des heyligen leidens Christi*. Strasbourg: Knobloch, 1519; [Prüß, 1520] [Flach, 1520]. Benzing 326; Chrisman P2.1.9; WA 2 (131):136–142; Aland 408; Benzing has the 1519 and neither of the 1520 editions which Chrisman lists; Chrisman does not have the 1519; after 5 April 1519; also in *mancherley büchlin* (Strasbourg: Schürer Erben, 1520).

――――. *Ein Sermon von Ablaß und Gnade*. In *mancherley büchlin*. Strasbourg: Schürer Erben, 1520. Aland 5; WA 1 (239):243–246; W2 18:270–275.

――――. *Ein Sermon von dē Hochwurdigē sacramēt des heiligen waren lychnams Christi, vnd von den Brůderschafften D M L A*. Strasbourg: Flach, 1520. Chrisman P2.1.6; Benzing 507; WA 2 (738):742–758; W2 19:426–449; Aland 655; LW 35 (43):49–73; after 29 Nov. 1519; also in *mancherley büchlin* (Strasbourg: Schürer Erben, 1520).

――――. *Ein Sermon von dem Elichen standt vorendert vñ corrigiret durch D. Martinū. Luther* . . . Strasbourg: Knobloch, 1519. Aland 177; Chrisman P2.1.1; Benzing 370; WA 2:166–171; also in *mancherley büchlin* (Strasbourg: Schürer Erben, 1520).

――――. *Ein Sermon von dem gebeet vnd procession. yn der Creutzwochen. Auch sunst von allem gebet durch dz gātz Jar wie sich der mēsch dar in haltē sol, allen christen mēschē nützlich vnd selig zů wissen*. Strasbourg: Flach, 1520; (Knobloch, 1519). Chrisman P2.1.8; Benzing 385; WA 2:(172):175–179; W2 10:1414–1421; Aland 392 [listed in Benzing as Knobloch, 1519]; also in *mancherley büchlin* (Strasbourg: Schürer Erben, 1520); after 1 June 1519.

――――. *Ein Sermon von dem Heiligen hochwirdigen Sacramēt der Tauffe*.

Strasbourg: Flach, 1520. Chrisman P2.1.10; Benzing 491; WA 2 (724): 727–737; W2 10:2112–2127; LW 35 (23):29–43; Aland 714; Benzing: Flach for Knobloch; after 9 Nov. 1519; also in *mancherley büchlin* (Strasbourg: Schürer Erben, 1520).

———. *Ein Sermon von dem Sacrament der Büß.* Strasbourg: Flach, 1520; Schürer Erben, 1520. Chrisman P2.1.5; Benzing 475, 477; (115) WA 2 (709):713–723; LW 35 (3):9–22; W2 10; Aland 115; Benzing has "Flach für Johann Knobloch" and "Ulrich Morhart"; after 1519; also in *mancherley büchlin* (Strasbourg: Schürer Erben, 1520).

———. *(E)yn Sermon von dē nüwen Testament: das ist vō der heiligē Mesz.* Strasbourg: Flach, 1520. Chrisman P2.1.3; Benzing 679; WA 6 (349): 353–378, 631; LW 35 (75):79–111; Aland 502; after 3 Aug. 1520; also in *Drey Biechlin.*

———. *(E)In sermō von dem Bann Doctor Martini Luthers . . .* Strasbourg: Flach, 1520. Chrisman P2.1.4; Benzing 580, 581; WA 6 (61):63–75, 630; LW 39 (3):7–22; W2 19; Aland 60; also in *mancherley büchlin* (Strasbourg: Schürer Erben, 1520).

———. *(D)Ie syben Bůsz psalmē Mit teütscher auszlegung, Nach dem schrifft-lichen synne . . .* Strasbourg: Knobloch, 1519. Benzing 78; WA 1:158–220; Aland 116.

———. *Teütscher Adel. (A)N den Christēlichen Adel teütscher Nation: von des Christenlichen stands besserung . . .* Strasbourg: Flach, 1520, Flach, 1520, Beck, 1520, Köpfel, 1520. Chrisman P3.1.3; Benzing 691, 692; WA 6 (381):404–469, 631–632; LW 44 (115):123–217; Aland 7; Benzing has only 2 Flach editions; after 18 Aug. 1520; also in *Drey Biechlin.*

———. *Theologia teütsch.* Strasbourg: Knobloch, 1519 (Sept. 16); Knobloch, 1520 (Aug.1); (Knobloch, 1520 [Aug. 1]). Chrisman P1.1.1; Benzing 165, 166, 167; WA 1 (375):378–379. 711; LW 31 (71):75–76; Aland 719; Chrisman lists only 2 editions, one in 1519 and one in 1520.

———. *Verklärung D.M. Luthers etlicher Artikel in seinem Sermon von dem heiligen Sakrament.* In *mancherley büchlin.* Strasbourg: Schürer Erben, 1520. Aland 656; WA 6:78–83 (82Z.10ff. *Kurzer Lebenslauf Luthers*), 630; W2 19:452–459.

———. *vnderrichtung, vff etlich Artickel die jm vō seinen mißgünnern vff-gelegt . . .* Strasbourg: Flack, 1519. Chrisman P3.1.2; Benzing 302; WA 2:69–73; Aland 738.

———. *Von dē Bapstum zů Rom Wider den Hochberümpten Romanistē zu Leiptzck.* Strasbourg: Knobloch, 1520. Chrisman P3.1.4; Benzing 663; WA 6 (277):285–324; Aland 548; after 26 June 1520; also in *Drey Biechlin.*

———. *Von den guten Werken.* In *mancherley büchlin.* Strasbourg: Schürer Erben, 1520. Aland 761; WA 6:202–204*, 204–276 (Druck), 631.

———. *Von der Babylonischen gefengknuß der Kirchen, Doctor Martin Luthers.* Strasbourg: Schott, 1520, 1520, 1520. Chrisman P3.1.6; Benzing 712, 713, 714; WA 6 (484):497–573, 632; LW 36 (3):11–126; Aland 120B apparently has one more edition than Chrisman; after 6 Oct. 1520; translated from the Latin edition.

————. *Von der Freyhayt Aines Christenmenschen.* Strasbourg: Prüß, 1520; Beck, 1520; Knobloch, 1521; Schürer Erben, 1522; Köpfel, 1524. Chrisman P1.1.3; Benzing 740, 742, 749; WA 7:20–38, 888–889; Aland 227. Note that Benzing has only 3 editions (Prüß, 1520; Erben ca. 1522; Köpfel, 1524), Chrisman 5 (Prüß, 1520; Beck, 1520; Knobloch, 1521; Schürer Erben, 1522; Köpfel, 1520); after 16 Nov. 1520.

Marcellus, Johannes. *Passion D. Martins Luthers, oder seyn lydung durch Marcellum beschriben.* Strasbourg: Knobloch, 1521; [Prüß, 1521]. Chrisman P3.9.3, P3.9.4; Tü 1566/4061; Ho 3908.

Mensing, Johannes. *Von dem Opffer Christi in der Messe: Allen Christglaubigen / Teutscher Nation not tzuwissen Denen zu Magdeburgk in sonderheyt / tzu gut geschriben vnd auszgangen. Beweret mit Götlicher schriffte.* Leipzig: Schmidt, 1526. Klaiber no. 2104; Tü 996/2529

Murner, Thomas. *An den Großmechtigsten vnd Durchlüchtigsten adel tütscher nation das sye den christlichen glauben beschirmen, wyder den zerstörer des glaubens christi, Martinum luther einen verfierer der einfeltigen christen.* Strasbourg: Grüninger, 1520. Klaiber no. 2220; Chrisman C10.1.4; Pfeiffer-Belli 7:56–118.

————. *Antwurt vnd klag mit entschuldigung doctor Murners wider brúder Michel stifel weyt von eßlingen daheim, vff das stüfelbúch so er wider meyn lied gemachet hat, daruß er des lieds den rechten thon erlernen mag.* Strasbourg: Grüninger, 1522. Klaiber no. 205; Chrisman C10.1.10; Pfeiffer-Belli 8:31–42.

————. *Ein Christenliche vnd briederliche ermanung zú dem hoch gelerten doctor Martino luther Augustiner order zú Wittemburg (Das er etlichen reden von dem newen testament der heillgen messen gethon) abstande, vnd wider mit gemeiner christenheit sich vereinige.* Strasbourg: Grüninger, 1520, 1520, 1521. Klaiber no. 2217; Chrisman C10.1.1; Pfeiffer-Belli 6:31–87; Tü 1292/3326, 1473/3871. Chrisman has only 2 entries, one for 1520 and one for 1521.

————. *Uon dem grossen Lutherischen Narren wie in doctor Murner beschworen hat.* Strasbourg: Grüninger, 1522. Klaiber no. 2228; Chrisman C10.1.11.

————. *Von dem Babstenthum das ist von der höchsten oberkeyt Christlichs glauben wyder doctor Martinum Luther.* Strasbourg: Grüninger, 1520. Klaiber no. 2219; Chrisman C10.1.3; Pfeiffer-Belli 7:1–55; Tü 620/1630.

————. *Von Doctor Martinus luters leren vnd predigen. Das sie argwenig seint, vnd nit gentzlich glaubwirdig zú halten.* Strasbourg: Grüninger, 1520. Klaiber no. 2218; Chrisman C10.1.2; Pfeiffer-Belli 6:91–122; Tü 1483/3889.

————. *Wie doctor .M. Luter vß falschen vrsachen bewegt Das geistlich recht verbrennet hat.* Strasbourg: Grüninger, 1521. Klaiber no. 2222; Chrisman C10.1.7; Pfeiffer-Belli 3:1ff.

Spengler, Lazarus. *Schutzred vnnd christéliche antwurt ains erbern liebhabers gotlicher warhayt. der heyligen schrifft. auff etlicher vermaint widersprechen. mit anzaygúg warumb Doctor Martini Luthers leer nit als vnchristenlich verworffen. sonder mer fur christenlich gehalten werdē*

sol . . . In *mancherley büchlin.* Strasbourg: Schürer Erben, 1520. Laube
1:501–516.

Stifel, Michael. *Von der Christförmigen, rechtgegrundten leer Doctoris Martini Luthers, ein überuß schön kunstlich Lyed, sampt seiner neben vßlegung.*
Strasbourg: unknown, ca. 1522; Schott, 1522; Kerner, before 1525. Chrisman P3.9.6, P3.9.7; Ho 2935; Tü 1093/2773; Tü 315–316/900; 364/
1024.

———. *wider Doctor Murnars falsch erdycht Lyed: von dem vndergang
christlichs Glaubens. Bruoder Michael Styfels von Esszlingen vßleg vnnd
Christliche gloß darüber.* Strasbourg: Prüß, 1522. Chrisman P3.9.8; Ho
2934; Tü 249/695.

Sylvius, Petrus. *Eyn klare beweisung wie Luther würde seyn eyn vrsache, des
steten eynzuges des Türcken, des vnchristlichen yrthums, zwitracht, auffruhr, vnd empörung des gemeynen volckes* . . . Leipzig: J. Thanner, 1527.
Klaiber no. 3046; Tü 1183/2965.

———. *Die letzten zwey beschlissliche vnd aller krefftigste büchleyn M. petri
Syluij, so das Lutherisch thun an seyner person, von seyner geburt, vnd an
seyner schrifft, von anfang bis zum end gründlich handeln, vnd seyne
vnchristlickeyt schrifftlich entplossen.* Leipzig: M. Blum, 1534. Klaiber no.
3059; Ho 3430.

———. *Eyn Mssive* [sic] *ader Sendbriff an die Christliche versamlunge und
szonderlich an die oberkeit Deutzscher Nation zu wegern den untthergang
irer herschafft, vnd das iemmerlich verterbnis der Christenheit, Eyn iden so
durch tzeitlichen vnd ewigen friden, syn leib vnd szele sucht zu bewaren
nutzlich vnd itzt nothafftig tzu erfarn vnd zu lesen.* Dresden? Leipzig?,
1525. Klaiber no. 3038; Tü 996/2528.

*Uerkündungs Brieff der hochberüempte Uniuersitet Erdfürt, zu schütz schirm
vn handhabung des Christliche gots diener vn lerers. D. Martin Luthers.
Durch Wolffgang Rüßen verteütschet.* Strasbourg: J. Prüß, 1521. Chrisman
P3.9.2; Tü 258/3223.

*UF das Fürhalte so durch Keyserliche Maiestat Vnd des heiligen Reichs
versamleten Churfürsten, vnd stände, Dem Hochgelerte Doctori Martino
Luther. etc. durch des Reich Redner zu Wormbs erzelt. Ist diß sein personlich (Zum kürtzistenn) begriffen antwort* . . . Strasbourg: Knobloch, 1521;
Prüß, 1521; Schott, 1522. The Schott title is *Handlung so mit doctor Martin Luther Vff dem Keyßerlichen Reichs tag zu Worms ergangen ist, vom
anfang zum end, vff das kürtzest begriffen* . . . (Strasbourg: Schott, 1522).
Benzing 919, 920, 924; WA 7 (814, etc.):815–887, 898; LW 32
(101):105–131; Aland 775; German translation by Georg Spalatin.

Vadian, Joachim. *Karsthans.* Strasbourg: Prüß, 1521; Prüß, 1521; Köpfel,
1521. Chrisman P3.3.3.; Ho 8897; Clemen 4:1ff.

Wulffer, Wolfgang. *Wider die unselige Aufruhre Merten Luthers.* Leipzig:
Landsberg, 1522. Klaiber no. 3444; Tü 119/323.

Zell, Matheus. *Christeliche verätwortüg M. Matthes Zell von Keyserßberg
Pfarrherrs vnd predigers im Münster zu Straßburg, vber Artickel jm vom
Bischöfflichem Fiscal daselbs entgegen gesetzt, vnnd im rechten vbergeben.*
Strasbourg: Köpfel, 1523. Chrisman P3.11.3; Tü 217–220/613.

Index

Designer: U.C. Press Staff
Compositor: Asco Trade Typesetting Ltd.
Text: 10/13 Sabon
Display: Sabon
Printer: Malloy Lithographing, Inc.
Binder: John H. Dekker & Sons

26201892R00140

Printed in Great Britain
by Amazon